CANCER, KINTSUGI, CAMINO

A Memoir

Shoshana D. Kerewsky

Lockweed Press/Shoshana D. Kerewsky, PsyD, LLC

Publisher's Cataloging-in-Publication Data

Names: Kerewsky, Shoshana D.
Title: Cancer, kintsugi, camino : a memoir / Shoshana D. Kerewsky.
Description: Eugene, OR : Lockweed Press, 2022. | Summary: A memoir of breast cancer and the Camino de Santiago, including Jewish identity, atheism, AIDS, COVID, and meditation in mixed lyrical prose and poetic forms.
Identifiers: ISBN 9798428812329 (pbk.)
Subjects: LCSH: Kerewsky, Shoshana D., 1962 -- Health. | Breast -- Cancer -- Patients -- United States -- Biography. | Christian pilgrims and pilgrimages -- Camino de Santiago de Compostela. | Camino de Santiago de Compostela. | Spain -- Description and travel. | BISAC: BIOGRAPHY & AUTOBIOGRAPHY / Personal Memoirs. | BIOGRAPHY & AUTOBIOGRAPHY / Medical. | BIOGRAPHY & AUTOBIOGRAPHY / Women.
Classification: LCC RC280.B8 K47 2022 | DDC 362.1969 K47 C —dc23

For

Nancy, Paula, Arlene

CONTENTS

ABOUT THIS MEMOIR

This is a work of non-fiction. It includes fantasies, dreams, and loose associations, and creative expression based on lived experience. Some events are reordered, abbreviated, or lightly fictionalized to simplify the narrative or provide privacy. Descriptions of clients and students are disguised. Descriptions of others are simplified or composite to the extent possible without sacrificing enough verisimilitude to tell the story of my own experience. While my intention is to be accurate, I would not be surprised if I have misremembered some details that I did not record in my journal.

I have used the names of public figures. Other names are used by permission or are pseudonyms. Frederic Evans required me to use his name in this form in every publication in which I refer to him.

Some of my own writing, such as letters and published poetry, is reorganized and reworded for clarity and relevance. Brief fair use quotations from other works are used transformatively. They appear in quotation marks, italics, or both. In Notes and Sources, I provide citations and influences, as well as original publication and presentation information for my own work. I translate some words and phrases. Non-English words are typically italicized only on their first appearance in the text.

PREAMBLE: BRIGHT AND INEXPLICABLE MOTIFS

It's dark on the plane, which is not as clean as "dingy," but not quite as disturbing as "dirty." I want to be calm, but I'm tense both from what came before and what will come later. On arrival at Delhi Indira Gandhi International Airport, I had learned that not only was my flight to Chennai canceled, but my entire airline was, at least for now, terminated. About two hours of pushing into crowds, waiting for the tour company representative as he argued for a ticket, driving to the international terminal, waiting outside for the representative while he dickered inside, and finally paying over $600 plus $50 in *bakshish* to get on this night flight had been a challenge to my equilibrium. Anticipating trying to find the ashram's driver on the other end, whom I had no way to contact and who would be looking for me at the wrong terminal, did not relax me. Well, I thought, I've made my way to unexpected destinations before. I'll lose myself in my book.

"A zoom like growl by my ear, then a starfish of pain in my breast. The first time I was punched on the street, the men were on motorcycles." Katherine Russell Rich, a breast cancer survivor, was describing an incident of "Eve-teasing," a genial-sounding euphemism for sexually assaulting women in India. I closed the book.

I was an unescorted woman in India, making my way in the night to the ashram where my students were midway through a study and service-learning trip. I was there to observe the program, hear how the students were doing, help them navigate the intense emotions of an immersive cross-cultural experience, suggest ways that they could bring their learning home to their lives and work. I had been to Gandhi's *ghat*. I had had red string tied around my wrist, although I didn't want it, although in Cambodia I had declined it. I didn't want to make a fuss. It's difficult to be a moral atheist when opportunities for idolatry abound, when one does not want to give offense. I still wore the red string. If there were no god, it was superstition, or misplaced politeness. If there were indeed, it was an offense unto the lord. It brought me no comfort, though I wished it did. I had seen fortresses, camel-drawn carts, trucks with bright and inexplicable motifs, light- and dark-skinned people, men with and without turbans, women with betel-stained teeth, smiling, a gaunt *hijra* begging at the van window, children sorting spices on a dirty cloth between lanes of traffic, cows lolling in the road, *Coracias benghalensis benghalensis,* peacocks, common moorhens so far from what I thought of as their home.

In northern India, we were never alone. Not in Rajasthan. Not in the rain at the Taj Mahal. Not at the Delhi hotel where armed guards shone light on the undercarriage of our van, mirrors flashing, not where we were scanned for dangerousness, X-rayed, wanded, patted, locked in, surrounded by razor-wire perimeters. I thought that maybe, but did not yet know, I carried my own ordnance in my breast. As it would turn out, it had already exploded. I was allowed one walk. I don't know if a man would have been permitted to take more chances. As for me, I had been cloistered for safety, as if safety existed.

At Chennai, I found my way to the domestic terminal. My incorrect flight arrived later than the ashram's driver was expecting me. He might or might not know about my airline's catastrophic failure. I walked back and forth in front of the terminal with my one small backpack, searching for a sign bearing something approximating my name, resigned to an all-night boustrophedon if necessary, ox working but going nowhere, so that at dawn I could arrange a ride. I inquired of the other drivers, "Sri Aurobindo?" They shook their heads. After an hour or so, my driver found me. I hoped he was my driver. He seemed to know where I was going. He spoke little English, and I had four irrelevant phrases in Tamil. I got in this man's car.

We drove for hours beside the dark sea. I comforted myself that I was too old and insufficiently thin to be trafficked. Wordlessly, the driver dropped me at a locked gate on a quiet street. I rang the bell and the night security *wallah* let me in.

Pondicherry was calmer. I walked at dawn, careful where I put my feet, dogs barking, a few men here and there going I don't know where, barefoot on the pounded trash, vegetative scraps, cow and dog shit. The sewer ran across my way, under the street, burping fetor, stink, ghastly exhalations against the early morning breath of the sea. It was a disturbing metaphor, rank dead stench of former living things. Later with my students, I would smell wood smoke, monkey urine in the crevices of rocks, ghee-smeared statues of deities in small, hot stone rooms, simmering *dal,* sweat and awe and unwashed feet. I was quiet in my potential sorrow.

My room at the ashram was monastic, slightly less austere than a college dorm room ready for a class reunion, with sheets, a blanket and towel, soap. This room also had dull brown gingham curtains, two wire hangers, and pamphlets on Sri Aurobindo's spiritual practices. It had a Western-style toilet. I meditated in the wrong tradition. At dawn, breakfast around the corner, a giant conical *dosa* with unidentified condiments, cost about a dollar.

After a long bus ride to the temple, we found the women's room boarded up, locked, obscured by weedy vines. The defunct-restroom wallah said sadly, "But what can I do?" I pissed in a field full of goats with my undergraduates. I like to pretend that I'm the kind of faculty member who can nonchalantly piss in a field with her undergraduates, but it does not come naturally to me. At the entrance to the temple, my Indian colleague mocked me gently for refusing to take off my sandals, but I felt too vulnerable to exotic pathogens, though I didn't tell him why. *Namaste.*

I walked by a small city park, overgrown, wild and undifferentiated tangles, nothing in flower. It was an herb garden as well, but seemed to be denuded of medicinal plants. I passed a billboard warning that Eve-baiting was a crime. I scanned for motorcycles and monitored my breasts.

I had deferred a biopsy for four weeks, until my return from India. The radiologist accepted this delay, mentioning that "80% of these are benign." He was accurate statistically, but not for me, a single-case study deviating from the mean. A person is not the aggregate data set in which her probabilities are located.

When I was in college, my best-paid job was as a life drawing model. I would take off my clothes for a community art class of legally blind sculptors, a community painting and sketching class, my classmates taking studio art. Sometimes on campus I would fail to wear a shirt for free, because I've never cared for them or seen the point. After my return from India, I would become so used to stripping off my blouse for medical personnel that sometimes I would forget that this was neither necessary nor welcome at the dentist or ophthalmologist. Still, the goddess in me salutes the goddess in you.

When I was in college, I wrote a poem about modeling for the blind sculptors and sitting shirtless in a goatless field. It included the lines

> "I like this more than paint," one says,
> "because with sculpture I can feel
> if your breasts are the right size."
>
> my breasts are the right size

and in the right place
and when I check later
they are still there

Soon, this would no longer be true.

ORIGIN STORIES

Yin and yang

Yes, my parents
were there
that year,
hard by
the Trylon
and Perisphere.

Clay

No, she's my mother. My sister's younger. Though we do look alike; you wouldn't mistake us for strangers. We're twins separated at birth—my birth—by 23 years, cast from the same mold. But talk to us a while; I'm the storyteller, outgoing in my shyness, queen of the semicolon, as easy in language as she is in clay. I make my artifice in words, render figures in illusory perspective. I hold the syllables in my mouth, caress them with my lips and tongue like—

Well. I first said "lesbian" when I was twelve. That doesn't mean I didn't think I'd marry a curly-haired New York boy and have two girls. Which is what she did. And no. I have no earliest memory of her—always I imagine her at the kitchen table—later, in her studio—hunched over something, calculating or mixing or sketching. In my head, I know she cooked and cleaned, did those house and mommy things, had friends and conversations. In my heart, I know this cloistered scene: Mother at her alchemy, mother with packets of powder that melt into colors, bring forth patterns hidden at inception, mother with a handful of small brass weights. In my dreams, she is the fixed interior, silent and serious as an oyster, soft inside a closed shell. Pearling all irritants, transforming edges to the luminous and smooth. In the cathedral of my mother there is a hush, expectant susurrus. Only the tiny stained glass windows shout their reds, exult their blues and golds. A noisy child, turned noisy woman, but even now my speech goes still, I am dumb with the mystery of my mother.

Later, in her studio, she would wedge the clay, making it look easy until I tried, strained against the medium and air. At her wheel, she would center and throw, her upright cigarette slowly burning to the filter as she worked, extinguishing itself. Sometimes there would be a row of them, ranked ash and yellow, dead regiments. My mother, up to her elbows in grey. It makes me wonder, how do separate forms emerge from single lumps of clay, how are they fixed and fired, made hard and distant and distinct? When the vessel is fully formed, is it truly empty, or does it cup some memory of fullness, some recollection of itself?

At night she would fire a kiln, sometimes both kilns, in the studio next to my room. Midnight, three AM, I would still be reading, hieroglyphs, the myths of Sumer, verbs in ancient Greek, galaxies distant, inverse square, anywhere but here. The dry air carried ropes of sulfur, a fine, burning dust that even now holds memories of home. In the black hallway I'd hear footsteps, creaking stairs. Turning off my lamp, I would creep to my door, open it silently, peer into her lair. There she was, bending to the peepholes, checking the cones, haloed in orange, wreathed in smoke, silhouette and casting shadows, reeking of brimstone, this demon my mother, not Savior, not Mother Mary, not Satan the adversary, but Lucifer, bearer of light in an odorous glow. So there we were, mother and daughter in darkness and flames, doing our duties: Making and watching, creating and casting into words.

Sometimes I wonder, if we are separate and singular, why not more so? If we are one and joined, why this terrible clawing to be free? In our mingled dreams, I am Daniel, interpreter and judge, but which of us is Nebuchadnezzar's idol with its feet of clay? What does this curl of lip mean, this twisted handle? Why green markings on a charcoal field, why their mirror and reverse, just on this side? Why one leaf pressed into the slip; why not three, embedded fossils of once-present beasts? Why these ashes, why the subtle textures of the glaze? Clay is not a unitary thing; there is porcelain and terra cotta, river clay and Egyptian paste, greys and whites that bisque to whites and reds. While words are not a product, tangible, stackable, they can still feel rough against the lips, they can still shatter or explode.

So it's true that we hold each other to impossible standards, measures invented to push away and pull. That there's a taxonomy for everything, including us. That we stack each other up, make sets and sentences, sometimes find each other wanting. As for myself, there I am twice as hard, harder than hard words, harder than fired clay. Imagine the master, her even breathing, the perfect stillness of the studio, gold motes in the morning light. In her mind's eye, the bowl turning; she knows without words just where her fingers go. How to cup the clay and just what touch will let it blossom, just where the gesture stops. She kicks the wheel to set it spinning, lowers her wet hands—

Girl bursts in, nasty goblin with a mouthful of sound, I want to poke the clay, I want to investigate its properties, I want to speak reams on it, I want to give a learned lecture, I want to make a lovely poem so she will praise me, I want to write a dozen dozen haiku, I want to coat everything with an oil slick of language; even now, I want to say the clay is like a breast, even now, I want an avalanche, an echo, a flashing radar screen of words to bounce from every surface and tell me what I see, I want to make the air between us thick with thoughts so I can see and rend it, get to her, I want, I want my mother, I want my mother to talk to me.

I am the idol, gold-tongued, clay-footed monster, golem grunting, fumbling for speech, hauling buckets of syntax out of a burning, a steaming, a stinking linguistic sea. I flood the *shtetl;* the villagers flee, but who remains behind? Mother at her craft, calmly setting out containers for my stories. Jars for the organs, jars for the heart. In ancient Egypt, they threw the brains away; unnecessary. There are maps and incantations, scrolls and good advice. Nothing is lost.

First there was a girl and another girl, only one day the girl grew up to be a mother. It was her cellular destiny. After everyone was a woman for a while, or at least an older girl, there were other girls, sometimes so many it was impossible to keep track without a chart. That was a good use of language. As time went on, there were fewer girls, until one day the girl discovered that she was a woman too, and the only other woman there was still her mother. Which was disappointing in a way, but not her mother's fault. Her mother, after all, had kept a sort of promise, not the kind that is spoken or incised on tablets with a pointed stylus, but the kind that lives in physical things that say without saying, *I am,* and *I am here.*

Stelae and sentences, accounts of the flood, memoirs of the fallen queen, a basket of potsherds, fragments and whole. We tell stories with our silences as well as speech, our gaps and mistranslations, the archaeology of our ruins. You make the vases, the flower pots and dinner plates. I will say which way the sand blew, how the sunlight fell, mosaics blue and red. People used to live there, joining piece to piece. People are still living there today.

Origin stories

I didn't spring full-formed from Zeus's brow, suddenly shift from nothing to something. Planck's constant need not be invoked. Dependent arising suffices. I ceased to not exist. But what I have to report about my childhood is not an interesting story of drama and conflict. Yes, there was distress, yes, there were heartaches and disputes. But I've always been optimistic, always seen the possibilities, always squirmed through the rubble, noting, "That apocalypse wasn't so terrible." In the version of my story that I tell myself, my childhood is mostly zeros and white space, though I remember almost everything. No abuse, no neglect, no abandonment. No lost parent, divorce or death, no bullies or horrible teachers who couldn't ultimately be survived. I never had mumps. I never fell off a horse and broke my arm. With whatever anguish or pleasure I experienced, I always had broccoli, books, quilts, and cats. My sense of my being tends toward the resilient.

The slightly older girl who walked me to elementary school said I would burn in hell because I wasn't a Baptist. I had no idea what she was talking about. It seemed incorrect. She said someone called "god" was in the sky. It was a cloudless day but I imagined an attenuated cloud-man, horizontal and parallel to the horizon, elongated, featureless, a Giacometti bronze figure. This is still my image of God, a figure at home in the Dreaming, perhaps with a snake friend or kangaroo. I tend to picture metaphors and similes literally, vividly. I'm glad I was much older when I first heard that "Jesus is a door."

When I was a child, a friend's family invited me to join them for church, so I did. Soon people began filing to the front. My friend pushed me forward, so I went. Following the actions of the others before me, I opened my mouth and the wafer was placed on my tongue, tablespoon of grape juice in my mouth. When we returned to our pew, my friend's mother triumphantly exclaimed that I had eaten the body of Jesus, and since I wasn't Catholic, I now needed to convert and repent or I would burn in hell forever. I was more confused than upset. "But Jews don't believe in hell. We don't even really think there's an afterlife. We don't believe that Jesus was the Messiah. Why would I need to convert?" She stared at me and said nothing. That look was becoming familiar. It was a look that said either, *I don't know what Jews believe, but I don't like it,* or *I didn't know that children read adult books, and I don't like that, either.*

My father gave me a children's illustrated Old Testament. We were a non-observant family. He had already advised me not to tell the Christian children that there was no Santa Claus because this matter was between them and their parents. I've only heard my mother mention God once. She said, "God doesn't intend for me to work on weekends." The joke was that at his *bar mitzvah* my father said, "Today I am a man, so now I'm done here." We lit Hanukkah candles on the menorah with one blessing and not quite the right tune, eight nights of small presents. A handful of Passover *seders* with relatives, hiding the *Afikoman* with my mother's cousins, perhaps once asking the Four Questions in English. Neither *Rosh Hashana* nor *Yom Kippur.* No Hebrew school on Sunday morning or Wednesday night, at least until later, when I was teaching them. No *Shabbat* candles or Friday night services. No *Havdalah,* the Sabbath's conclusion.

The bible had beautiful images, dark-eyed, dark-skinned figures who looked like my family, olive and brown, not white and pink. I'm sure the artwork was the impetus for my father to choose this book for me, probably at a book sale at the school where he was the principal. Maybe there was more. When he needed a liver transplant later, he seemed moved by my offer to ask a rabbi to say a prayer for the donor. Perforce, a typical organ donor has died a sudden, quick, non-toxic, and violent death.

I read the children's bible many times. I considered the Patriarchs as my grandpas, Sarah and Naomi as my aunts. I was most provoked by Nebuchadnezzar's visions. *Mene, mene, tekel, upharsin* spoke to my delight in counting more than to an appreciation of divine evaluation, of souls measured in feather-weights.

Now my greatest empathy rests with the idol with feet of clay. As a child, this image held my fear of everything going awry, crumbling. Now that things have gone wrong, I am sad for the idol, trying its best to cup a measure of divine light, an imperfect and reviled vessel losing its footing, stumbling, disintegrating into itself and down like the World Trade Center, pillar of clay, pillar of salt and smoke, black hole collapsed and gone. How can the idol rise from the slag, not as golem, not as sacred alphabetic smoke, not new or renewed, born or born again, but gold-veined, here—still, here?

This place is like a

My father was a storyteller. He especially liked to tell me about interesting ideas he had gleaned from educators' meetings and workshops. He recounted Claude Steiner's *The Warm Fuzzy Tale* when I was sad, describing the exchange of warm fuzzies, cold pricklies, and the coming of the Hip Woman. He described games designed to illuminate aspects of power dynamics in a workplace, including one that involved participants crawling on the floor. I enjoyed imagining my teachers doing this.

My father gave me a model for exploring metaphor. It was actually structured around a simile, but they're really the same thing, a way to compare the salient characteristics of two subjects in order to highlight similarities. The exercise, which probably originated with someone else, was a fill-in-the-blanks framework that began with the statement, "This place (a school, in his example) is like a _____." On that basis, it moved on to invite assertions related to the simile: "The principal is the _____. The teachers are the _____s. And the students are the _____s." *This place is like a zoo. The principal is the zookeeper, the teachers are the lackeys who clean up monkey shit, and the students are animals.* I use this activity frequently in teaching and psychotherapy. People like it; it's fun. They like hearing other people's imagery, expanding on it or offering a contrasting vision.

The second part of the activity involves a closer look, first asking, *Does exploring this symbolism reveal something important about unconscious assumptions? Does it explain otherwise puzzling behaviors?* If this psychiatric hospital is like a prison, if the therapists are guards and the patients are inmates, why wouldn't the patients' goal be to figure out the right thing to say in order to get sprung? Why would they trust the therapists with their vulnerability? This part of the exercise encourages exploration of the metaphor and discussion about how it is enacted.

As with so many incantatory processes, the magic comes alive in the third part. Metaphors compare like features, yes, but often drag dissimilar aspects into the mix, incorporating overextensions of the presumed similarity and mistaking points of contrast as if they support rather than limit the comparison. This is a game about the blind men and the elephant. The school may be similar to a zoo in some ways, but this metaphor does not support the conclusion that therefore children should be kept in cages or fed raw fish from a rusty bucket. What if the school is not just like a zoo, but like a garden, a solar system, a lifeboat, a dung beetle, the periodic table of elements? What if cancer is a journey, but also a school, a stone, a labyrinth, an ocean? What if pilgrimage is a cancer? What do I learn about my assumptions; which incongruities are revealed?

This is the spell my father taught me. This is the enchantment he conjured, bringing the girl of broom, meadowsweet, and oak to life.

Not the boy himself

At that time I longed for a tattoo of Icarus, but a tattoo capturing the story, not the boy himself. At my left scapula: The indifferent ancient sun, stiff red cardinal points, regular curvaceous diagonal rays of yellow and green. The unbending universe, a rigid, ordered world. At my right hip: A small, curved black feather, also scapular, in a circular ripple of black water. The absent boy an afterthought, less disruptive even than his plashing legs in Bruegel's *Landscape,* unnoticed even by a bird. The tragedy is personal, minuscule, not catalytic. Though the Fallen Tower crosses the Hanged Man, the world itself is not distorted. Assimilation, not accommodation. Life goes on, which is both comforting and horrifying. The world persists when I no longer exist.

I don't know why this image drew me. Perhaps for the same reason I considered a Yin-Yang tattoo, the tight symmetry disrupted by the omission of a smaller yin circle in the dark swoop of yang. The reductive either/or, the formal duality, felt constricting rather than encompassing. Yes, there's a little zero in every one and vice versa, but are they so tightly encapsulated, narded over, separate shells and pearls with no interpenetration? I was not the boy, but apparently I was not entirely a girl. I already knew this model was too simplistic, like assigning a color to a geographical direction, phlegm to this temperament and blood to that, a *mitzvah* to each bone or organ. I already knew that reflective symmetry was not harmony or balance, that the map was not the terrain, that metaphor was not the thing itself.

Now I have 6 tattoos, dots forming an unknown constellation, an indeterminate astrological sign.

Two half-moon haiku (Card XVIII)

Two dogs make more dogs.
Two half-moons don't make a whole
moon, just two whole halves.

Half-moon gloats in a
purple sky. Flirtations,
crustaceans, frustrations.

Picking up trash

My first experience of conscientious responsibility was after reading Baba Ram Das's *Be Here Now* in high school. I was walking back to school, having sneaked away to buy a better sandwich and a ginger beer for lunch. As I passed a trash can, I threw away a piece of paper. A wrapper? A brown paper bag? A receipt? It hit the rim and fluttered to the ground. I would have picked it up anyway, but now I realized that being more intentional required that I notice the litter, that in pursuing a more mindful course I obligated myself to pick it up, not because there was a rule but because it was the right thing to do, and because having noticed the litter, I could not un-notice it. I could no longer be oblivious, walk myself to the edge of oblivion. With a Jewish education, I would have understood this as an aspect of *tikkun olam,* repair of the world. Since I didn't yet have that framework, I just felt proud of myself, but also faintly annoyed. This mindfulness was going to take a lot more effort.

Out of bounds

My grandparents' living room prominently featured a large reproduction of a Lascaux cave painting, a message from the people of the Paleolithic to me, an adolescent visiting Greenwich Village in the 1970s. A bison or bull, ochre and umber, black and clay, running in an attitude unnamed by common heraldry, not quite a beast *courant.* Fat yellow horses, hematite blotched, black-shaded, on the white and dun rock communicate continuity, passion, motion, survival, calling the food gods down. No one is sure when the painting first appeared in my grandparents' apartment, precisely which bovine dominated the image, whether there were people, or when it disappeared. There are few of us left who might know that story. Someday I'd like to see the handprints, brown and white and orange, the being-human across all the generations.

Christopher Street was one of my walking perimeters, the allowable boundary. Though my sister notes that some of us adhered to the restriction and others did not, because the good record stores were on St. Mark's Place. I was a good girl. Within my irregular polygon of freedom, there was still plenty to see. The sex toy shops with their intimidating window displays took my breath away. As for the men, it was warm in August for so much black leather. Chains and pyramid studs glinted. Polarized sunglasses reflected me back to myself, lightly distorted. A store's window sign offered "piercing with and without pain." Women with short hair appraised me from barstools facing Bleecker Street. I still had long hair then. We nodded: I see you. We are here and we have always been here, in some form, even if we are not depicted.

Was it Lascaux? Or Altamira? I remember ruminants. Were there ungulates as well? Definitely no red ochre thylacine from Kakadu. Stories blur, ancient bison thunder right to left and gone.

A rejection letter

Michelle Cliff, co-editor of *Sinister Wisdom* and lover of Adrienne Rich, rejects my interpretive translation of Lorca's *"La Casada Infiel."* She includes a lengthy, pleasant note asking if I don't think the attitude and tone are patriarchal, too romantic, not really lesbian-feminist enough. I didn't know how to reply. I was a real lesbian feminist when I wrote it, a lesbian feminist with a broken heart.

Q & A

Is it a memoir?
Más o menos. It is a memoir but not the only possible memoir.

What is its form?
Peripatetic, peregrinative, wandering, exegetical. Assemblage and commonplace. Cornell box. Mosaic, bricolage. Not otherwise specified. It might be a travel narrative, a *seder* plate, the Game of the Goose.

Is it chronological?
Generally, though time isn't always linear.

Is it thematically arranged?
Perhaps it's thematically infused.

What is the organizing structure?
Associative. Playing with metaphors. Scattering tesserae, re-collecting, recollecting.

In what way is it a memoir?
In some ways, including the Way.

Is it all about the Camino?
Isn't it all about the Camino?

Is all of it true?
Yes, depending on the flexible dimensions of "truth."

Are names changed?
Where it matters. Would you like your name changed? You can change it.

Were once you lost and now you found?
At some times and in places. Mostly I continue. Progress on the ground measured in kilometers, not a skyward light-year leap.

When is the cancer part?
It's possible that we're already at the cancer part. Who knows how long the body can keep a secret?

Is the journey the central metaphor?

Not being sure if the journey is the central metaphor is the central metaphor.

WHEN THEY COME FOR THE JEWS

Jesus is a door

It's a great conversation, my friend and I sitting on a dorm bed eating Doritos, taking our short break while a different group of counselors manages the middle schoolers' evening activity. Jesus is a door, we agree. Is Christ a metaphor? No, she says, He is real, not a symbol, not a stand-in for something else. The *door* is a metaphor. It is not the same. We cannot bridge our chasm between real and symbolic.

Parts

You say the text is a woman's body,
broken. Poor boy. She still won't sing to you.

Let me catalogue how I'd caress you,
an alphabet lonely for its language.

I refused to handle or be touched by
the boy who let me play with his glass eye.

The two men entertain a wish to be
bestial with girls, cigarettes, coffee.

Everything I eat becomes myself: Squid,
garlic, butterfly, flames, salmon mousse, lort.

Who needs metaphors, figures of speech? Here,
we find blood and teeth in the stolen car.

Speak to me a boy-poem, full of snot and pus,
spit as far as you dare from your body.

She kissed my neck. I pressed her to the wall.
N.B.: This is not about your girlfriend.

Carp, waterfall and wind, the floating moon:
That's a big tattoo for a girl like you.

With one eye closed, I can see my nose. I
didn't used to see my sweet little nose.

The quilt cradles your bare foot in its folds.
Fragment. Undated. Private collection.

Dinner with Susan Sontag

"What?!" asks Martha. "You had dinner with Susan Sontag?!" Yes. Frederic and I invited her to join us at our apartment in Providence. I cooked Vietnamese pork chops with diced scallions, sticky rice, and broccoli. Frederic cleaned. He may have made cucumber salad, seasoned Japanese-y. We ate at the coffee table in the living room. It was spring, and sunny. Our apartment looked really nice.

I dream of Susan Sontag. She is dressed in black slacks and turtleneck. She looks tired. We are in the audience at an event in an amphitheater, sitting on the ground in a hillside section with grass and seats. The action is some way off, an opera? A period drama? She's only half-watching; it's the end of a long day. Her assistant is there, to the side, organizing something, whispering into her phone. I am there, though whatever my role was—driver from the university? Event escort?—has ended. When I helped her settle in, I dropped one of my short stories and an essay beside her, which I saw her notice. I sit slightly downslope. I haven't been invited, but I haven't been dismissed, either. I see her bare feet and scoot a little closer. I touch her toes, ask "May I?" She agrees and I begin to rub her feet. They're neither ugly nor attractive, just feet, adult feet with calluses, dry skin, several knobby joints and a few toes that don't quite straighten. She makes a sound of approval and contentment, relaxes. I massage her feet and watch the distant opera. Eventually I fall asleep with my head beside her knee. Her assistant wakes me; they're about to leave. My bag, shoes, and other small items have been gathered into a haphazard pile. My manuscripts are there. I stand to say goodbye, hold and kiss the back of Susan's hand. She kisses me briefly on the mouth. It's not romantic, but an acknowledgment. I wonder if I should ask, "Do you remember me? From a fiction workshop at Brown?" but I decide against it. She and her assistant depart for their car to the hotel. In twilight, in a light breeze, I kneel to collect my things.

I was 21 when I cooked Vietnamese food for Susan. I didn't know she'd visited Vietnam during the war. She had traveled at the invitation of the North Vietnamese government in Hanoi. Why Vietnamese pork chops? Because I only knew how to prepare a few dishes, and this was a meal my mother sometimes made. I didn't know that years later I'd visit Vietnam with a delegation of psychologists. We toured a psychiatric hospital in Ho Chi Minh City, though we still thought of it as "Saigon." Rusting barred gates led to an outdoor courtyard where patients and their families sat all day, just sat. Young women with terrible ear-to-ear gashes still healing, sultry air, paint flaking off the metalwork. I played a counting game with a patient, my minimal Vietnamese meeting her better English. What must she and the others have made of us, or were they used to foreigners' intrusions, our inexplicable inability to converse coherently? Upstairs, we met with a group of psychiatrists, who were introduced, and other men who were not and said nothing, just watched us all. The doctors described psychiatry in Vietnam; we presented to them on post-traumatic stress disorder. When we asked if there were ways we could be helpful, they told us that they had a Russian ECT machine but it was broken; would we give them money to fix it? This was awkward because our current standard of practice was to use electroconvulsive therapy only for severe depressive disorders, but this hospital was using it for other diagnoses, such as schizophrenia. We demurred, saying that we would have to discuss it, but might be able to send additional personnel, postdocs to rotate through. Susan published "Trip to Hanoi" in *Esquire;* I published "Professional Travels and Ethical Travails: A Psychologist Abroad" in a specialized newsletter. It was concrete, an account of actions and some of my thoughts, not highly philosophical. I don't think Susan would have liked it. She didn't like the story I workshopped, which was about wrestling a drag queen in a

Jell-O pit. It was mostly autobiographical. The best detail was the realization that lime Jell-O stings when a drag queen has scratched up your arms and throat with her long, sharp nails.

We were just becoming scared. We didn't know much; he didn't know much; there wasn't yet much to know, or ways to know it. The big concern was still Hepatitis B. Frederic hadn't yet received the gift of a silver-colored pendant, oval, depicting an angel on one side. A kindly Christian guardian angel, with long hair, flowing robes, a beneficent expression. Not at all a Jewish angel, tangle of six flaming wings, too many supernova eyes glaring out. On the obverse was a quote from Psalm 91, promising that angels sent by God will hold you up so that you won't hurt your foot on a stone. Just before this, verse 10 of the psalm promises that no plague will come to your tent, but the pestilence was already in our camp.

Frederic had a beautiful singing voice. Sometimes I listen to recordings. When Susan visited, he was working as a singing, dancing, balloon bouquet delivery clown, taking a break between college and graduate school. At work he'd learned to curl extravagant falls of colored ribbon. Did Susan talk to him at all? He was so talented, so sparkly. He had spent a semester at Gallaudet, sometimes had to look at his hands to see what unvoiced thought his fingers were signing. In ASL or English, he was one of the most liquid conversationalists I have ever known.

While writing this essay, I devour Moser's 800-page biography of Susan, the two available volumes of her journals, several book reviews and essays, and her son's account of her final iatrogenic blood cancer and horrible death. I already know this essay will be called "Dinner with Susan Sontag." This will turn out to be one of those funny and eerie coincidences of naming. When she came to dinner, she hadn't yet written an essay subtitled "Tea with Thomas Mann," nor will I learn that it exists until months after I draft this piece as I search for information about the period in which she taught my workshop. Further, in the online catalogue of Brown's Rockefeller Library, I am startled and briefly dislocated when I discover the narrative "Your Dinner with Susan Sontag." "[Gustation] with Susan Sontag" is clearly an archetypal title. This "Your Dinner" reminiscence, by my then-classmate Joanna Scott, both raises questions and provides some corroboration. Joanna says that Susan had dinner with all of her students. I don't remember this. She writes that the workshop students referred to Susan as "the Duchess." I didn't ever hear or do this, but Joanna and others evidently did. Her description of the Armenian restaurant dinner she and two other students ate with Susan is comfortingly confirmatory. Susan holds forth while drinking wine. She dominates, name-drops, is expansive, orchestrates the discourse. Joanna remembers that they shared pistachios. Nice detail; evocative, sensual.

At dinner, Susan was talkative, somewhat abrasive, competitive. "How many books do you have?" she asked me. "About 2000?" I ventured. I have had more than one conversation with worried landlords who fear for their structures' load-bearing joists. "I have over 10,000," she responded, an edge of triumph in her voice. This might have been intimidating, but instead I felt defensive. I was 21, for God's sake. As an undergraduate just a year before, I had had a $10 a week allowance, with most of what I earned on campus going toward my tuition. My spare money went to books— okay, books and one pair of black leather pants—and I was in love with my library. And also, desire. I longed for Susan's 10,000 books, no matter which books they were. I still do. I assume she collected even more. I hope so.

I had experienced Susan's edginess before. At a party, after a poetry reading? By Marilyn Hacker? Which I remember as if it took place in our tiny living room, though it did not. I offered an opinion about George Bataille's *L'histoire de l'œil* or Pauline

Réage's *Histoire d'O*, some *histoire* about which Susan had written. I complimented one of her remarks. She criticized my praise, making a point about feminism and the pornographic gaze that I didn't absorb while I berated myself for sounding unsophisticated. From my current vantage, I don't disagree with her. I do wonder if her extensive amphetamine habit and much-remarked-on lack of empathy contributed to her general aura of aggressive superiority. Now, I could hold my own in that conversation, but now, I am older than Susan was that day, almost three times my own age then. Frederic died at 33.

Oh, no! Should I have served wine? Did I serve wine? I didn't write about the dinner in my journal, and Susan and Frederic are dead. I ought to have served wine. What's good with a sweet pork entrée? I hope I did. Let's just say I did. Who is left to contradict me?

Frederic and Susan held their proximate deaths that night, already clenched in their cells. Frederic deeply, privately feared that he had AIDS. It was the early 1980s, and his had been a joyous and extensive sexuality. We were young and rarely had reason to speak of illness.

Susan had been diagnosed with metastatic breast cancer about a decade before. She received a Halsted radical mastectomy, such a brutal procedure, had other lesions extirpated, more than two years of chemotherapy. Maybe my tumor was already with us, too. The next year, I would move to Israel for work and acquire tuberculosis, or at least a positive antibody response. Later, back in Rhode Island, living again with Frederic and before the Internet laid out its smorgasbord of excessive information, I was tested, quarantined, not allowed to visit the library to search a reference work. All I knew about tuberculosis was that Susan had contrasted its cultural meanings and representations with those of cancer in *Illness as Metaphor*, and that I would now go to a sanatorium to die, coughing up blood. Half a year of treatment stained my urine, sweat, and tears bright orange, transformed four thimblefuls of Passover wine into a violent Antabuse-like poison. I didn't know until recently that as an adolescent, Susan had been electrified by *The Magic Mountain,* had visited Thomas Mann and written her essay about that meeting. For his part Mann wrote of that day, "Afternoon interview with three Chicago students...." For mine, I noted, "Write about dinner with Susan Sontag." Later, of course, there was my own cancer efflorescence. Who can say if it was already imminent, unfurling tendrils in my breasts?

Susan's journals make me feel inadequate. I find at age 16 her comments about Lucretius. My journal at 16, randomly opened, invokes Talking Heads, a string of *"fa"*s, in my irregular hand, large, green.

I was supposed to graduate college in 1984, but I was ready to run off and be a lesbian more thoroughly, so I finished my high school requirements a year early, leaving for college at 17. Susan went at 16. Had we discussed this, I'm sure she would have pointed out that she was younger than I when she left home. Photos of me and my high school classmates appeared in a special edition of *LIFE* magazine focused on the college class of 1984, though, so I win that point. We all thought about Orwell then, but by 1984 I was free and chatting with Susan Sontag. Susan Sontag! In my living room with my best friend and my cat! Eating my mother's Vietnamese pork recipe! What was Susan's life in 1984? It seems she was teaching here and there. A commentator characterizes this period in her life as unproductive. She had already written *Illness as Metaphor,* but had not yet published *AIDS and Its Metaphors.* If we had talked about AIDS, would she have competed for most friends dead? Not an honor I would have coveted. In my city I saw bumper stickers that proclaimed: AIDS: IT'S KILLING ALL THE RIGHT PEOPLE.

While we ate, bright sunlight filtered through the luminous blue curtains Frederic had sewn. Gravity rolled around on a bare section of the wooden floor, catching the last glow, watching us with her emerald eyes. She was so gorgeous. It turns out that Susan didn't like cats. That would be a deal-breaker.

Susan asked me, "Have you been to Vietnam?" She didn't ask Frederic. I said I hadn't. By 1984, I had lived in Switzerland for a year as an infant, but had no memories except of green, and cows. I hadn't even been to Canada or Mexico. Things are different now. A few years later, Frederic and I drove to Canada one day, singing "Albatross" and "Farewell to Tarwathie." Frederic always cried when he sang "Albatross," gripping my right hand while I steered with my left, as shining metal-roofed churches flashed by.

Susan told me that the Vietnamese peasants cooked sticky rice on their backs while they worked their paddies and fields. Did she mean "in a pannier on their backs"? For decades I pictured a rice plaster on the sweaty shoulder of a deeply tanned, loincloth-wearing man, wet grains naked to the sun or loosely covered with a black-and-white checkered shawl. He wears a conical leaf hat, *nón lá*. Some have lines of poetry inside.

We had a lot in common—Jewish though not religious, lesbians (I more, she less), writers in mixed forms. We each had striking dyed hair, hers the distinctive black-with-white stripe, mine at the time a fierce hot pink, which looked fantastic against a background of lime Jell-O. We would have breast cancer. Her name in Hebrew would have been *Shoshana*. We were interested in metaphors, though she argued against them for obscuring reality, whatever that is, and I adore them for illuminating similarities and distinctions. We were interested in diseases, in AIDS, she writing critical theory and I writing a journal article about the meanings Frederic ascribed to the AIDS Memorial Quilt. We would seem to have had a lot to talk about, much pleasure to find in each other's company. We loved reading, travel. It's strange to have visited enough ossuaries to make comparisons: I admired the human bone chandeliers of the Capuchin Crypt on the Via Veneto, and finding St. Clementaine's remains in Brno was serendipitous. Susan was formidably attractive—a storyteller, a pontificator. She held the room. Her gestures raked the air. Her anecdotes were larded with rich adventures. It was my first apartment. She looked damn fine there. I'd have cooked her dinner again if she'd wanted, perhaps artichokes with drawn butter to lick off our fingers, something lush and sticky for dessert.

I'm usually not afraid to contemplate my death, at least abstractly, though I still think it's a very bad idea. I have moved from an abstraction to the present moment. Of Susan, her son writes, "She who could talk about anything could rarely really speak of death directly, though I believe that she thought about it constantly." I can't say what our conversation about mortality would have been in 1984, but now, as a psychologist who works with people with cancer, some days I talk about little else. Susan and I both experienced our breast cancer treatment through the imagery of the Vietnam War. I imagined the surgery as combat, slaughter, the severing of the body; chemotherapy as napalm, a wholesale destruction, Kim Phúc denuded and screaming on a South Vietnamese road; the targeted local search for enemies that is radiation, and of course, the nearby Nagasaki shadows. The allegory breaks down at tamoxifen, a selective estrogen reuptake modulator that is statistically my most effective treatment in the five years after mastectomy. It was developed the year that I was born. It wasn't available when Susan was treated, but I have no doubt she'd have taken it if offered. Susan and I both used *Harrison's Principles of Internal Medicine* as a home medical reference. Many of the illustrations still make me queasy.

I've seen *Alcedo atthis,* the Eurasian kingfisher, in Hanoi, fixed on slight movements below the clouded surface of Hồ Hoàn

Kiếm, tensed to cleave the waters of the Lake of the Returned Sword. I've seen the photos, Agent Orange, landmines, poisons and amputations, monks in flames, people already shot, still kneeling upright. I've see bodies dissected and preserved. They don't enchant me. I've read my own pathology report. It's a very good appetite suppressant.

At that time, the dominant postmodern writing stance was *the text is a woman's body, so chop her up, boys!* I enjoy the resecting and reorganizing of the story, but not the analogy of the dismembered female body. I struggled, tried to write reordered and reconstructed stories in which characters retained their interiority, had secrets, psychology, still inspired empathy. Susan's journals are filled with observations about her tendency to flatten and distance, punctuated by her recognition that her fiction was often abstract. She wrote that she wasn't oriented toward plot; instead, it seemed, she tried to create a mood. I would have liked to hear her elaborate on this, give examples from her work. Neither am I attached to plot, but I like to experience accrual, collage, image on image, irritants and pearls. Susan's fiction interests me, but I haven't felt engaged by most of it, not as much as her essays. She didn't care for what she saw of my short stories. Too linear? Too rooted in interaction? I don't suppose she would have liked my poetry. She might have liked this memoir, with its references and disjunctions, its discontinuous collage of description, observation, speculation.

I search archives, online indices, the tables of contents of special collections. I learn that two boxes of Susan's papers and journals may not be accessed until December 28th, 2029, 25 years from her date of death. I learn that there is a spiral notebook for 1984. What did she write about her time in Providence? A biography quotes her blunt, unflattering descriptions of her students at another university and their work at about that time: "pathetic... endless pedestrian ms." Would I want to know? Journals are rarely laudatory, so infrequently capture our admiration and respect.

I consider donating my papers, my postcards, my juvenilia, my journals. But why? Who would want them? So many sonnets copied out by hand with only the placement of a comma to differentiate the drafts. I don't want to be famous. I don't want to know important people. I don't want to set the style for my generation, the tone and color. I am not a head on a stick. I like being my body, even as it deconstructs itself.

When Susan discovered books, she approved of their neutral and objective nature. In my childhood and adolescence, books were the verso of this coin. When I first read Hans Zinsser's *Rats, Lice and History,* C. W. Ceram's *Gods, Graves and Scholars,* Thor Heyerdahl's *Aku-Aku,* I knew immediately that the authors' intentions were directed to me. Me! And I was only 7, 10, 15 years old. I knew how earnestly they hoped I would be fired with their passions, I saw the care they exercised to prompt my understanding. I was a citizen-scientist, not even junior. If I understood it, the book was meant for me. I learned about cuneiform on clay tablets, studied transliterations of ancient, sacred texts. Now I recognize more meanings: M-L-K, the consonants for my holy king. Jean-François Champollion, only 5 years old when he first began decoding! The utility of the cartouche. What a virgin is, what lives in a drop of pond water, details under magnification. Karl von Frisch's apian shivers and dances. Not Lucretius. A little Ovid, a little Catullus. Forbidden fiction and science from the restricted adult section of the library. What they all implied was *I love you.* What they all suggested was *I will wait for you.* Before I was even admitted to Swarthmore, Frederic and I met in a hallway there and quickly discovered our mutual obsession with bee communication, vectors for bubonic plague. This was when we found each other. I love and I hate. Sometimes he was a handful. Sometimes I am, too.

I dream about Frederic, not often. Usually we have an ordinary conversation, and I'm so glad to see him, to have the time together, knowing in my dream that he is dead. He died in spring, 10 years after our dinner with Susan. The petals of cherry blossoms floated across Boston Common, came to ground in drifts against the wall of Arlington Street Church. Whenever I read *AIDS and Its Metaphors,* I cry.

The pork was delicious. The secret is good fish sauce, *nước mắm nhỉ.* I had no idea I'd visit Vietnam several times, Cambodia, too, lecture at their universities, contribute to a travel guidebook, accompany my students to women's shelters, villages of banana trees and red clay roads, to learn about the effects of groundwater arsenic on children. After cancer, my fear of insect bites, heat, puffy extremities triggering lymphedema, and the threat of having to navigate emergency medicine in dictionary-dependent languages ended these excursions.

I dream that Susan Sontag claimed to have discovered the Higgs boson particle. An apologetic voice-over explains that this wasn't her own research, but a superficial pattern she said she'd noticed in other people's descriptions of their scientific work. She was going to report this finding, but first she and the fictional scientist had to determine who would be attending which party. She wanted to make her announcement without being in a room with the scientists who had conducted the work, and whom she disliked. The dream's protagonist is Susan; the magpie pattern recognition is mine.

In the labyrinth of indexing, Ariadne's golden thread unrolled through online meanders and sudden blind alleys, I pursue Susan to Sarajevo. As I investigate her Balkan visits, I encounter archival evidence of my anthropologist relatives. Were they all in the region simultaneously? Did they know each other? Sidetracked, I explore family mysteries. They take me no closer to Susan. Susan wrote of her trip to China that she wouldn't write exposition about her visit. Susan, I didn't stalk you, but I've been to China, too.

Soon after Frederic and I moved to Providence together, he picked up my soda and took a sip, set the can back on the table. It wasn't a symbol. It was a test. I drank the rest, aware of the sharp metal lip, the potential for blood-to-blood contact, weighing the risks of cola-transmitted disease. Even early in a pandemic, when we hadn't yet heard the up-to-the-minute warnings, I chose love over threat.

Susan's sparing journal comments about her cancers suggest not a disregard for metaphors, but a deep respect for the terror they may evoke. Fanciful language may breed goblins, *nomen est omen.* I, too, fear calling out their names and attributes. I, too, fear being eaten by myself.

Sticky rice is considered to be a good offering to the ancestors, but at that time I'd never put anything on an altar, lit a candle, said a prayer. Tiny bunched bananas and a pack of Marlboros smelled too much like offerings to foreign gods, like bowing down to gold-headed, clay-footed idols. *Oryza sativa, var. glutinosa.* Susan wrote of a friend's vision of the world that body parts might change into "demonic creatures." She had three cancers over time. Susan wins; mine were simultaneous and similar. She referred to her uterine cancer as "spiked 'like a sea creature,'" perhaps a sea urchin, as I came to think of my breast cancer as well, but I understood it as food for a shark, and I was the shark.

Susan, I have the advantage. I can read your journal but you can't read mine. I know what became of you; we do not know what will become of me. When she died, her son kissed her mastectomy scar. Annie Leibowitz photographed her dead. I can't believe that illness is only metaphor, or that metaphor is only illness. Susan wrote, "Whenever I travel, it's always to say goodbye." Today I cry for her death. It is the 27th anniversary of Frederic's. Susan, *odi, amo.* I miss you, in all your incarnations.

The wind blows Frederic's ashes east. I have to get upwind of it, west of it, not to be constantly gulping my sorrow. Next century, in Finisterre, I will open my breath to the currents above the ocean. Frederic used to comfort himself by repeating, "Nothing is lost," fingerspell it, too, right hand at his side, left hand holding mine. Driving to Montreal in a borrowed car, no radio. You take the Judy Collins part, I'll sing the humpback whales.

After one

After one, asleep.
My futon dips. He's come home,
redolent of men.

Being Jews

Rachel and I sit on the concrete steps of my apartment building. I talk for a long time about being a Jew, how I'm not really a Jew but a person of Jewish extraction, not theistic, not religious, not sharing certain important Jewish values. Sure, I'm Jewish-ish, but really more of a Buddhist, an atheist with a philosophical world view most similar to Buddhism, though without the demons and prayer flags of Tibet, more a Buddhist practice than beliefs, but with at least some Jewish perspectives—

Finally, Rachel responds. "It doesn't matter whether you think you're a Jew or not. When they come for the Jews, they'll come for you." Despite reading many Holocaust memoirs as a child, I hadn't quite put that together.

When he took a job at the Board of Education, my father was praised as the first person of his race to ascend so high in the county school system. Board meetings began with a prayer and invocation of Jesus. When they come for the Jews, they'll know to come for you.

VERBS OF MUTUAL RELATIONSHIP

Five airports

I'm dating Zahava. Sort of. But she says she's not the woman for me, she's Israeli and she's going back to Israel. Rachel had said the same: She'll return to the Land, go up to the Land, ascend, elevate, perhaps become a citizen, make *aliyah*.

Rachel sends me a small classified ad from *The New York Times,* teachers wanted at a school in Israel. I apply. I interview. I get an offer. I haven't been out of the U.S. since I was a year old and my parents taught in Switzerland. I take the job. This proves to be an efficient way to end my relationship with Zahava. I will learn over time that following people to other countries is not an effective dating strategy.

The school in Israel tells me to arrange the cheapest flight I can. At the student travel service near Brown, I book a 23-hour transit on Tarom, the Romanian airline. I've never heard of it. It stops in Bucharest. Nicolae Ceaușescu is head of state. I don't know who he is, what we will later learn about AIDS and the fate of Romanian orphans. When I arrive at the school in Israel and submit my receipt for reimbursement, they are horrified. "No, we didn't mean *that* cheap!"

I move out of the apartment Frederic and I share. He keeps Gravity, of course. I will be floating. I store everything in my old bedroom at my parents' house, construct a ziggurat primarily composed of boxed books. I ship several bags of clothes, books for teaching, and household items to myself. I pack two large suitcases with my immediate necessities. Now I travel lighter, but I didn't yet know what I needed, how to equip myself. I didn't quite know that I could buy a frying pan, a spiral notebook, a toothbrush when I arrived.

Paula had spent a summer in Romania between college terms. I tell her that I'll have a layover at Bucharest Otopeni International Airport. "Ah," she says. "Be sure to take a handkerchief." She doesn't say why, but I pack a bandana in my carry-on.

I must have left from Friendship International, south of Baltimore, but I don't remember it. Too many subsequent flights have blurred the memory, thin phyllo tissues of familiar gates and sometimes a waft of Old Bay Seasoning in a restaurant where the waitresses call me "Hon." By 1985 it had been renamed, but it is still "Friendship" to me.

The voyage to Switzerland was on Holland America Line, the S.S. Statendam. The return a year later was on the Rotterdam. I have one vague memory from the second trip. I've flown twice, once as a child, once as a college student. I've never flown through JFK before. It's intimidatingly large, but I feel expansive, cautiously at ease. I might like airports, their purpose, determination, motion, optimism. I eat a bad, expensive cheeseburger. I board my flight.

The stewardesses are grim, almost silent, the passengers contained, subdued. As the sky darkens into night, I lose my view of the grey Atlantic, nothing but waves, a vertiginous descent. I sleep. Thump. I awaken. We have landed in a driving rain. Uniformed men storm the plane. They shout at us, *Achtung! Schnell, schnell!* Off the plane quickly! You—left! You—right! We clang down slippery metal stairs in a frigid deluge. Exhausted and alarmed, I wonder if they're herding the Jews into cattle cars. Which is the better direction? To the death camp, or just get it over with? Buses whisk us across the apron to a terminal. A man in an official-looking jacket grabs my ticket, peers at the rain-smeared red print, and says to me, "Be back at this gate in an hour and thirty minutes" before stalking off. Then I am alone in an airport. Evidently this is not Romania. Has there been a mistake? I am drenched and shivering. I inch around the terminal, looking for a restroom. I don't know where I am. I don't want to get lost in the maze. Store windows sparkle and glitter, coruscate, throw tiny disorienting rainbows dancing on the walls, refracted from.... Crystal. Austrian crystal? Though it did not appear on my itinerary or in my ticket booklet, we have a layover in the Vienna *Flughafen.* I hover close to my gate until we reboard, afraid I'm too tired to remember its unscribed number.

We continue to Bucharest, a shorter hop. As we descend, I see tanks by the runways. We bump down and taxi to the gate. The pavement is cracked, weeds nibbling at the edges. I enter the terminal, passing truculent armed soldiers. The terminal is really just one large chamber, no currency exchange, little to eat or do. I find the restroom but have no money. I'm not sure if this means I can use the toilet but don't get a square of paper, or if I'm not allowed in at all. The toilet paper *babushka* and I regard each other. I am mystified; she remains inexplicable. I return to the main area and find a seat. I will need to wait several hours until I'm on the next plane, but I have no other options. I hear soft cooing and look up. Pigeons are clustered on the overhead support struts. I open my bag, take out my bandana, and drape it over my head. Now I am a babushka, too, a babushka with a babushka, a thin blue *shmatte* between me and the birds.

Another taciturn boarding. We cram into an unnervingly decrepit plane. Everyone is tense. As we loft and the landing gear folds in, the exit sign at the front of the cabin falls off the wall. The stewardesses leap up before we are even level. They move to the galleys. Suddenly it's a party! The passengers clap enthusiastically and the cabin crew are all smiles. They pass through the aisles with large wicker baskets of fresh fruit.

Everyone gets a glass goblet, which they fill liberally with clear spirits, plum brandy? Our next stop is Tel Aviv!

At Ben Gurion, there are also tanks, also armed soldiers. But here, as we walk toward the security screening, the soldiers smile.

Flora

No one told me Israel had palm trees. It makes sense, I just never considered it. That summer I live in Jerusalem, center of the celestial map, omphalos of the universe.

"I'm sorry," my Israeli wife would say

"I'm sorry," my Israeli wife would say, solicitously smoothing the sheet of crumpled paper with its jumble of claws and ants, "it hasn't been translated into your language."

"Tell me about it," I begged on more than one occasion. "Just give me the gist."

"It—" she waved her hand, shrugged, seemingly helplessly, but was it with a touch of pride? "It's untranslatable."

Postcards and aerograms

The landscape looks just like the postcards. There are green and brown trees, but it's amazing how close the desert is. I look at the next hill and it's dun and white, little Arab houses clustered together. The cities are an admixture of developing and developed. Palestinian men smoke tobacco beneath a plastic sign, *Hadash! Qoqa-Qola Diet,* New! Diet Coke! Everyone carries groceries in sacks or plastic baskets, orange, yellow, and purple. No Kraft paper bags. To my eye everything is slightly dirty, but that's my ethnocentrism. The people are very nice, beautiful, and the cottage cheese tastes nothing like U.S. cottage cheese. The *New York Times* Sunday crossword puzzle appears in the Friday *Jerusalem Post.*

The adjustment isn't bad, though I'm lonely despite the number of people in the flat. Two of us taking over the lease, two in and two out. No one has enough room or time, either alone or with others. Rachel and I think part of the problem is that we are all waiting to start work or school, but not yet working or studying, and living in vacation mode when none of us are really on vacation, nor would we choose to live like this if we were. Avimelech finishes his army reserve duty, moves into the flat; I learn my way around enough not to need an escort to point me to the correct bus.

A strange and pragmatic place. Soldiers everywhere, more reassuring than threatening. Conical hayricks of submachine guns, harvested black stalks in the vestibule of the cinema. I've already been on one bus with a suspicious object and have learned to say "Bomb!" in Hebrew. Unattended bags are illegal and the bookstore at Hebrew University of Jerusalem on *Har HaTzofim* requires two security checks to enter. The tomatoes in the market this morning were so beautiful that I bought three, even though I didn't want to eat them. Refrigeration isn't terrific; we shop every few days. Israelis consume an amazing amount of yogurt, milk, and cottage cheese. I don't know if this is true for Arabs.

Since arrival, no one has mistaken me for a boy. Is this physiological? Do Jews know what Jewish genders look like? Or maybe I lack the external cues for Israeli masculinity—yarmulke, sideburns, *tzitzit,* black suit, beard? In the U.S., you are male if not marked female. In the U.S., the unknown if mysterious is female, if threatening is male. But here I'm not threatening, not a maybe-male, not a darker assertive stranger but a normally complected person in this setting, one who doesn't yet speak the language.

In your sleep

They told me (I was told)
that in sleep your face would smooth
and soften, liquefy, show
me the level of the land.
In darkness,
light on still water.

We followed each other here.
Each stayed and saw the city on her own.
The desert you see is finite.
The sky I see is ended.
Now what do you want from me?

Black flies that do not glitter
squat on the glittering
olives in the trough.

Our separation

She is trying hard to experience something and she is bewildered by its elusive presence and absence.

I am experiencing nothing and am bewildered by its absence and presence.

Together we are mystified by opposites. In this mystery, we discern our separation.

Walking in Jerusalem

There are so many places to walk in Jerusalem. The Via Dolorosa, Stations of the Cross, through the narrow and crowded mercantile ways, the business of the city's quarters only rippled by passing pilgrims. The Church of the Holy Sepulchre with its easily anticipated winding queues to visit the tomb. To the *Kotel,* the Western Wall, the Wailing Wall, abutting the broad plaza where a woman in an alarmingly flimsy carmine dress and heels stalks rapidly from the direction of Al-Wadi Street, whipping on a broad white shawl that covers her from the top of her head to below her knees as she strides, fetching up on the women's side of the Wall to *daven.* Up the ramp, through the security checkpoint at the Mughrabi Gate, and into the Temple Mount area to appreciate but not enter Al-Aqsa Mosque and the gorgeous geometrics of the Dome of the Rock, blue, yellow, white, green. I admire the use of written language as a decorative element, unable to read the flowing script even alphabetically. Back down to the city, exploring the Armenian Quarter, green ceramic work everywhere. The Roman Cardo Maximus excavations, right where the mosaic Madaba Map said it was, near Jaffa Gate, four meters below the contemporary surface of the city.

> I feel nothing at
> all, Western Wall, don't daven.
> Sun strikes sun-struck rocks.

A bus to Yad Vashem, monument and name, the Holocaust memorial. Trees for the Righteous among the Nations. None of my family's more distinctive surnames appear in the database of victims, despite my attempts to use phonetic and approximate spellings. The more common names, the color surnames imposed on the Jews, are too numerous to sort, all the linguistic variants, black, green, red. A general strike is called. There is no bus. Another walk, the long and hot way home.

No Hebrew education

Ah! ZVV is *zivuv,* fly; ba'al is lord, so Ba'al Zivuv is Beelzebub, is Lord of the Flies! I would already know this if I'd had any Hebrew education.

A letter to my great-aunt

I don't mean to give you the impression that I want to practice Judaism. Any time I'm drawn to *any* religion, no matter how appealing, I run into the problem of my atheism, which at its most religious shades at times into an extremely shallow agnosticism. Celebration I understand. Worship I don't. Rules and social contracts, and the appeal of ritual, yes. Belief in a higher intelligence dispensing forgiveness, no. Perhaps I read comparative mythological studies at a crucial time in my development, and perhaps I take too psychological a view of the whole thing. To me, to desire to believe in deity is weird— I already *have* a mother and father, and I've internalized *their* rules and expectations quite nicely without dragging God into it. While I sometimes think it would be very reassuring, as well as compensatory, to believe in God, I am more bewildered by others' belief than concerned by my lack of it.

I am nervous in synagogues. I think this anxiety derives from having only a partial knowledge of Judaism's intentions and rites, and that with or without having been brought up with that specific indoctrination, I am still more a Jew than anything else. My values and morals and methods are more Jewish than Christian, and I am curious to explore that. When I say "Jewish," how much of what I mean is "Diaspora Jewish" and how much reflects the majority of Jewry? I have very little concern about whether there continue to be Jews. I can understand dying to defend a way of life or an ethical code. I can't understand dying because you believe God is One, because I don't believe God is anything. I don't feel like *my* choice is the essential feature here, though, because I don't think Jews have a true choice to assimilate versus the external mandate and pressure to do so.

I think of myself as "American" before "Jewish." I can't say what religious observance I'd be engaged in under other circumstances or at another time, but I realize that the

Holocaust keeps me from assimilation and forces me to examine my relationship to Judaism. The problem is not that I am opposed to Judaism but that I resent this very present reminder that assimilation can be rendered moot by stirring up a mob. I sometimes long for a relationship with Judaism that I suspect cannot exist for an atheistic feminist, a kind of emotional engagement with Judaism that would explain or ameliorate the effects of this external hatred of the Jews. But what there is is silence. Silence about Judaism, silence about family history. A tremendous silence about American Judaism, so much so that I know more about what goes on in synagogue than I know what B'nai Brith does. I know when our family came to America—that's about all I know of my family tree. I'm not even sure I could produce documentation for an orthodox rabbi in Israel to show that I am indeed Jewish, of Jewish descent, for at least four generations back.

I'm realistic enough to know that I wouldn't last long in a concentration camp. I'm strong and adaptable but I get respiratory infections easily. I have no idea who stayed in Europe and Russia and who died there. I know nothing about what impelled our family to come to America, or whether I have relatives in Israel. I saw an appliance store or factory in Tel Aviv called "קירוסקאי." If that's not "Kerewsky," it's pretty close, but I can't even go in there and ask if there's a Kerewsky to go with the sign, because I have no idea how we might be related. I live in a flat with *mezuzot* in each door frame. Because I read something in a novel, I know there is a strip of paper inside, and I might recall what is written on it. By observation, I know they're always to the right of the door. But do I know what to do with them? Do I touch them? Are women allowed to? Am I supposed to say anything? I have no idea. Perhaps I don't want to do any of these things, but I want to know, and I want to have a choice. Secular as I am, reading is the only way to find out, because to learn from people quickly slides into religious indoctrination, as I discovered this summer when I tried to study *siddur* and instead got instruction in prayers I must say and an injunction to rush home and say them. If I'm to be treated as a Jew, I would like to have this knowledge, because even the non-religious Jewish community assumes I comprehend.

It's certainly not the emotional struggle many of my religious friends engage in, but I'd like to find my relationship to the community of Jews. I don't want to be a religious Jew, but I want to understand the generation of ideas: Okay, you put a *mezuzah* on the right side of a doorway. *So what constitutes a doorway? That* interests me. *Mishna* and *Gemara* interest me but until about a year ago, I didn't know they existed. When I walk into a synagogue, I don't even know what to call the guy who's reading from the Torah. I'm not so concerned about the Torah; I'm concerned about his relationship to it.

I'm not sorry I was raised without religion, but I do wish more of the history and culture that formed my personality had been explicitly available to me. I have the end results without much awareness of where those values and ideals come from, and this isolates me.

An unintended pilgrimage

I sat in the common kitchen of the Benedictine monastery at the Church of the Heptapegon, where Jesus multiplied fishes and loaves, with no keys to my flat, my right hand swaddled in gauze and Betadine to protect the five tidy stitches holding the edges of the knife wound together.

After work on Friday, *erev Shabbat,* I jumped into a *sherut,* a multi-passenger taxi, from Tel Aviv to Tiveriya on the Kinneret, the Sea of Galilee. The other passengers were Arabs, all men. They were pleasant and respectful. None spoke English; the passenger in the front spoke about as much Hebrew as I do. He asked me to tell a story to pass the time. Who would turn down an invitation to be Scheherazade in a taxi? I had just read a short story translated from Arabic to English about a blind reciter of the Qur'an. I begin to tell the story in aleph-level Hebrew, present indicative, much pantomiming. This reciter was a second husband who recognized his wife by feeling her wedding ring. I hold up my hand and grope at my ring. This needs no translation. We go back and forth through the story, Hebrew, Arabic, gesture, occasional question interjected: Arabic, Hebrew, gesture. I remember too late that the story is about infidelity, with ring switcheroo activities that result in step-incest and might be offensive or provocative, but the men are engaged and animated, working hard to discuss the implications as we progress. Did the man know his daughters weren't his wife? Surely he must have—it's ridiculous to think he only knew his wife by her ring. By acceding to the deception, was he complicit in the crime, a witting partner to the infidelity? Was he now unholy, or did his sensitivity in not confronting his wife amount to an exquisite sacrifice on his part? Is the silence that hangs over these acts an analog to his blindness? Is his blindness really blindness, or does it symbolize a different way of perceiving? We entertained ourselves all the way to

Tiveriya. In English the town is Tiberias. While Jesus still lived, it was named for the Emperor Tiberius, not a pleasant person, possibly syphilitic, definitely sadistic, the "T." of Captain James T. Kirk, commander of the U.S.S. Enterprise.

Rachel and Tanya met me at the *sherut* stand and we ambled to the youth hostel to drop our bags. We ate at an outdoor café, where we were hassled by every man passing by on the coastal road. Could we sit in peace for even a minute or two? We returned to the hostel hostile.

Saturday is Shabbat. Nothing is open and no buses run. We hitchhiked northwest around the lake to Ein Gev, a *kibbutz* with what turned out to be a very pleasant beach. We rode with two soldiers past fields of bananas and cotton, the Golan Heights an outrageous, too-big and too-close backdrop to the east. The soldiers warned us about "men who do bad things to women." Some holy land. Even a blind man would know the score. We walked several kilometers along the road until we reached the kibbutz and its beach.

We swam and played, watched the sun set behind the mountains across the Kinneret. Then we hitchhiked back to Tiberias with some *kibbutzniks* from a different kibbutz, and descended to town for pizza, champagne, and apricot popsicles. Drunk and silly, we sat outside a restaurant called "Fish on the Roof" and listened to an embarrassingly poor singer. We stumbled up the hill, collapsed in our beds, and slept until daylight.

In the morning we bought provisions for the day. Rachel and I drank *kaffei hafukh*, "upside-down" coffee with foamed hot milk on top. Hopping on the bus to the mystical city of Sefat (Safed, Sapph, Zephat, Sfad), we soon came to the Capernaum junction. We walked down dusty agricultural roads, stopping at the Church of the Heptapegon to see the mosaics. In early Christian art, Orpheus is a cipher for Jesus, hides him in plain sight, loses Eurydice in the analogy. In mosaics of Orpheus, animals and birds gather to hear him play his cithara. Peacocks, loaves and fishes, cormorant, snakes, lotus, oleander, a heron spearing a snake, ducks, mongoose, quail holding a ribbon, orange and cream waves, mosaic meanders, a Nilometer. We admire the church built around Mensa Dei, the rock where Jesus ate with his disciples.

We continued our walk toward Capernaum, a city where Jesus did some of his major agitating. It was lovely in its tumbled disarray, Corinthian capitals strewn over the ground, a partially reconstructed synagogue, carved posts with flowers, *Magen Davids,* geometric designs. We decided to continue walking, find a beach, and eat and swim. Many beaches on the Sea of Galilee are rocky, with nowhere good to sit. We kept walking, passing a Greek Orthodox monastery, bright clay-red roof-domes topped with crosses, astonishingly beautiful against the misty blue Kinneret and the yellow-grey Heights across the water.

We finally found a beach with easier access to the lake, where the only people we could see were two Bedouin boys herding sheep and goats. We swam in the Sea of Galilee. We sat on the rocks, careful to avoid sheep and goat droppings, pulled out our apples and Swiss Army knives. On my second cut, my apple split completely in half and my blade slashed directly into my palm, just between the pad of the thumb and my lifeline. I said to my friends, "This is a bad injury," and applied pressure with a dishtowel, holding my hand over my head. I did eat the piece of apple I'd cut, which Rachel fed me, no need to waste it. She helped me pull my clothes on over my bathing suit. We clambered up the rocks to a field where a man and a woman with a car sunbathed and refused to drive us to the monastery for aid. Burdened with food, sleeping bags, and knapsacks, not to mention a stigma that bled when my hand moved, and which was turning blue and squashy around the edges, we crossed black rock fences and fields of dried briars and nettles to the Greek Orthodox property. No one answered as we banged on the gate shouting, "Help us! Someone is hurt! We need medical attention!" in Hebrew, English, and French. Inside the wall, a distant man saw us, paused, and vanished.

We resumed what was becoming a Kafkaesque journey. Regaining the road, we flagged a man sitting in a car full of military gear. We decided later that he had pulled over in order to hallucinate more effectively. He agreed to return us to Capernaum. He wouldn't pull his handbrake and his car ran over the strap of my pack. I had to throw my weight against the rear bumper to roll his car. When he dropped us at Capernaum he drove off, unintentionally, we decided, with the net bag holding almost all of our food, two of our knives, and the key to my flat.

We approached one of the Christian tour buses in the parking lot to ask if they had a first aid kit. I was increasingly concerned to get some antiseptic into the cut, which was beginning to throb in the awful way of deep gashes. Yes, someone was medical on the Morning Star Christian Tour bus, and he swabbed some alcohol into my palm, improvised a butterfly bandage, and wrapped my hand in gauze. The tour leader offered us a ride to the Capernaum youth hostel, which was reputed to have eucalyptus trees and peacocks. First, though, we would stop at the Mount of Beatitudes. Tour guide: "You see how unspoiled and beautiful it is here? Pilgrims, ready your cameras. It's because this site is too important to too many people to let it be anything else. Where He walked here always looks like it did two thousand years ago." Everyone piled out of the bus and took photos. One of the guides orated the Sermon on the Mount, then people walked around the site. We got back on the bus. I was still holding my hand over my head. A man worked on Tanya, trying hard to convince her to accept a tape of religious music. It was a refreshing change from offers of fucking.

The tour bus finally pulled up at the Church of the Heptapegon, where Jesus hailed St. Big Jacob and his brother John from the shore. I wanted a second opinion on my laceration, and possibly a telephone to call a taxi so I could get to a clinic. Someone led me past the "private" signs into a parklike back yard, where a shirtless doctor guest admired the makeshift butterfly bandage, examined my wound, pronounced that it did indeed need stitches. "Too bad I don't have my kit with me or I'd do it right here." He escorted me inside and made a call to a doctor friend. In Hebrew and Arabic, he told the doctor that there was a little problem here, a young woman had cut herself, not really badly but it needed stitches right away, and she was worried because she didn't have her teacher's insurance card or much money with her. Would he take care of it as a favor? They chatted a little, then Father Wolfgang arrived and handed me a note for the doctor and bottle of wine. He called a taxi and rode with us to an army field hospital, saying he would visit a friend and pointing us to the surgery. He instructed me that the doctor was Russian so I should give him the wine.

In the grungy reception area, two nurses snatched the note from Rachel's hand. "Brusque" would be putting it mildly. One yanked at the bandage, trying to force it off rather than untie it. I jerked away and unwrapped it myself. They poked the wound, which began to bleed again. Gesturing me to a tiny cubicle, they ordered "Sit!" I sat. "Open!" I opened my hand. The other nurse poured Betadine into a plastic emesis basin and pushed my hand in. I kept up a steady monologue in present tense Hebrew: "Ah! Well, I feel that! It hurts but I want it because it is good for me. Oh, yes, I feel this in my hand! It is not pleasant!" In came the Russian doctor. I handed him the bottle of wine. "Lie down!" barked the nurse. I did, and flexed my fingers on command. "Little injecta!" cried the doctor, poking into my hand while I babbled, "Oh, I am scared! Ow! I feel that!" The Novocain made a nauseating little hillock under my skin.

The suturing hurt less than I expected. I watched the last two of five stitches. "Five for a girl to look attractive, only three for a boy," the doctor commented. I remarked, "Oh! What an interesting sensation! My knife is very good. See," I continued, "how my hand looks like a cat's belly after you keep her from making baby cats!" Rachel asked the doctor why he didn't use a more attractive thread color, but we all agreed that black was becoming against my skin. As the doctor prepared to depart, I asked if he was from Russia and said, *"Spacebo,"* He asked, "You speak Russian?" and I replied apologetically with the only Russian I could remember from my high school textbook: "Attention! Attention! I have an extra sleeping bag. The flight for Leningrad leaves in 10 minutes! I am your stewardess, Beverley." Okay, "Natasha." I am sure he treated me better on account of this display of linguistic prowess.

With Father Wolfgang, we returned to the church by taxi. "You must stay the night. You cannot camp like this." After some discussion, the offer was extended to Rachel and Tanya as well. We put down our bags and went to dinner, chiefly yogurt and bread. We eyed each other as nuns shouted *"Achtung!"* and other commands in German, which hasn't always ended well for the Jews. Intimidated, we ate in silence.

As we prepared to bed down at the monastery, a tall Nordic woman approached us and carefully explained, "You are safe here, except under the trees here, sometimes the branches fall down. Also, there is a kind of snake, but not a snake, but it is very poisonous, but it is okay. The priests have a serum, well, no they don't, they have a kind of rock and they cut you and put a stone on it, and take you to the hospital, so is okay. Good night!" She left, though Rachel cried, "Wait! What?!" Despite the warning, no snakes or rocks disturbed our sleep.

The next day we returned to the Mount of Beatitudes. It was peaceful. My hand throbbed. We watched mist over the Sea of Galilee. Our plan was to bus to Jerusalem that night, then return to Tel Aviv. There was no late bus from Tiberias; not safe enough to travel through the West Bank at night. Another youth hostel.

Arising early in the humid heat, we succeeded in finding a bus. What a desert! I was fascinated despite my motion sickness from the swift, abrupt driving. Hills crumbled, hills worn so smooth it seemed impossible for them to erode further, grey and yellow and white, folds and laborious twists, all sides pressing in too close to the road, the road itself an intrusion loomed over by cracking boulders and sand. Deserted communities, seeing right through the houses because the windows were just holes. Heaps of brick and stones, an occasional small group of Bedouins with tattered black tents that made me wonder what constitutes reasonable shelter or a "dwelling," goats at impossible angles in niches, on shelves of rock. To the left, mountains and the Jordanian border. Patches of crops here and there, each vegetable poking through a plastic mulch strip, shreds of plastic from the previous crop clinging tenaciously to the dry, furrowed earth.

Back to Jerusalem since I was keyless, cashless, so heading to my place in Ramat Aviv would do me no good. I called my landlord, let his wife know I'd need help opening my flat the next day after work.

I took a bus from Jerusalem directly to work the next morning. When the school bus dropped me at home in the late afternoon, there was no landlord. With my one phone token, I called. His wife screamed at me in Hebrew, having misunderstood when I would arrive. I cried. I yelled back in Hebrew. My vocabulary was definitely improving. As I sniveled on the public telephone, a man rode by on his bicycle and blew a leering kiss, so I kicked his rear tire as hard as I could. He wobbled but didn't crash. Probably just as well. I walked to a coworker's flat. She gave me a towel for a shower and fed me dinner. Her husband drove me to my landlord's to get the new key.

My stitches itched. I was supposed to have them removed by a doctor in a week or so, but I had no doctor and I had no money, so I pulled them myself with a pair of boiled nail clippers and my teeth. I was learning how to function in the world.

Mene, mene

I am a woman without shekels
without love for you
with a mouthful of words

mene, mene

another land's words
nowhere to spit them out
to see them flower

I look the other way

Frederic *Motek Habibi,*

I was just thinking how nice it would be to have a baby or two and live on a kibbutz and keep a kosher home, but then there was a great flash of light and Jesus appeared and there was a tremendous battle between ~~the sun and moon~~ ~~Arthur and Mordred~~ good and evil. You'll have to discern which won.

Azure sky, white and yellow stone. Golden stone, Jerusalem Stone. The line between cultivated areas and desert is alarming. From the university I can see Jerusalem, green, yellow, blue. Walking across the road I look the other way and see as far as Jordan, maybe, on a clear day. Dust and yellow, chalky, yellow-grey sky.

It's hot, it's Shabbat. No way to go, nowhere to go. Lorca, O'Hara; I miss their green and blue.

Jumped in Jerusalem

Zahava arrives from the U.S. With Rachel, we take a Palestinian bus to the Mount of Olives. We walk through the old Jewish cemetery, so pebbled we cannot tell which of the graves have been visited by people and which are visited by the wind. We sit on a gravelly slope and watch the sun set over Jerusalem, the Dome of the Rock a brighter gold and blue, ornate against glowing yellow stone. We walk slowly toward the Jaffa Gate, the long way past Gethsemane, follow the road toward the Dung Gate. Near a blocky section of old stone wall, perhaps of the City of David, we stop to look at an excavation. As we resume walking, someone grabs me from behind in a bear hug. This is a show of force. Stay steady, don't give ground. I yell, step backward, drop my weight and smash out with both arms. My follow-through is weak but it surprises him into letting go. I wheel on him and advance shouting, fists raised, Zahava running up beside and passing me, shouting as well, multilingual rage. Two men, one with hands held up placatingly, "He was joking!" but as Zahava, who is formidable, advances, he turns and runs after the first, the one who grabbed me, both jumping into a *wadi* and vanishing into the Kidron Valley.

We look at each other. We continue walking. Does it count as a mugging if you break free, break into a torrent of abusive Arabic and Hebrew? Feeling that aftershock of vulnerability, though I was satisfied with the outcome. On the walk home, Zahava teaches me how to shout, "Don't touch me!" in idiomatically correct local Arabic.

Postcard to Frederic

About the assault: No, you have to write your fantasy narrative of it first before I will tell it to you. Maybe I will like your story better and will never tell you, but you'll have to take that chance. Here is a bit of dialogue to spice it up:

Zahava: "I still wish they would have stuck around so we could have killed them a little bit."

Navigating by the stars

Cassiopeia seems too close to the horizon. Should I be looking for different constellations? It's all still circumpolar, isn't it? How will I tell sidereal time when I'm lost in the Negev? Do I remember how to determine the plane of the ecliptic?

Verbs of mutual relationship

In Hebrew class today we learned about Martina Navratilova, who is a *lesbit.* This was mentioned in order to teach us about verbs of mutual relationship in the feminine plural, "They [female] marry each other."

SHOSHANA D. KEREWSKY

We kiss like wasps

We kiss like wasps on fruit
our mouths are never without buzzing

You are here

There you are
six years ago
looking at your
passport photo

In the Old City

I sip Turkish coffee near the Damascus Gate. "You want a nice pigeon or bunny rabbit for eat later perhaps?" The stones are too hot to sit on. I have a lunch date in an hour at the intersection of El-Wad and the Via Dolorosa. Dust, spices. Hot stone and hot wool. A group of Spanish pilgrims, one carrying a gigantic wooden cross over his shoulder, the bottom dragging on the street as merchants shout in Arabic for room to bring donkeys and carts of fresh stacked pitas through the narrow ways, through the *suq,* swaying brass vessels and colorful sheer gauze dresses billowing close to either side. I point to a huge burlap sack of pistachios, receive my small plastic bag. "How do I say it in Arabic?" "*You* don't say it," says the Palestinian pistachio merchant. "You just point."

Outside Sultan's Pool: If you want specifics—a fragment of blue-glazed ceramic, a milky opal shot with pink, mint leaves not more than 2.5 centimeters from stem to tip—I can find these, too.

History is fuzzy, geography a palimpsest of visions—yes, here is the True Cross, a handful of nails, on this exact spot, build the Church to which pilgrimage has brought me. I am looking at the wall of the Old City of Jerusalem from Wadi er-Rababi, Henom, Gehenna, the valley of the shadow of death, where Rachel reports it is thought children were sacrificed by means of an infernal mechanical idol to Baal, a Caananite Semitic god incorporated into Israelite Semitic monotheism as "Lord." As, any number of child sacrifices across the region and the inland sea. Firstborn sons, boys dancing in the oven? This kind of oven? Or maybe Moloch, M-L-K, that bull-headed god, both king and sacrifice. Or I Am That I Am, the tetragrammaton storm god who won; though there are no other gods—say, the manifestation that ate up all the others, burping out more attributes and names. These are contentious topics. Perhaps we *should* fear evil despite the psalmic attestation to the contrary. Vision is so easily contained and is so little of what can be discerned. Flat vistas, unencumbered except by the occasional structure, a distant blue.

"Allo, Lady, how you are, excuse, welcome, allo-o.... Bitch!"

Night is full of moths and bats and glass on glass. I pimp the city, show you her dressed stone blocks, dolomite, limestone, *maleke* at the Wall, crumbled passageways, beneath. I show you the gates we have no keys for, layers and underlayers too inaccessible to describe. I cannot show you the city unclothed. I cannot say she adorns herself in one style to the exclusion of others. There are no statues of the aniconic God. Nothing to topple or smash.

The city swallows her tongue and it

The moon defines the hills and balustrades by her absence and reappearance, easing into black almost green velvet. The moon is fuller than full, inedible salmon. The moon is nearer the city than strictly necessary. The moon is a satellite to many small villages as well. We are not given to despair.

I admit that nothing much is crumpled on the lip of darkness. I refuse your entreaties. There is little stillness between breezes. Now the grasses fumble and sway.

Cinnamon might have twisted in a powdery cloud several hours prior to the encounter. There should be nothing overhead, but stringy blackness cuts the moon. *Hoshek,* darkness, *yareach,* moon. As more details become available, you will be notified. We are waiting for a formal invitation. We must stand on flat stones and ceremony. Fainting on the foothills. Hebrew behind me, digging like fingers into a day-old bruise.

Here a woman must always be deeply involved in something significant but of complete disinterest to the men who observe. I am sick of people. I am sick of the moon and stars. I gave thousands of shekels to beggars today. We walked among excavations under yellow-blue haze. Too bad there's no smog so we could say, *Too bad there's smog.* Glaring white buildings, earth newly turned, dirt-sweet, faintly nauseating. I wanted to stay there in the cool reconstructed rooms, under the seen level of the city, down in the tel.

One of the functions of the Messiah is that he not show up.

Shabbat

I illustrate an incomplete Tarot deck: I of Walls: Possessions. The Suit of Arbitrary Signifiers. V of Systems: Gradations of grey in a thunderburst over the Kotel. VIII of Transgressions: Feet on the Pillow.

The single Shabbat candle I lit (and blessed, I note) sways and loses its black smoke, a net scarf. Glutinous soup foams and shrugs in a battered aluminum pan. Chopped parsley limp in the gold glass bowl, its cut stalks, its crushed leaves a darker, wetter green.

In East Jerusalem, we eat in a restaurant called Philadelphia. We walk to the suq for dessert, back though the Jaffa Gate and home via Derech Beit-Lechem, Way of the House of Bread, the House of Meat.

The landscape itself is abrupt; vistas change with no transition to the next one. So there's desert and stone and sun and Bedouins with goats for hours. Go around the hill and there's Jerusalem.

Titsy the Wonder God

Whenever I hear the god name *El Shaddai,* I think "Titsy the Wonder God." It's a more or less literal translation. At least this being of gendered expression or syncretic appropriation doesn't seem to have hurled children into the flames.

It's hot in Jerusalem. I don't know how hot. For much here, I have no index: The temperature, my weight, cooking measures, today's exchange on the dollar. I'm learning to live with approximations. For Israelis, to compromise, admit fear or uncertainty, show vulnerability, is to lose. Yet they will invite a stranger to dinner.

I've been attending Friday night services at an Orthodox synagogue near our flat. It's a game to try to follow the prayers and psalms in Hebrew. It's noisy; everyone rocks, reads aloud, stands and sits according to ritual, but not in unison. It's formulaic but individually paced. A *mehitsa,* translucent but still a divider, separates men and women. It is pulled back during spoken sections, then into place for singing. The women of this congregation sing loudly and participate fully in prayers. It's an interesting experiment for me, with my flatmates: Synagogue, keeping kosher (vegetarian), talking interminably about religion. I don't feel any more religious, but I do feel much more Jewish, much more that I am participating in a cultural and ethical community. I realize that wherever I go in the world, I will find Jews chanting the same prayers in the same language.

Sunsets are crimson, cream, and plum. Development towns like ammonia crystals on the hills. Iridescent blue hummingbirds chirp and buzz in the orange trees outside the window.

Jerusalem stone

Dun and bone,
bone and dun.
She will clothe you
golden like no one

A visit from Lilith

Waking dreams that speak to me in tongues. Tongue of tongues, tongue of our fathers by day and our sisters by night. Of our mothers there is no word. They are rumored not to speak. Perhaps they merely do not speak to *us*. Does Lilith say she's visiting? Do I?

Exotica

I fit "pretty" here better than in America, where I'm "exotic" or just interesting, so men don't pester me much. "Pretty" is new to me; in America I've rarely been approached by men who don't care if I'm engaging. The women talk to me only about having babies or difficult *halakhic* points concerning menstruation, which is more interesting but soon loses its charm.

Encounters on a beach at Ashqelon

Sunday morning we went to the beach in Ashqelon, the water a lustrous turquoise, silk colors. Even the rills and runnels as the waves hit the breakwater were edged in bright bluegreen, and the water was clear enough to see the ridged sand of the bottom. Crabs, fish, barnacles.

Two men bothered us on the beach, upsetting Rachel. Recently she has had eggs and rocks thrown at her flat by neighborhood boys, as well as her breast tweaked when she went out to confront them, so she was ripe for explosion.

The first man was one with whom something was clearly wrong. He was on a bicycle and wearing slippers. He sat on the sand next to us and began talking. I answered shortly. He approached Rachel, who was trying the I'll-ignore-him-and-he'll go-away technique that doesn't work. He sidled up next to her and began touching her arm while he spoke: "Yes, hello? We come here tonight to sleep, yes! Hello?" She told him to go away and leave her alone. He kissed her arm. She sat up, said, "That's it, go away!" He looked at me and I walked toward him, *"Achav! Lech! Lo, lo, lo! Lech! Zeh lo tov! Anachnu rotzot l'hiyot lavad!* Now! Go! No, no, no! Go! This isn't okay! We want to be alone! I said it over and over and dogged him away from our towels until with a mournful "Tonight, yes?" he slowly rode his bicycle into the sea, turning southward in the knee-deep waves.

The second man was just some guy. He was walking north along the beach, saw us, so dropped to a squat and started with "Hello? You speak what? *At yisraelit?* Are you Israeli?" again to Rachel. Finally, after much ignoring (I watched surreptitiously from under my bangs), she said, "If I wanted to talk to you, I would talk to you." They switched to Hebrew. He kept telling her not to be nervous; she kept saying, "Leave us alone, I don't want to talk to you, you're bothering me!" Finally he said, *"B'seder, slicha,* Okay, sorry" and walked away. Rachel fuming. We discuss alternatives—what to do? It is a social situation that is exploited, one where the woman can't make any negative response and still be considered reasonable. I suggested that we neither ignore nor ask rhetorical questions, but rather should stick to short, declarative statements: "I don't want to talk to you. Leave us alone. Go away." The alternative, to move, to be driven from our place by this behavior, makes my stomach churn to contemplate.

I wear a gold wedding ring in the Land. When I was preparing to leave, I mentioned to one of my mother's friends that I'd heard that solo women were frequently hit on. She said, "I have just the thing," and disappeared into her bedroom. She returned with the ring, a nice chunky one with an engraved mesh-like texture, clearly a wedding band. "Here," she said, dropping it into my palm. "I'm collecting them in a jar by my bed." The ring doesn't stop anyone. Older women appraise me at bus stops: *"Nu,* are you Jewish? You married? I have a son, he's a captain." Men still press against me at the market, at the bank. "If you're married, where is your husband?" If I say he's in Rhode Island, they chide him for not protecting me, question the importance of the relationship, persist. If I say he is at work or in the flat, they try to shame me for venturing out alone. I learn to say, "He's parking the car. He's buying falafel. He went in back to look at a carpet. He'll be here any minute." What I never say is that there will never be a man.

Your weapon

"Your weapon is your girl," the soldier said.
"You grease her up, and you take her to bed."

Questions about the relationship

I came to work at the school with a bad dream on my mind and walked right into a conversation about AIDS. I spoke a little about Frederic, and Jenny started asking me questions about my relationship with him. I told her that I'd known him since I was a prospective student at Swarthmore and had lived with him the previous two years, about the suspicious moles he had had removed this spring, about how he would like to have babies with me. She asked how I felt about that; I said I didn't want babies at present and was also wary of having a child with him until there is a cure or preventive for AIDS (for the child's sake more than mine). She said, "Ah, but the heart doesn't work that way, does it?" A misunderstanding, but also true. I told her that if there were any chance he had AIDS, I would return immediately and make a home for him. The whole conversation was very sad, and I told her something she didn't know—that funeral homes in the states are even refusing to bury people who have died of AIDS.

At work

I spend my Shabbat cutting out potsherds and making mosaics with construction paper. It is my turn to decorate the bulletin board outside the elementary school office. I also make a cutout of a bronze pre-Yahwistic Canaanite goddess named Asherah, of whom I have been fond for many years. I don't reproduce the Canaanite fertility goddesses because they're always presenting their breasts on cupped palms, and this seems inappropriate to the venue.

My colleague Aisha wore pants again today. I ask if she usually wears her skirts from religious conviction or personal preference. She answers that it is neither; rather, a requirement of her previous job, so she owns a lot of skirts. Also that her husband heads a religious school and the reputation of a school like that includes observations such as whether the director's wife wears halakhically correct clothes. She says she wears pants when she's driving door to door or being rebellious. She says, "Right now, I'm rebellious."

One of my tasks is to ride the school bus, monitor the K through 12 students. When the high school boys give the driver a cassette of the Violent Femmes to play over the speakers, I ignore the first three tracks, then leap forward and eject the tape at the precise instant between *"Why can't I get just one"* and *"screw,"* saving everyone's virtue and arousing their admiration: "Wow, *Geveret,* you know that song?" "I know the whole album, guys, I'm a *punkistit* from way back, so don't try any Sex Pistols, either!"

One of my other tasks is to check the school's lockers for unauthorized use. I make my rounds every week or so, looking for locks that shouldn't be there. When I find them, I sever the hasp with the pair of heavy-duty bolt cutters that I get to keep in my shared office. If there's anything inside the locker, even a small paper bag, I don't touch it. Instead, we call the bomb squad. I've learned the names of many explosives in Hebrew.

A week in the Negev

Dear Frederic,

I'm spending a week in the desert with 22 high schoolers and another chaperone, a spring break field trip. We're staying at an old army base/kibbutz, now converted for tour groups. Metzoke Dragot ("the Cliffs of the Dragot [River]") is on a twisting, steep road above the Dead Sea, near the oasis of Ein Gedi. This may be where David hid from somebody or other in a possibly semi-historical biblical narrative. We hike in two canyons, Wadi Mashash and Wadi Khatzatza. There was a one-day delay since it rained in Jerusalem and flash floods threatened. No one else eats the halvah at breakfast so I get plenty, and we rappel down cliffs of up to 50 meters. My mother says I'm counterphobic, and she's probably right.

The landscape is beautiful: Yellows, whites, dusty greens, with the Dead Sea visible at times, deep light blue or darker green. The birds are mostly black-and-white, or golden brown, or, in the case of the Dead Sea starling, black with yellow-orange wings. Our tour guides and group are shades of Caucasian, some more Semitic than others.

- Nubian ibex
- Vulture circling overhead
- Geckos

We are swarmed by houseflies at Wadi Mashash. The glare off the canyon walls is harsh and yellow.

- Tristram's grackle (Dead Sea starling)
- Carpet viper
- Egyptian eagle
- Storks

- Coneys
- Rock hyrax

We take a tour in Sedom, that is, Sodom, a City of the Plain. We trek in what looks like a dry creek bed between sheer walls. The walls taste of salt. Hey, it's Sodom. It cries out for me to transgress. I'm sorry you aren't here. We enter the cave in Mount Sedom. This isn't a euphemism. It's cold, an arching salt dome, striated tabby cat white and grey, in many places smoothed by water or hands. During the Great War there was a movie theater inside the dome, but people found it too difficult to return to the heat and oppressive atmosphere of the Dead Sea Rift afterward. A photographer from *The Jerusalem Post* accompanies us.

Oh, Frederic, I'm engaged in some first-class spying. I'm sitting in the dark outside the guest house at Metzoke Dragot, under the bright stars, near the Dead Sea. Another group staying here is Christian. They're outside, close together in a pool of lamplight, taking notes while a British man speaks. He tells them about the Antichrist and that when you contact a spirit, it's always an evil spirit because good dead people are sucked up to the Spirit of God. He warns, with citations, about false teachers and those who bring evil to scriptures. Bats swoop in and out of the light. He admonishes, "When the alarm bells go off in your head, that's the Holy Spirit talking to you and telling you the man you are talking to is evil." Admire my restraint. I do not run shrieking like a banshee into their midst. It wouldn't be kosher.

Earlier, our tour guide was bitten by a snake, specifically, a carpet viper, possibly the painted saw-scaled viper. Based on what I've witnessed so far on this trip, our guide or one of the other Australian guides probably poked it with a stick until it struck, providing an excuse to kill it, then turn it over with the stick and argue about whether it's poisonous. I could be wrong, but this has already happened several times. The guide seems to be all right. Not so much the snake. And they ran out of schnitzel at dinner. Oh, signs are not only following; they're running ahead and falling into canyons.

I thought the point of Christianity was love, but we seem to be more worried about evil here. The worst, though, is that earlier, one of the women in this group asked an Israeli kibbutznik who lives here, "Have you heard about the son? Not the sun up in the sky..." which is a Star Trek quote from Season 2, "Bread and Circuses." I had to step away so I wouldn't laugh.

Now the group is led in prayer against "the devil, a defeated foe, who is leading our own country, Great Britain, into evil." Frederic, are you *allowed* to quote different gospels like this: "Further, Matthew says..." and then repeat what a different apostle said as if it's substantiation rather than the same text? "In the name of Jesus, we have a victory!" They sing: "Who can tell what God can do?/Who can tell of his love for you?" What do you think the kibbutzniks think?

Basic rappelling is very simple. There are two wide straps that one knots into a chest- and waist-harness, attaching the two with a carabiner. To rappel, you take a figure 8 and pull your rappelling cable through it, then over the second section. The second section is attached to the carabiner: Basically, you've made a friction slide. You hold the bottom of the rope at the small of your back and step backward off the cliff. It's wonderful! Our cliffs alternated positive and negative surfaces so sometimes we were walking down the face at an almost perpendicular angle; other times, we were hanging free. The view was strange and gorgeous. In a wadi, the rock shapes and channels are determined by flash flooding, so they're smooth and twisty. It's hard to adjust to the scale—you look up and cliffs, canyons, and mountains fill your whole field of vision. It's difficult to focus or measure perspective.

I am over 430 meters below sea level, afloat in the Syro-African Rift. I am at the lowest land in the world. The Dead Sea tastes more bitter than salty. Salt floes dot the surface like crystallized icebergs. The salinity hits every scratch and mucus membrane, much worse than citrus Jell-O! The article is out in

The Jerusalem Post. This is the best photo of me that will ever be taken.

In Ramat Aviv

Frederic calls. I know it's Frederic when the phone rings because I've just talked myself out of calling him. We have no new news, just want to hear each other's voice.

Several nationalities

It's 8:25 AM and I'm drinking Turkish coffee at a hole-in-the-wall outside the Egyptian Embassy, waiting for them to open so I can get my visa. The office staff at my school has made four trips here on my behalf, so far unsuccessful. I hope that being here in person will resolve matters. With me is a scrofulous crew of British and Germans with oily bleached hair, tattoos, and Grateful Dead tee shirts. And that's just the women. All are carrying dirty frame backpacks and travel brochures for Egypt. One reads a copy of Dreiser's *An American Tragedy* in German. "Sherry" is on somebody's transistor radio. Everyone flips their passports restlessly. They discuss the sunburns some acquired on the ferry decks between Greek islands. Some may be Scandinavian. It's already hotter and more humid than southern Maryland on a summer morning, those days when the rugs began curling with damp at around 6:45 AM. The Egyptian flag hangs listlessly in the slight breeze; the middle stripe is snagged so it's puckered at the edge. The man opposite me at the next table is wearing a St. Christopher medal. A pregnant grey-striped cat shuffles through the traffic. Fortunately it's Sunday, so I, happy employee of an American institution, don't work, though the rest of Israel does.

We form two lines in front of the embassy—"Israelians" and "Several Nationalities." Inexplicable and beautiful sign:

PLEASE WE DON'T REÇEAVE
ANY APPLICATION
IF ALL THE APPLICATION
WITH DETAILLE WILL
BE "OK"
THANK YOU

Into Egypt, out of Egypt

Yesterday morning, U.S. forces bombed Libya. Memo to school staff: "Washington has informed the American Embassy to advise its agencies that all travel to the West Bank, Gaza and the Golan Heights should be avoided until further notice."

The bus takes us through Gaza. From Gaza on, the houses are made of crudely fitted, undressed cinderblocks, roofed with palm fronds, corrugated tin, ragged plastic, held down by more cinderblocks, rocks, armfuls of branches. Sabras delineate field boundaries. Scruffy white donkeys. The rebar on the uprights protrudes even on "finished" structures, rusted. Women in black bent over in the fields, indistinguishable at a distance from goats and sheep. Impossible to tell if many buildings are still being built, have been abandoned, or have been pirated for materials. The fields are much smaller than Israeli kibbutz or *moshav* plots. Crushed cars, plastic trash by the side of the road.

Testimony to the love not lost between nations: Our Israeli tour guide tells us the black market as well as the bank rate for dollars to Egyptian pounds.

A bird with dusty-orange wings beneath, very angular, like origami. Another Dead Sea starling? Too far off to say. The Suez Canal. We wait to be ferried west. This is a sandy desert with dunes, not like the rocky Israeli wastes. Camels, goats, chickens in the buildings and lots. One small settlement gives way to the next. Mine fields. We're on the edge of Passover. Out of Egypt, into Egypt.

I travel solo so I am paired with another female traveler, Midwestern American, decades older, a deep snorer, and prone to answering in Hebrew, which doesn't seem safe. There have been incidents recently. When a waiter brings her a napkin, she responds, *"Todah!"* while simultaneously I call over her, *"Shukran!"* The *ful* and *shakshuka* don't agree with her; she gurgles. I try to be amiable, a good if reluctant companion, as she makes fun of me for drinking a liter of bottled water every day: "I brought a pint from Israel days ago and I'm still drinking it! What do you need all that water for?"

Cairo. In the suq, I buy sandalwood oil and a box with very nice mother of pearl and bone inlay work. I walk alone at night. What seems to be an unpaved road is actually crushed detritus, the thick smashed trash of the metropolis. Buildings crumble into piles of rubble, surmounted by goats. I suddenly understand: A city is never done. This is a revelation and a metaphor. A city is a garbage midden. A city is a garden. A city is the body, blooming, decaying; invasive, colonized; host and symbiont. Men in sidewalk cafés smoke tobacco from *shishas*. No women are present. I stop at a café serving beer and sit. The waiter tells me apologetically that I can't have beer. If I were a blonde Norwegian I could, but a beer for me might be construed as giving alcohol to one of our women. I drink mint tea. I hear people breathing all around me in decaying concrete buildings, stuffed to the gills.

The Temple of Queen Hatshepsut. The figures are defaced. She wore a false beard and ruled as a man. Waiting for guide and group. Some of the others are feeling the heat, but not I. It's bright, though; can't open my eyes fully except when facing away from the sun.

Karnak. I sketch hieroglyphs and statues in my journal with a purple Le Pen, a gift from my friend Paula. A man approaches, gestures for my journal, which I hand him. He rapidly draws the cartouches of Hatshepsut, Ramses II, Seti I, and Amenofis III, hands my journal back. I dig a couple of pounds from my pocket. He gestures no, *la, la*. Points to the pen. *Aiwa*, of course! We are both satisfied. After dinner, the group walks through the market. Donkeys, sugarcane trampled underfoot, spices, dust, excrement. Guttural shouting, carpets flapping. Artificial light glints off the brass, copper, mother of pearl.

The temples at Esna, Edfu. The Nile grey-blue. Smell of lanolin.

Jellabas, saffron, spangles. Dust blows up from the street.

We take a *felucca* to Kitchener's Island to see the botanical garden, hundreds of ibis nesting in the trees. The drive from Luxor to Aswan is bumpy but fascinating. Houses of mud brick or cinderblock, some painted turquoise or mustard and displaying stylized blue representations of a *hajj* to Mecca. Mud retaining walls. Goats, ducks, geese, a reddish ox in a yard, scrabbling in mud and straw. Boys drive a donkey in circles, water wheel spills into an irrigation ditch. Men cluster on the sidewalks of larger towns, smoking. Some towns are narrowly surrounded by very lush greens, the desert visible through the fronds.

Night train return to Cairo. How my *wagon-lit*-mate can fart! Mercifully, the antiquated air conditioners mask her superhuman snores.

A man says "how

A man says "how
a man says "how nice
"how nice to see
"how nice" a man says
"to see a girl"
"a girl"
"reading
"reading
Hemingway
on the train."

Yom Hashoah

I'm talking with another teacher in the corridor. Suddenly at 8:00 AM a loud, piercing siren. Everyone ossifies, heads down: They don't stand, they freeze, like commuters' shadows smeared against the brick by nuclear flash. The siren goes on and on; the dog Elaine keeps at the school howls and jerks. My jaw is clenched so tightly.

I hope the Second Coming doesn't come.
Let me wander here,
wander in Jerusalem.

Educating

Student: "Was Adrienne Rich a lesbian?"
Me: "She still is, dear."

Ostraka

You feel that if you could just interlock the fragments, you would decipher the message. I leave that to you; you have been reconstructing pottery from potsherds all your life. Wondering if this will be the sentence, as if the one sentence held any absolute power of encoding and decrypting, even when its absence is so sharply defined, pungent with jasmine and aluminum. How your body conflates absence with desire! As you squat on the gritty terrazzo tiles, blue towel draped quickly over your shoulder (long end trailing on the floor), your hair moist and spiked, fingers twitching around the pen because just now in the shower it drifted through your peripheral awareness: *The skin, the skin breathes too;* and the ghost flavors: *Jasmine, aluminum.*

Ostraka, aluminum, towel, blue. Crumbly toeholds on the sheer face of abstraction. Let us agree, for the sake of fiction, that you are the one for me. That one ostracon fits gently into place and that, for the instant, there is nothing to attain.

Descent

Going to Israel from diaspora is *aliyah,* going up. Leaving Israel is *yerida,* descent.

When I drop down to American soil, I will buy tracked shelving. And a mannequin! And a teal or light brown rug to match my futon cover. And I will dance like some kind of demon.

When I arrive at Washington National, even the city landscape looks shockingly green from the sky. My family is there to meet me. So is Frederic, down from Rhode Island as a surprise. He is standing beside my mother, dressed as the Statue of Liberty.

THE BUDDHA'S SMILE

Interludes

Over the year in Israel my weight drops ridiculously. I earn a total of $5000, half in shekels, half in U.S. dollars. Most of the time I eat instant chicken broth, nuts, cheese sandwiches, a hunk of halvah once a week. I am praised for this weight loss, but I feel fragile and unsturdy. My diet secret: Desert and not dessert.

I get a teaching job at an Orthodox Jewish *yeshiva.* Skirts below the knee, elbows covered, modest neckline. As a joke, Catherine sews me elbow pasties with tassels. I'm hired in part because I can read Hebrew well enough to tell if the students are cheating in their secular classes by writing test answers on the chalkboard in Hebrew letters. I get another job at a Conservative Jewish *midrasha* teaching Jewish history. This is how I formalize what I have learned from reading on my own. These positions will later cause consternation when I apply for a teaching position at a rural community college, my CV creating the assumption that I am deeply religious. That and a dissertation on meaning-making by gay and bisexual men with HIV handily remove me from consideration.

Carrying my gear in a small backpack, I fly to England, ferry to France to join Laura, Frederic, Catherine, and other musicians in Frederic's group Melusine. A picnic lunch by the river near Chartres Cathedral, busking at Notre Dame, walking with Laura on winding lanes beside cow pastures. Three decades later, she and I will walk in Europe again.

Victoria, 5:00 AM

My photos of vagrants
asleep at the station
came back dark grey.
I was too eager
in too little light.

The Buddha's smile

When I visit my friends' dojos, I nod but don't bow to images of the Buddha. I don't believe he was a god, can't *salaam* or *daven,* touch my forehead to the worn wooden floors. I take in the swastikas, forward-wheeling and reverse; "forward" from a Western, left-to-right perspective. I consider the triskelion's spirals, rotationally and not bilaterally symmetrical, triquetra legs, an awkward half-bug running from itself. Mostly we all agree that three is a magical number.

I retrain, work as a mental health therapist in hospitals, catch the Gulf War in quick snatches on the group room's television. I realize that if I want the power to influence therapeutic policy, a master's degree is not enough. I will need to get a doctorate.

My new classmate has just returned from India. A group of my other new classmates clusters around him to ask questions about the ashram. He has been there several times. He often gets hepatitis. "Did you experience enlightenment?" one asks. I admire that he answers "no," and "that's not why I go."

My hypnosis instructor says that everything is a trance. As he walks behind me up the stairs to our classroom after a break, I hear him whisper, "Now we are in the walking-up-the-stairs trance," "Now we are in the settling-down-in-the-classroom trance." I don't remember much from this course because we learn by doing, and I am frequently hypnotized, asleep on the floor or in the graduate-student-travels-inner-space trance. He talks about the Buddha's smile, an involuntary twitch of the lips. He teases us toward it: "Ah, I see the little Buddha's smile in Shoshana," and indeed, I smile as if I am ridden by that evoked *orisha.* Reversing time's arrow, I now recognize this as one of my most valuable classes as a person and in my work as a psychotherapist.

I sit on a stray ledge or part of the structure around the outside stairs, some architectural excrescence, at Coffee Exchange on Wickenden Street, late afternoon, a sliver of Providence Harbor shining beyond the buildings and trees. I am drinking a small Sumatra, medium roast. I am overcome by a feeling of rightness and peace. I set my cup down carefully on the uneven concrete edge. I feel the muscles of my cheeks pull up, the curve of my lips. It is the Buddha's smile, cajoled in class by my instructor, but for the first time I experience it spontaneously. I will see its mirror on the lips of the Buddhas and Brahmas of the Bayon Temple in Cambodia. Everything is calm, intrinsically hilarious, brimful with its own being, entire and still. The trance fades. It's another state, not an altered state—altered from what? I finish my cold coffee and walk home.

Frederic and I no longer live together. The next time I see him, I tell him about this moment. He beams. "Oh, good! I was hoping for something like this for you!" I am startled and stay silent. He has never expressed such a wish to me, never talked with me more than briefly about his personal faith. That was all that we said of it, then or ever.

I talk on the phone with a college friend, now distant, now Jewish. When I tell her I'm meditating more, she bemoans how many young Jews are falling away from the faith and being seduced into Buddhism. Decades later, a rabbi will express the same concern, but about Christianity, as if religion is an innate characteristic rather than a choice, as if belonging matters more than belief.

Meeting the Buddha on the road and killing her because the Buddha is not separate, is inherent in us all, is useful advice, but if we meet the Buddha in the other who is us, what then? I clap my head with one hand, a smack in the forest of my dendrites that no one hears but me.

Four drives

Frederic calls from New Haven. "I have pneumonia and I probably have AIDS." I call the other college crisis intervention specialist and arrange for her to cover my on-call shifts. I set out extra cat food, take a shower, pack a bag. I stop to get drive-up fast food as I head south on Route 95. I don't speed. There is no rush. He will still have AIDS when I get there.

A universal barrier precaution sign is posted outside Frederic's hospital room. On the door of the next patient over, the sign says "NOTHING PER OS," but it is damaged and reads "O THING PER OS," which seems like the opening invocation of an epic poem about a global pandemic. Frederic complains that his lesbian and bisexual women friends keep crawling into his hospital bed and offering to marry him. I am among them. Catherine, Laura, and I clean his apartment, adrift in used tissues, and comfort a wild-eyed Gravity.

Frederic, Catherine, and I decide to circle around a Great Lake or two and drive north. Being together all day, I can see how depleted his energy is, how he lets us set up the tent then crawls inside to rest. How we do everything else while he breathes and continues to live.

I drive to Cambridge to see Frederic, to pick up his prescription in Boston. He draws me a map to his pharmacy on the back of an envelope. He perseverates on the street over the Longfellow Bridge, extending it beyond the right edge of the envelope. He looks puzzled for a moment, then returns to the left side and again draws a long line. When I next see my therapist, I say, "He looks like a concentration camp survivor," thinking of the photo of Elie Wiesel and other skeletal men, most lying on shared wooden bunks, one nude but for a wad of clothing over his genitals in the foreground, all gaunt, surprisingly alive.

I drive to Cambridge to see Frederic, to take him to a medical appointment. He exerts all his will to get slowly, slowly, out of bed, to draw on his clothes, to move his body to the elevator, to open the door, descend the stairs, deliberately fold himself into my car. He is underdressed for the weather. There's ice on the road. He doesn't buckle his seatbelt and I don't ask him to. He thanks me; it is too painful on his bones. At the clinic, I pull the nurse aside and describe the issue with the envelope the previous week, ask her to work a mental state exam into their conversation. If he is, as it seems, increasingly impaired, we will make extra efforts to be available to him and his partner. She reports back afterward that while I may well be right, it's too subtle for that cognitive function screen. He has reported that he is "fine." I drive him back to his apartment. When I next see my therapist, I say, "He looks worse than a concentration camp survivor." That is the last time we see each other before I get the early morning call.

Boy becomes

Boy becomes body,
empty, entropy. Where goes
the light he walked in?

Boy becomes ashes,
phlogiston to flames. What burns?
What is unmade here?

Boy becomes astral,
unearthly glow. Well. So. That's
how the story goes.

Boy becomes fractal,
ubiquitous in nature,
algebra for star.

Boy becomes wavelength,
inverse square: Photon boy who
is no longer there.

Boy becomes light when
these galaxies collapse, boy
is the next Big Bang.

AIDS quilt with Icarus descending

A stitch in time saves none.
I wield my needle through
landscape and floral, clouds,
borders, raspberries. Air.

This counterpane is my
country of loss, world's-edge,
insect whir, what ocean?
What sky? What absent son?

I quilt cartographies,
mapping I don't know what.

To hold the place of loss in joy

Like Jesus, Frederic dies at 33, though he might prefer that I compare him to Evita. I ask if I may have his angel amulet. Over time, Catherine and I throw some of his symbolic jewelry into rivers, lakes, oceans. This would have amused him.

I drive a long commute from Providence to Keene for my doctoral classes. Especially in winter I have to keep my hands on the wheel. I cultivate the habit of composing and refining one haiku on my drive. Then I release it. If I remember it when I get to Antioch, I write it down. If I don't, I appreciate having known it. Sometimes haiku return as I drive home, a fine example of state-dependent memory.

> I let haiku go
> as a high wind blew in New
> Hampshire in the snow.

I have never thought about living in Oregon but after two years, I can't stand to be quite so close to his ashes, lambent in every speck of dust.

I dedicate my dissertation to Frederic, quoting in Hebrew the lines of Psalm 91 that include the fragment on the back of his angel amulet. No one has ever asked me to translate it or say what it means to me.

I dream that Nancy is eating snack bees. I ask her what snack bees are, but she just smiles.

Nancy proposes on Valentine's Day. Our extrajudicial union, conducted in the exclusionary umbra of the Defense of Marriage Act, is well-attended. Frederic is evoked by the music played by Laura and the remaining members of Melusine. My father speaks. He describes the destruction of the Second Temple in Jerusalem and why the groom steps on and breaks a wineglass at a Jewish wedding. It is to remember this tragedy, to hold the place of loss in joy. He suggests, though, that perhaps the destruction of the Temple was a good thing; our Jewish officiant gasps a muffled "Oh, no!" My father talks about the importance of change, about shifting traditions and values. I hadn't known what he planned to say and I am moved by this iconoclastic sentiment, his celebration of a union where two women shatter the glass together. Nine days later, my mother calls us in Jamaica. "I think you should come now." The next morning, my father dies. Though we had seen him thin and pale at our wedding, he had minimized how ill he was.

Nancy and I take what she calls a Lesbian Cruise to the Holy Land. It is the first time the tour company has run this itinerary. Athens in the heart of a heatwave, the huge statue of a runner composed of jagged, stacked grey glass painful to view in the grainy dry air. We keep leaving the Museum of Cycladic Art to buy bottled water on the street, return to the figures with their flattened faces.

At Port Said, we board a bus to Cairo, a long ride in the desert with a tour guide and an armed guard. In the seat ahead of us, Alison travels solo. We get to talking; she has had breast cancer with bilateral mastectomy and no reconstruction. It's years before I'll have to think about this more personally; I'm engaged and interested but don't know how to further the conversation. The tour guide asks at large, "Are you ladies... together?" with clasped hands demonstrating the quality of "together." "We are!" we chorus. "I've heard of that," she replies, not seeming fazed. Later, she asks if we know about Queen Hatshepsut. *Yes, yes,* we say, *of course, she ruled as pharaoh, she wore a false beard as a sign of office.* The guide is impressed, but really, if you're on a lesbian cruise to the Holy Land, you may well be familiar with Hatshepsut.

After the enormous and echoing Egyptian Museum, grandpa's treasure heap and junkyard of dusty antiquities in the high-ceilinged gloom, we visit the pyramids at Giza. Some take camel rides. It's 110° Fahrenheit, excellent practice for a future excursion on the Spanish Meseta, the air sandy grey, and only two of us leave the bus at the viewpoint. On the trip back to the ship, the guide exclaims, "You ladies are okay! Who needs men?" Well, my wife and several others are bisexual, and most have fathers and brothers, but we respond in good spirit.

I decide to read a book from every country. It's a way to learn about the world. DHL delivers stained, heavy boxes from France, from the University of the South Pacific. What is most easily available in English translation is war, rape, religious conflict, oppression, horror, and sometimes if I'm lucky, a cookbook.

I visit the National Cathedral and the Church of Jesus Christ of Latter-day Saints in Washington, D.C., Notre Dame, Chartres, the Church of the Holy Sepulchre, Sagrada Familia, the Church on Spilt Blood, St. Peter's, the Basilica of Our Lady of Guadalupe, St. John's Co-Cathedral in Malta. I find it hard to shake my lingering historical distress. Being in these buildings disturbs me, splits my attention. I want to learn about flying buttresses; I want to engage with the artistry; I want to feel the colored light through the stained glass on my skin. I want to be part of the Mass, part of the celebration.

Instead my mind goes to the history of the Jews, the lack of welcome I would receive in most eras in these houses of Christianity. *Hep! Hep! Hierosolyma est perdita!* in the background of my consciousness, ancient and modern pogroms. I don't experience this at Karnak, Angkor Wat, the Hypogeum and Tarxien Temples, Talum, Wat Pho with its enormous reclining Buddha. I might be more comfortable walking the pilgrimage of Shikoku-Henro, visiting 88 temples and not bowing to statues, walking in traditional Japanese pilgrim's garb, more at home than in my neighborhood Baptist church. I want to believe in peace. I want to reconcile, hold both associations, let it go. I want to look at flowers carved on fonts and rose windows without seeing genocide. Not that most peoples do better, not that the biblical Jews were such terrific neighbors. But it is my own history I see first in the worn stones.

We visit the Bardo in Tunisia, not the liminal Buddhist state but the museum with its huge collection of intact Roman mosaics, provenance of the Muses. Gold smalti is more luminous; which is the glass, which is the gold? The Bardo will be the site of a deadly attack in 2015, reminding me that tensions between primate troops are not restricted to Jews and Christians. In 2015, I will be preoccupied with other matters.

I don't know what to do in church or a Buddhist temple, and still have only a little more sense of what to do in a synagogue. In Catholic places, I pay my dollar or euro to light a candle, don't take Communion.

It's afternoon. I'm at a bar in Santiago de Querétaro with Benito. We're each working for pleasure, parallel play. I'm slowly reading a collection of short stories in Spanish by Esteban Mayorga, my Ecuador book. It's a step in the quest to read a book by an author from each country. There's no Wi-Fi. I have a little pocket dictionary, not very useful. I puzzle it out from context; I ask him, "Does *tenia* mean 'tapeworm'?" He's not sure. I seem to be reading a story about a man and his parasite.

After Mass with Krista and Benito at the Basilica of Our Lady of Guadalupe in Mexico City, I ask Benito why he thinks it's harder for me to participate in other religions' rites as an atheist than it is for him as a Catholic. He thinks it's because Catholicism is syncretic and can find itself in other traditions. That as an atheist, I answer to myself, not an external authority. It could be true. I tend toward monotheistic atheism, though intellectually I think it's more likely that there are gods than God, if there is such a thing, about which, I think not.

I continue to consider this as we visit Frida Kahlo's house with its eclectic and attractive courtyard, as we walk nearby to the building where Leon Trotsky was assassinated. They enter; I decide to return to El Zócalo, La Plaza de la Constitución, on my own, to look again at the Diego Rivera mural "Man, Controller of the Universe." I accelerate through earth that clenches the pre-Christian artifacts we will also admire from the open-air walkways of the Museo del Templo Mayor, the vestiges of Teotihuacán, where we will ascend the pyramids of the Sun and Moon.

I once watched the December peregrinations in a different Mexican city, in different company. I have climbed the stairs to the crucifix at the Shrine of Our Lady of La Salette, though not as a pilgrim, not on my knees.

"We are," says my Cambodian host carefully, "not completely Buddhists. We are really animists." Spirit house in an empty lot; a little nature shrine of two oak galls and a stub of incense on a leaf at the base of the tree. At Wat Phnom, rooms stuffed with Buddhas in tiers and lines, metal, painted wood, plastic, stone. The enormous shrill and endless klaxon of insects, so loud that at first I thought an alarm was blaring.

It is hard at times to answer "Are you married?" It was easy when the answer was "No," though this often led to attempts to set me up with a very nice young man. It was easy when the answer was a lie, "Yes." It was easy when my marriage wasn't legal, when I could say, "Hmm, it's complicated," warding off further inquiry, or "Yes and no. We had a community service but didn't file papers with the state," which tended to suffice. Or as we said to a Canadian immigration officer after we married in Massachusetts but the whole country was not yet on board, "Should we fill this form out for your side of the border or ours?" Now we are legally married across the nation, but not in some countries we visit, not safely in some where I travel alone. I have never been in the closet, but I sometimes avoid pronouns in gendered languages, switch to

English though I know how to say what I want to say. I speak generally in Botswana, Thailand, China. When we are together, our astute fellow travelers sometimes notice our matching wedding rings. Sometimes we wear different ones.

After reading a book from every country, I am fascinated by Malta. The only English language book I could find by a Maltese author was Professor Sir Themistocles Zammit's *Prehistoric Malta: Tarxien Temples and Saflieni Hypogeum.* Though it was a book of necessity not choice, I'm intrigued by the megalithic temples Zammit described, illustrated with poorly-lit black-and-white photos. We plan a vacation with a day in Valletta so we can see the underground temple, the Hypogeum, for ourselves. This requires booking admission online three months in advance. The Hypogeum, rediscovered during the course of cistern construction above, is pleasingly mysterious and largely inexplicable. It is a mirror of the sacred in the world below the world. Shadows on the cave wall. After we re-emerge to light, we visit Malta's National Museum of Archaeology and comment to the ticket clerk that we'd just admired the Hypogeum. He says we were lucky to get in since they are booked months in advance. I reply that I'd indeed booked in advance. He asks how we knew about the temples, and I tell him that I'd read Professor Sir Themistocles Zammit's book on the Tarxien Temples and Saflieni Hypogeum. "Ah, my great-uncle! There's a bust of him on the second-floor landing!" St. John's Co-Cathedral is floored with memento mori, pensive skeletons, ravens, candle stubs and skulls. Caravaggio's *Beheading* still hangs.

When it becomes a thing, we begin paying carbon offsets for our flights.

> Stinking of Thai wine
> and bad behavior—sadly,
> my drunk countrymen.

> No sweat. The hotel

van is late. A rare cool breeze
ruffles the palm trees.

I name native birds:
Anastomus oscitans.
You spot a *farang.*

Minutes trickle by.
Shrikes in the frangipani,
back of my neck burnt.

Flooded muddy fields
seen through the clouds: Blue and white,
brown and green and blue.

Sometimes on my own for weeks at a time, I volunteer in Cambodia and Vietnam. I teach, write, wander, sweat, ride an elephant, use chopsticks poorly with my right hand, slurp velvety vanilla-scented mangoes in the shower to evade ant attacks. I turn down the offer to have a red string wrapped around my wrist, made by a monk at a Water Ceremony. He sits on the old wooden floor, his robes a nest for three kittens. I wander the Siem Reap night market, out of the sun unlike the Jerusalem sun, with the watchful attention of a woman on her own. My fingertips snag on the loose raw silk weave of a $3 scarf. I stand on the roof of a boat as it motors across Tonle Sap Lake, stirring up a wake that gently rocks the houseboats of the indigent Vietnamese, watching for bee-eaters on the shoreline's bending reeds. At Angkor, a bas relief of the churning of the sea of milk, *apsaras* wearing castles on their heads. Below the boats, crocodiles and geese chew fish. Only the crocodiles chew the sailors' legs. I watch the monkeys clamber over the hot, ancient stones of the Bayon Temple's four-faced Buddhas. The Buddhas' smiles are serene though they are swarmed by nature, as we will be when we are gone.

In Vietnam, my hosts order me a "very special" drink. "What do you think is special?" they eagerly ask. I consider the glass, layered green, blue, and clear, a few colored tapioca balls and obscure fruit shapes in suspension, rough green vegetal stalks protruding above the rim. They are delighted when I correctly perceive that it is intended to represent a swamp.

In India the students *ooh* over the farmer who offers them botanicals and herbs. Should I point out that they can also get this wisdom at home? That plant distillates are still drugs, that one might want to research the interaction effects of a leaf purported to gentle menstruation before eagerly eating it from a stranger's hand? I do not. It is theirs to learn. I hear rumor that the Eye Hospital has eyeballs floating in vats. Fortunately I have a scratchy throat, so I beg off, wait in the parking lot with zippy little birds. I'm not in the mood to see disassembled body parts.

Between inconclusive imaging and a scheduled biopsy, the radiologist reassures me, "80% of these are benign."

KNIFE FIGHT WITH
A MERMAID

What tiny seeds
the genome holds
and breeds

These calcifications appear on 95% of mammograms, and most commonly represent fibrocystic changes. After the second mammogram, 70% can be called benign, 5% are clearly cancer, and 24% cannot be determined without biopsy.

January is fine for biopsy. Call PCP for anxiolytic. Okay to go to India with students.

I've visited 55 countries, including some without standing as sovereign states, such as the Caymans. A train trip in Europe with Nancy may bring me to 70 by year's end. I feel mixed about organizing another trip to Cambodia with students this year. My vulnerability and uncertainty about the pending diagnostic process make me reluctant to initiate an offer to take students away *in loco parentis,* even a year from now.

Breathing in the golden light, the protective light. Couldn't hurt to douse myself in psychic honey, imaginary Manuka honey for hypothetical wounds.

I am in a holding pattern, waiting until the Friday biopsy. Sleep increasingly disrupted by bad dreams about the procedure. I have to challenge my idea that somehow it's better, more honorable, to decline Xanax.

No, I do not want to see five pink-and-white worms of my

cored breast tissue. But she displays them without asking. My body makes of itself a parasite.

I lose one of the earrings I wore to the procedure. Golden Murano glass from a trip to Venice, to evoke a healing light. The clinic can't find it. This is not a sign.

After the stereotactic biopsy; bored, uncomfortable. It is a lie that I won't experience much post-procedure pain, or that Tylenol will be at all useful or sufficient. The equipment: Painful and not woman-shaped, straining ribs and arms. The procedure: Unpleasant. Deep tissue injection: Painful. Biopsy: Uncomfortable but not painful. Sequelae: Painful. I don't mean to kvetch. Frederic, Nancy, my father: All managed not to complain aloud. Me: Trying, but irritable and nervous waiting for results. Placebo: I thought I'd popped an alprazolam just before going in for the biopsy. No—it was one of my usual morning medications by mistake. I did feel calm; my unconscious gave me the best of both worlds: I didn't take it and I received its effects.

The wait for data is tiring, anxiety-ridden. Give me my news —*my* news—while I can manage "plucky and determined"! I secretly fear that the medical student who participated in the procedure dropped the samples in the wrong bin—they're spoiled, rotted over the weekend even more than they had already rotted inside me; we'll have to do this again. I soldier on. My work bores me and any request for my time is a burden. I can't think what I'd like to eat. My breast is still swollen, pores near the biopsy site bruised, skin yellowing around purple stippling, Pointillist porn. Hot pink outlines of bandages. I told them I'm allergic to standard surgical adhesives, but I have become an object, not an agent, in this intervention. Puncture scab. Both shallow and deep pain.

How expository should a memoir be? Can the first-person narrator claim privacy even in a memoir? Can there be subtlety? Must everything be stated, or can emotions be evoked and relationships between events inferred by the reader, as it is in haiku or *haibun?* Is it sufficient that unlike a fictional character, I do have an interior life, or ought its display be the privileged form of communication? Well, *ne Jupiter quidem omnibus placet.*

I am as upset as I've ever been. Not as sad as I've ever been, because here I am, and here Frederic and my father are not, which matters. Wednesday the radiologist called (the wrong number, my work number). He said the diagnosis was ductal carcinoma in situ, low grade, that I'd need surgery and maybe they'd want to take lymph nodes, too, which is not what I've read about DCIS. He said there were four local breast surgeons; which did I want? Well, how would I know? My nurse practitioner recommends a different surgeon, not on the list. I go with her suggestion. Nancy sends an email to Martha and I go into the faculty meeting I'm late to and supposed to be running. I tell my colleagues, details pending, hugs from the right, please; the left is sore. I tell them it's not a secret—if I had a disease requiring shoulder surgery it wouldn't be, so that it's my breast should be no different in terms of disclosure. I am distressed by the idea of surgery, more so at this point than by the diagnosis, though that's bad, too. I begin handing off responsibilities. I call my nurse practitioner for the pathology report. No lunch. Not hungry. I schedule an MRI of both breasts.

"And Rabbi Yohanan said: 'Whoever asks for what he needs in Aramaic—the ministering angels don't accede to him, for the ministering angels don't understand Aramaic.'"

Not hungry. The pathology report does *not* indicate a low-grade cancer. Although it is stage 0, it's "grade 3" and "solid pattern" as well as diffuse and possibly multifocal. DCIS has a good general cure rate, but who wants to be in the bad 4%? Martha reviews it at my request, cautions, "You're looking at a mastectomy." There are some other issues like proximity to my nipple that push the recommendation further in this direction. This was not a possibility I had considered, and isn't what the radiologist told me. She goes on to suggest genetic testing and perhaps a prophylactic bilateral mastectomy, but I can hardly listen. I am floored. Cancer to surgery to mastectomy to *double* mastectomy? I spend the night shivering uncontrollably despite alprazolam.

I can't look at the clinical and surgical illustrations in the DCIS book. They make me gag, become lightheaded. Nancy sticks Post-its over them so I don't have to see these revelatory mirrors.

When I was a child, the only lesbians in books and movies came to a bad end. Now it's women with breast cancer.

I expect that as I get used to the idea of surgery, maybe extensive, I'll be in touch with the not-wanting-to-progress-to-invasive-cancer part that will make surgery seem like a good idea.

Nancy and I get the hell out of town, fly to Hawaii on a cheap ticket. Kona, North Point to Volcano National Park. Extensive tense conversations about diagnostic confirmation and treatment options. We see several new bird species, lizards that look like the anoles we got as "chameleons." They are apparently the same lizard, a species that escaped from pet stores in Hawaii in the 1950s and naturalized. Five mongooses, a number of humpback whales, green sea tortoises. We also see the active crater, though not up close. I have better things to do than inhale a lot of sulfur dioxide. Whenever I lie down, my teeth chatter. I'm trying to get used to the idea.

My breast still hurts from the biopsy, arousing my alarm about the soft-pedalled and inaccurate information: "Many women are back at work the next day!"—unlikely for lumpectomy and not at all the case for mastectomy. But he read me the wrong patient report, didn't he? That is the only explanation.

I buy a soft pima cotton shirt for after surgery. It features a large shark, toothy mouth open at my left breast. This will entertain me once the breast is gone. It's as good an explanation as any: [Sad expression]: "There was this shark, a Great White, I think...." Shipwreck is everywhere. I am a hero!

I wonder if I can find a Harry Potter tee shirt that says "KILL THE SPARE."

We cancel future travel. How shall I construct my classes for the end of the term? Much depends on when the surgery is scheduled, how long the lead time is from genetic testing to treatment decisions, including, on a scale of 0-2, how many breasts I come out of this with.

The biopsy hematoma is more pronounced today, or the rest of the swelling is down. I try to express hope and love toward my breast, which itches. But also, to say goodbye.

This breast is like a winter avocado. It looks great and feels firm, just ripe, but it's going bad on the inside. A surgery that is also amputation.

Cancer is a failure of organization. Cancer makes me expository, strips me of poetry. I think of E. M. Forster's distinction between story and plot, the difference between "and then—and then—" and a causal explanation. I can't answer the *Why?* of cancer. I can hardly formulate the questions. What I can do is record, document, write the history bare of reflection, *this, then this, then that.* Later, if there is a later, I will seek out a context, an overview, better metaphors, transitional phrases. For now I gather information and opinions, transcribe statistics, chronicle unfamiliar words. This is testimony, not a saga. If I consume enough data, digest enough anecdotes, I might guard against narrative twists: *But what she didn't know at the time was—; And if only she had asked—; It was a damned shame because—.*

Codeine Plus Benadryl Plus Xanax Plus Melatonin: A Case

Study. In other words, could I possibly get one night of sleep? It is more difficult to keep my emotions in check at work today. I do want my body, my emotions and thoughts, to harmonize. My teeth still chatter at night.

I dream that Nancy sends two emails, one to a doctor asking a question about cell type, comedo or cribiform? She has it in the wrong message window and sends it to the entire university. The adrenalin of this (though in reality, I'd be more chagrinned than alarmed) wakes me after two or three hours, and I do not sleep again. This is my first cancer dream.

I'm practicing to have my breast cut off. Not what I intended for my spring break. On the other hand, being alive is something I enjoy. I am fortunate, and slightly self-congratulatory, for having already had a lot of psychotherapy, much of it grief work; being trained as and practicing as a psychologist; having good habits that can also be improved; not having an addiction so I can take opiates if necessary; having a strong appreciation of the absurd; and having great relationships, including my smart and loving wife.

I am half full, an optimist. But also completely full: I am filled with my life. I am also saturated with my death. Whether or not that means cancer cells, I picture myself as simultaneously replete and empty. This is a dilemma. How do I imagine myself free from cancer, yet possibly containing the seeds of my own end? Death and life inhabit all my cells; I know this, yet *timor mortis conturbat me.*

"Cancer" is a word to wrap your mouth around, not because it's savory but to get to know it, feel its contours on the palate, mouthful of jagged pebbles. As Demosthenes, I carefully and lucidly articulate: *Is there an effective treatment for this quality of cancer? Is there a cure?* For this crab, this spider, this knot that roots between my cells, cracks its ground to shoot out coarse and spiny stems? In Israel, I began each day by shaking out my shoes, sometimes expelling a tiny scorpion or two. I tried not to shudder. *In my shoes!* Fuck! Scorpions! A breach, a violation, a misunderstood deal with nature. I thought nothing would eat me until I was already dead.

We've compiled our list of questions for Dr. Corbin, and things he should know about me, including that I've never had surgery and that the biopsy bandage adhesive raised an impressive rectangle of welts. Are there questions that two smart women who already own *Harrison's Principles of Internal Medicine* might not think to ask?

Consider the Meditation on a Corpse. Also, the Buddha's smile. Simultaneous and competing pulls to look inward and be preoccupied, to look outward with great mindfulness and intention.

> If cancer were a
> just-discovered plant,
> I would name it
> Love Lies Screaming,
> Let Me Die Now,
> Enter the Dreaming.
> My body's acreage,
> black spot, blossom end rot,
> late blight.
> Tear out the wet fruit.
> Sow the fields with salt
> like Carthage, broil me
> under the sun,
> suppress, deliquesce
> *delenda est.*

I'm not hungry at all and the idea of meat is disgusting. I eat fresh vegetables and sneak in a spoonful of vegetable protein. I cannot bear to imagine a knife slicing into a chicken breast.

The MRI is easier than the biopsy. The clinic is calm, tastefully furnished, with well-trained staff. The MRI setup for breasts has breast-holes. Had anyone told me that, I'd have been less anxious about pressure on my still-tender biopsy site. I might have slept, or so I pretend. In goes the IV contrast; hold very still in order not to spoil the image. I meditate on my shallow breathing. The machine sounds are like a Mickey Hart *Planet Drum* track. I silently augment the percussion with a made-up tune, careful not to move.

Coconut crabs, grown enormous, clamp themselves around the ripe shells, husk them slowly, pierce an eye hole and suck the milk, crack the whole fruit open and feast on its silky meat. I remember blue crabs swarming over a raw chicken drumstick, carefully lowered on a string over the gunwale where it won't foul the outboard motor, on a hot, bright-grey day on an inlet of the Chesapeake. Using sympathetic magic, could I dangle a bit of flesh over the side of the stone boat of my life, lure the cancer to a substitute host or effigy instead? I do not think tofu would work for this purpose.

I weary of this. Another report worms into the online portal before the associated medical visit. *Harrison's Principles of Internal Medicine* open beside me at the kitchen table. "Washout," that's not good. The MRI confirms widespread DCIS in the left breast. More importantly, it shows an area deep in the right breast that does not appear on mammography. It's probably a malignant tumor, an invasive cancer.

Cancer is a question with inadequate answers. Is it "the" cancer or "my" cancer?

I tell Martha, "It was invaluable that you were direct with us about the biopsy report. We would have been shocked to hear it for the first time when we met the surgeon. As it was, I was able to say, 'We've talked about bilateral mastectomy and it seems to be the best option, so please don't worry. We already know.'"

The surgical clinic's parking garage uses animal symbols to identify the levels. Whose clever idea was it to make one a crab?

The right breast in general has "a lot going on in it," says Dr. Corbin, who calls me "the poster child for contralateral MRI." Lit up like a constellation. He shows us my most recent mammogram, zooms into the hidden structure of my body like the opening of *Fight Club* in reverse, like a cool science animation. I schedule an ultrasound-guided biopsy. Dr. Corbin assures me it won't be as bad as the stereotactic biopsy I already had on the left, though this will turn out to be incorrect. Goodbye to both breasts, then. Dr. Corbin doesn't think I'll need chemotherapy or radiation. To accommodate my wish to teach until close to the end of the quarter, we schedule surgery for late February with a dye injection the afternoon before. I will have one or more simple mastectomies with sentinel lymph nodes "harvested." *Eccchh!* I hope this terminology doesn't make vegetables seem disgusting as well.

The ultrasound-guided biopsy is only nominally less painful than the stereotactic biopsy, but still requires multiple injections and five tissue extractions at two sites. They offer no pain management option and seem angry that I ask. "Are you saying you want to cancel the procedure, then?" They have a hard time locating the IDC tumor. It requires a journey to the center of the earth, or deep into my breast, at least. I'm in a very tight compression wrapping that is to stay on for one or two days, to be followed by a "very tight sports bra." I will need to buy a very tight sports bra. The wrap is claustrophobic, uncomfortable, and slightly scratchy. I ice both breasts in alternation. I take Xanax, which has properties both medical and magical, since it has two Xs and is a palindrome. Results will be back toward the end of next week. I don't expect to hear anything that would mitigate the recommendation for a bilateral mastectomy.

Let's get on with it:

> it's mother of clam,
> it's a mess of stars,
> it looks like Orion;
> it's a diagram of a breast
> segmented like fruit;
> it's not an onion,
> but it makes me cry.

I remember a confectioner's window of marzipan fruits in Florence, delicately and intimately rendered, complete with blemishes, discolorations, intimations of soft spots and decay. My marzipan breasts, bruised from biopsy.

Later, I'll be in touch emotionally with what I know intellectually, that it's fantastic that the discovery of DCIS on the left has triggered a good look at the right, has revealed something worse and invisible to the mammogram. At the moment, though, grief and disconnection make it hard for me to appreciate this.

> I like the nuisance birds,
> starlings, grackles. I can't get
> angry at this crab.

How do I say "cancer" in Hebrew? *Sartan,* I correctly guess, meaning "crab." I know how to say "fish." I don't know the names of the other sea-*trayf,* the scallops and crustaceans. The Yiddish word "trayf," unclean, derives from a Hebrew word for mauled or torn animal flesh. The crab holds both sides of this equation perfectly: Unclean and tearing at my meat. Is cancer always "crab," a cross-cultural universal? One crab, many crabs, dipping claws over the lip of my torso and into the wet lymphatic channels of my arm.

I'll be able to go home the same day. Isn't that astonishing? Outpatient mastectomies. My friends in other countries are horrified. The surgeon says I'll be comfortable, oh—other than the Jackson-Pratt surgical drains in my torso, which no one has ever enjoyed—and should get up and move around for short periods throughout the day without taxing myself. They'll manage the dressings over about two weeks. There shouldn't be much chest pain. He tells us that opiates seem to drug the T helper cells, so not using them after surgery makes a 40% positive difference in future outcomes.

I gird myself for surgery, though surgery is not, or is not only, a battle. Humoral theory suggests: If you are choleric, eat rosemary, garlic, olives, and bunnies. If you are sanguine, avoid basil, butter, and peacock. I'm not sure what to eat if I am an amalgam of bodily types, choleric, sanguine, phlegmatic, increasingly bilious. Note to self: As a precautionary measure, avoid eating peacocks.

A colleague I don't know well calls me into her office, lowers the blinds, plunks my hands on her breast and prosthesis. "Guess which is which!" She lifts her shirt to show me the scar from a mastectomy that Dr. Corbin performed. It is a surprising and moving experience. Another colleague, on hearing that bilateral is now the likely route, replies, "That's good—this way you won't spin around in circles." A different sort of kindness.

Note to my family and friends: "First, please no pink, pink ribbons, breast-referencing iconography. It's getting me down. Second, I would like small images that will remind me to breathe, check my posture, think lovely thoughts, meditate, etc. If you see a postcard, or want to make me a postcard-sized image that would evoke similar reminders for you, that would increase my mindful attention, and, because it's an image that's also meaningful to you, bring our relationship to my mind as well."

I read about lymphedema and the vulnerability of the arm, exposing the lie under the allopathic promise which is, *If we cut it off, you'll be just fine.* Consequences and sequelae are spectacularly minimized.

Genetic test results will be back in a few weeks and the pathology from the surgery within the week after. If the surgical pathology shows the sentinel lymph nodes aren't clear, there may be a further axial dissection *(eccchh!)* and other intervention. If the genetic testing comes back positive for BRCA, which is much more common in Jews thanks to the founder effects that follow our historical dearth of exogamy, I'll need to have my ovaries out as soon as feasible. The medical oncologist gets to weigh in on all of this, too, but I hope for a finite sequence of interventions.

I am a fox in an atheist-hole. My experience is only more confirmatory. I don't believe in God, but I do believe in Jews. I don't believe in heaven, but I take comfort in the ongoing existence of carbon. General anesthesia is practice for death. My sister Becca says, "It's not a problem for an atheist. If you don't think there's an afterlife and you die in surgery, what is there to be afraid of?"

The Jewish afterlife arose as a murky derivative of Zoroastrian beliefs. There is no heaven or hell in the *Tanakh,* just *She'ol.* Everyone goes there. There's not a lot happening, at least until the End of Days, Gog and Magog duking it out in Jerusalem. Therefore, be observant, do good works for the sake of the world, tikkun olam. Do we have souls? *Two Jews, three opinions.*

It seems bizarre that in a few weeks I move from the shock of "Cancer?! Bilateral mastectomy?! But there aren't any lumps!" to "If all it takes is bilateral mastectomy, that would be a relief." I'm speaking about cognition, of course. All of my affect is still screeching, "Cancer?! Bilateral mastectomy?!" and my body is saying, "Everything tastes like salt or nothing. Best not to sleep when faced with the void."

We go to a prosthetic shop to look at vests that hold the surgical drains out of the way, since the current plan is that I'll have four drains for two weeks. The shop owner isn't in, and the clerk is quite inappropriate. She insists I needed a prescription for a corset-style post-surgical vest that "everyone gets" though my surgeon didn't mention it, can't remember that I will have a bilateral mastectomy rather than a lumpectomy, argues with me about my breast size. I am not a DD. She can't find two ancillary components in the same size and insists this doesn't matter, starts showing me silicone prostheses when I've said I don't want to look at them, states that I must buy prostheses of the same size and weight as my current breasts or "You'll get a hunchback because you're used to carrying them!" Wouldn't the physics of her story have me falling backward? Do transmen have to walk around with fake breasts to correct their posture? She keeps repeating that I'll be glad I am "having both of them off," thinks Nancy is my mother, and so on. We leave and try the other local prosthetic store. It stinks so badly of mold and water damage that we immediately turn around and head back out. These joyless cancer errands become worse.

We pick up soft, warm, leopard-print pajamas that I can wear home from surgery, a scrub shirt and vest, both with buttons and pockets to hold the drain bulbs, and two oversized men's undershirts. I order new earbuds because Zebulon fished my iPod from under my pillow and ecstatically chewed them up. His brother Jet, a cat of more pacific temperament, just snuggles against my hip, responsive to my distress. We set up the boxes of medical supplies and medications, things I'll want easily near the bed, and the oops-I'm-sleeping-at-the-hospital bag. All of my courses will soon be ready to run without me. Nancy massages my feet and legs. I take my blood pressure. No one is talking about pain.

I now have a Buddha image in every room to help me focus. It is intermittently useful. I am less overwhelmed and discombobulated. Or discomboobulated. I make myself eat, though salt and nothing remain the predominant tastes.

The lost earring is not a metaphor, or both would be gone.

Ursula Le Guin has been lovely whenever I've heard her read or interacted with her. When I once told her I use a segment of *The Lathe of Heaven* in my graduate ethics class, she replied, "Poor Dr. Haber!" *Left Hand of Darkness* is one of my favorite books. Genly Ai and Estraven on the ice makes me weep whenever I read it. And indeed, I have often said to myself, including in the last few weeks, "Light is the left hand of darkness/And darkness the right hand of light."

I'm just as glad I'll be wearing a compression binder for two weeks after. Looking at the bruising while trying to tweeze off the sticky Steri-Strips from the right breast biopsies made me nauseated and faint.

The story depends on where you stand.
Me: The biopsy site still hurts.
Surgeon: It's healing very well.
Medical oncologist: It's still quite inflamed.

It's hard to comprehend having breasts in January and not having breasts in late February.

There is nothing scarier than an outdated cancer book and discussion board threads with titles like *You CAN survive invasive breast cancer!!!* I am possibly done sobbing and screaming for the afternoon. So many painful, identity-distorting activities are required. It is hard to reframe this as "health." It is hard to feel optimistic, but I am not a hen in a foxhouse.

Taking the fucking alprazolam. It's intended for this, the creeping early evening panic, chest and shoulders tight, jumping up and pacing, hiccoughing sobs. Why not take it? To prove something about my resilience? If not now, when?

Frederic's Floris rosewater, which he would spray on his shirts while he ironed them, sometimes while he watched soap operas. Now, I anoint myself sparingly. If not me, then who, in memoriam?

From what I've read, the perisurgical, surgical, and three-week postsurgical period are important times to have good immune functioning, so I'm working on that in a variety of ways, not the least of which is positive visualization and exercising. I won't be able to have any interventions in the arms or hands for some time after, which is where most of my useful acupressure and acupuncture spots for nausea and pain are, but I'm sure reflexology can offer me some foot or ear options. I have referrals for several breast cancer-sophisticated physical therapists and yoga instructors. I'll probably go to Nancy's naturopath, who is empirical, and talk with someone who does whole-system health and chi work, but I don't want anything that will address one system and kick up a problem in another. First allopathy and complementary interventions, then the more systemic and holistic. Kill it first, then work on restoring balance, hot and toxic yang followed by cool, healing yin.

My ability to discriminate is faulty. There was no palpable lump, though I have checked the situation for breast lumps for decades, memorizing my breasts' particular contours, bumps, and fibrous masses.

I would like to outlive my father. Seven years is my first goal, then.

> Slow breath, a story.
> Mutineers have overrun
> the body. Slow breath.

Dr. Corbin calls with good news from the biopsies, in the sort of universe where this type of news now constitutes "good." Yes, there is a tumor in my right breast, grade 1, probably stage II, slow-moving. The tumor cell proliferation rate is "low," that is, the cancer is not growing quickly. The invasive tumor is estrogen- and progesterone-receptive; "I like that," says Dr. Corbin. The Her2 neu is +1, which he calls "functionally negative," also good. A positive lymph node in the breast, maybe another in my axilla. Other junk—it's a busy breast—is probably more DCIS. Surgery is still on for late February, with bilateral lymph node dissection, such a delightful way to think about my body. He calls the main tumor "indolent." This is good. Easier for a shark to gobble up. This report is better than I anticipated and feared.

With both breasts going, the shark tee shirt loses its meaning. But a better metaphor: *I* am the shark. I am the nurse shark (breast joke). I eat benthic creatures, sea urchins, stingrays, spiny lobsters, and crabs, my scuttling companion. I am generally not aggressive to people. I am adapted to my environment. I respire well. I thrive in these shallow waters.

> Tonic trance—nurse shark
> wakes, consumes a sea urchin,
> indolent tumor.

Q: Why can't you just have lumpectomies?
A: Because the result would look like Mount St. Helens.

The medical team needs to know that I vomit so much in any conveyance that my wife once gave me the gift of a thousand opaque Ziploc-style bags.

A new staff member sitting in on an appointment opines that Tramadol is an "opium agnostic." "Agonist," we assume, but I like the idea of agnostic medication.

A high point for Nancy is that because I have to use a disinfectant body wash and keep the bedding clean, Zebulon will not be allowed under the bedcovers for several days before surgery.

I breathe in golden, liquid light. I breathe out anything that doesn't belong. I contain and shrink everything unhealthy. I am well-oxygenated. My T cells are just right. In this moment, I am alive. My meditation evolves to rest on the phrase "I am still here." I am still, I am here, in this instant of life.

A harpy without tits is just a mean pigeon.

Cancer disrupts the ordered cells, promotes the gradual intrusion of random thoughts and poetry into the medical narrative. Will language disintegrate completely, or reorganize itself after the collapse of sense and certainty?

> This meat is not
> a shell, but me,
> and I am not just meat.

Awake after a dream in which a nurse insisted on giving me an injection though my clothing, though I protested that this wasn't sterile.

I scream into pillows while Nancy is at work. It's too hard on her otherwise.

We get ready to ready the house, the bed, the larder, the papers and lists. I am the Black Knight from *Monty Python and the Holy Grail.* Chop off pieces but I'll keep biting. May I be valiant and not pitiable.

A difficult evening and morning, with crazy blood sugars. I am eerily calm since Thursday morning, yet I have decided to take the fucking Xanax at night without protest or evaluation of my mental state. I assume I should be thanking my unconscious for this flatness, with only brief eruptions of existential horror. I'm still scheduled for the radioactive dye injections Tuesday afternoon, though damned if I'll let anyone inject my breasts until the surgery is confirmed.

My oncologist is able to get a verbal report that I am negative for BRCA1, BRCA2, and other tested markers for inheritable genetic forms of breast cancer. This surprises me, because *s'iz shver tsu zayn a Yid.*

Another colleague, also a patient of Dr. Corbin's, yanks down her waistband to show me her laparoscopic oophorectomy scars.

My mind is not a monkey, but sometimes there is a monkey in my mind, scrambling over the falling stones of Angkor Wat, jumping and screeching, afraid the strangler figs will vine over it and squeeze tight.

I never named or personified my breasts, but around the time I lose them, I find a small, sleek bronze-colored rabbit figurine, ovoid, ears back, compact. Nancy buys it for me. Since then, I've leporidomorphized my breasts as a pair of missing bunnies, returned to the moon.

"Our sages of blessed memory have said: 'A sign has reality.' We, therefore, perform symbolic acts as a sign for good—an expression of prayer...."

Becca and I do our part to stop genetic transmission by failing to reproduce.

Every step reaches the destination. Standing still reaches the destination. I resist the literalism of "I breathe in [X, which is desirable] and breathe out [Y, which is undesirable]." It associates the exhalation with a negative, makes it a deflation. And if there is no "no" in the unconscious, it makes half of the visualization a reinforcement of the negative. I recall the invitation to consider the Buddha's smile, which does cause a subtle smile of recognition and identity. Namaste, you. Constant attention to the breath is useful. I make this a part of my here-and-now substrate. Keep the brain's monkey safe and mindful. Find order in chaos. Don't fear chaos. Don't scare the monkey! Have compassion for the monkey. Contextualize the monkey. Love the monkey. Don't be angry at the body. Extend compassion beyond the body to everyone, to the world. Accept disorder as well. Ritual is important for focus, for diligence, but risks being mistaken for a thing, risks reification.

Maybe I don't hate this cancer enough. I am perplexed by it. I grudgingly respect it. It's good at what it does. I made it; it's a part of me gone wild, spiraling out of the control that is ultimately such a temporary physical state. Maybe it would be better if I actively loathed this cancer, sought to viciously extirpate it, had metaphors easily at hand to suggest that it should crawl away and die. Frederic was a Friend. He wasn't comfortable with military visualizations about killing HIV. Instead he would tell it, "You can't stay here if you're going to cause trouble." I don't know what kind of story to tell myself.

I'm pissed off about lymphedema risk. Even if it's pretty low, I still have to be very careful and restrictive, forever. No one can give me a good answer on how to do my glucose testing. You'd think no one with diabetes had ever had bilateral mastectomy.

So much for visualizing the fucking golden light. I'd like to write, but all I'm thinking about is dying, so this might or might not be the best time. I think of creatures with too many eyes, per Michael Jackson.

Much illness on campus, including several cases of meningitis. Even if I get strep, my surgery could be delayed by several weeks, and I can't stand that. Staying put at home. Resisting the urge to go be helpful.

I tell Nancy I'm getting in touch with my mortality and ask if I should be more afraid of dying of cancer. She replies that I'm doing all of this so that I *won't* die of cancer. That is something, but since the cancer seems unreal to me, abstract, it's hard to be in touch with the positives of intervention and not just my losses and willing acquisition of disability. I have to keep telling myself that cancer may have happened to me, but I'm choosing to take these drastic steps to stop it. I actively accept the consequences, including the pain and alteration of function, because I want to live.

I dream I suddenly and unexpectedly have flat tires.

I am scared, I am bored. I am only peeking at the enormity of it.

I think often of a haiku I wrote about my positive Mantoux skin test after I returned from Israel, "breast" substituted for "lung."

> My soft breast speckles
> like the cinnabar *netsuke*
> Wasp on Rotted Fruit.

Despite worrisome imaging, 6 months of treatment stopped the tuberculosis in its tracks, if it was even there, not a phantom or misinterpreted calcification. I am neither the visible nor invisible woman.

"It's taking so long to get to surgery" versus "surgery is hurtling toward me like a bullet train." I have never had an operation. Today is my last bath for some weeks. I'm trying to reframe it as visiting a country with primitive cleansing facilities and only recliners to sleep in. Both breasts still hurt from the biopsies, but last night I was able to sleep on my left side for a few hours. A small pleasure, soon to be lost once more.

How the body holds the damage of the cure. I will never need a mammogram again.

Getting my hands on myself.

Radioactive dye injection. This turns some people's breasts blue, *Cf.* the unfortunate case of Violet Beauregarde in Willy Wonka's chocolate factory. Only one dose was prepared, though, so I pace and wait for the second to be ordered, prepared, transported, ready to stick.

Last exercise with breasts. Last night with breasts. Tomorrow:

Last shower, car ride, last shirt. Farewell, Breasts. You've been good to me, but it's time for you to go. My wife has enough breasts for both of us, if we're judicious.

Sadly, the dye does not give me purple breasts. If I were a bird, I wouldn't be a blue tit or blue-footed booby.

> Men scratch their bellies
> in the heat before dawn. Blue
> kingfisher plunges.

I awaken from surgery crying. Apparently this isn't unusual after general anesthesia. I was polysyllabic and loquacious in the recovery area but I did explain that this is just how I normally am in a disinhibited state. I am told that I expressed a willingness to sign my own discharge papers. "I'm a doctor!"

My abdomen and whole torso feel as if I have been kicked by a large animal. I'm going to say a yak. I have only intermittent surgical site pain. This is remarkable since all that I am taking is a weak benzodiazepine.

I have a mild sore throat and hoarseness from the breathing tube and need to take it very easy with my arms or they become painful. No nausea. My surgical sites are compressed by a big elasticized cloth binder that looks like a cross between a tube top and a flexible medical cast, so I have not seen what my chest looks like. The cats are avoiding me. I probably smell weird from the hospital. Nancy is not avoiding me. Nancy is wonderful and I'm lucky, despite other evidence at the moment that seems to suggest other conclusions.

My surgeon comments, "You're tougher than you look!" Libido, life force, vegetables and walks, luck of the draw.

I have not had the time to think about what my body is going to look like, or even about whether this surgery got rid of all the cancer. I need a truffle-sniffing pig, a drug-sniffing dog, to suss it out. I expect that when I have more energy I will think more.

Moon rabbits return
to Luna. The pair up there
light the whole night sky.

I am not draining much icky body fluid at all into the disgusting bulbs. The surgeon used a harmonic scalpel, which he characterized as "fun." He told me that I only lost two vials of blood in the surgery. I don't know how big the vials are.

The unappealing cancer journey continues: One of my sentinel lymph nodes was indeed positive, and there is a positive intramammary node as well. This means further treatment is needed to eradicate the cancer. The nature and timing of that treatment is yet to be determined. Needless to say, we are distressed and disheartened, and still quite floored that this much intervention is needed with an early detection. I know that good immune function is important, and hope that my ambient optimistic nature will carry me through, since at this instant I have very little positive feeling available. I will presume that kale and slow walking can substitute for happy thoughts. My protest to the lymph node news yesterday was to eat a handful of regular high-glycemic crackers and a chocolate, which, as a licensed psychologist, I can attest is a pretty low-grade rebellion.

I haven't yet seen the incisions or the shape of my body. I have internal stitches, external Steri-Strips, dressings, wadding, the binder over my torso. Right after the surgery I had no interest in my appearance; I might or might not sometime soon. I've lost much of the peripheral edema I had immediately afterward; I still have a lot of abdominal bloating though I can now suck in my gut, which was impossible a week ago. Does this surgery make me look fat? I continue to take a low dose of lorazepam, which makes me feel less like I'm stuffed in a sausage casing, dulls the pain (variously achy, itchy, burny, prickly, and zappy, as well as sensations of pressure, effervescence, formication, and muscle spasms), and makes it easier to reframe all of this activity as curing rather than harming.

My dressings will be evaluated on Thursday and at least some drains may be removed. This would be more comfortable and might allow Zebulon to sleep under the covers again. Bite-y cat plus inviting tubes of warm body effluence equals trouble all around. We are not up for the Harry Potter movie. I'm not so into the "I'm ready to die" business. Instead, we watch *Monty Python and the Holy Grail* again. A) Left to their own devices, most characters are "getting better," and "feel fine," and B) As to actual devices, the Holy Hand Grenade of Antioch not only references my doctoral alma mater, but bears a great visual similarity to a Jackson-Pratt suction drain, of which I have a bandolier of five ("Four, Sire")—of four. I'm sure this narrative would be more amusing with hyperlinks to these references, or maybe that's just the lorazepam talking.

I'm not even interested in birds. I stare out the window, seeing but not taking in. The chickadees call, "Heeere, kitty," their sorrowful, self-defeating song.

The cat cries. Nancy says, "This is what the cat does when you're away." I am enormously gratified. The cat will miss me. And yet, I am also terribly sad. This is what the cat will sound like when I'm dead.

Physically I'm okay enough, with some aching and transient shooting pain. Strangely, I experience it as nipple pain, though I no longer have nipples. Phantom nipple pain! My underarms are very sore from surgery ("sacrificing the fat pad to harvest the sentinel nodes") and the chest binder, which makes me feel as if I've spent three days using crutches incorrectly. Physiologically, my body is calm enough in the three hours following a dose of lorazepam, then I spend the next three feeling vulnerable. Nancy points out that it's a lower dose than what I was taking in Xanax for anxiety prior to surgery. The drain sites ache. It's not too bad. This is as close as I will get to being a radioactive spider, or the Flying Spaghetti Monster, or Cthulhu, or any victim in the Aliens films.

Maybe it's different when you're dead, but when I was knocked out with anesthesia, I was not there, time wasn't there. There was no evidence of daddy peering down from heaven.

I want to see the actual genetics report—until then, I won't believe it's good. I have no sense of relief after surgery except that the surgery is done—no *Yay, they took out the cancer things* feeling, probably because I only had hidden signs without symptoms. I'm still at *What do you mean I have cancer and have to have a double mastectomy?* In college, I heard the Canadian lesbian-feminist folk singer Ferron tell a story in concert. Paraphrased, it went: *So I'm standing in the middle of the road and there's a truck coming toward me. My friends are shouting, "Ferron, Ferron, look out for the truck!" and I'm going, "What road?"* This is where I am existentially. Maybe after I get the pathology report, if the news is good, I will be able to grieve in more than 30-second blips, and become emotionally positive in addition to simply behaviorally compliant. Ferron also sings, "If it's snowin' in Brooklyn, I'd say snow's what we've got."

There are things that were done to me pictures of which make me want to vomit. I think, *I should do something about that. I should look at those photos. I should desensitize myself.* And then I think, *Why?*

The first time we change the dressings at home, I see myself in the bathroom mirror and start to brown out. It doesn't look terrible, but the amputations are shocking and my body is wrong.

The drain removal process is not unlike Jimmy Carter reeling out a Guinea worm from some surprised guy's abdomen. There's a lot of tail in there. It is only weird, and twice uncomfortable for an instant. I feel better immediately—less encumbered, clunky, or likely to catch on random knobs and objects. Zebulon signifies his approval by returning to the bed —I thought the drains smelled bad, and he apparently agrees. I will probably shower tomorrow night. Adhesive from medical tape can be removed with almond, coconut, or olive oil. Still bandaged up top, and using the tight binder. What I could get a look at during the worm-removal and dressing change was in better shape than I'd anticipated, with little bruising or swelling and tidy Steri-Strip-covered incisions. My abdominal distension is reduced enough for me to wear pants, which I'm sure pleases everyone.

It is not the best cancer, but it is a better cancer than many. For a long time, I didn't want to call it *my* cancer, though I knew it arose from myself. It wasn't my idea, though.

The end result is sufficient, more or less flat. It's not as good as trans top surgery. I could get tattooed nipples, 3D even, but that would just look weird on my flat chest, and I'm not interested in reconstruction. I had enough trouble not banging live, nerve-rich breasts into doorjambs and furniture, so I can't imagine the Mrs. Doubtfire-style trouble I'd get into with insensate artificial mounds.

Can't I be done with this, just get on with treatment without these infernal obstacles? I have to find a different medical oncologist. We already had concerns about the office staff; for example, one called me to ask why they'd scheduled me for labs at 7:00 AM, when the lab isn't open, to which I could only reply, "I don't know." When I go in today for my labs and politely decline to have a blood draw from my arm, since I had just had a conversation about this with my surgeon's staff, the phlebotomist quickly escalates to an urgent yet condescendingly delivered, "You have diabetes, so if we take blood from your foot you could get a blood clot and die!" which earns her a sharp rebuke from Nancy. The oncologist is patronizing, seems to be using a cookie-cutter approach to planning but suggests a specific treatment, then mutters that he hasn't reviewed my chart to know if this is the correct intervention for me. He hands us two poorly-constructed histograms, one showing mortality rates. They are uninterpretable, and we both have doctorates in psychology. "This shows that if you stop with just the surgery, you have a 59% chance. That may sound good—" "No!" I interject, "that sounds terrible!" He doesn't respond to several of our concerns, tells us he doesn't have time to answer our questions. Then he leans forward and in a false empathic voice, says, "Now, you're *going* to *lose* your *hair*," which on the hierarchy of things I'm worried about does not even appear as an item. He doesn't ask me any questions like, "How was your surgery? How do you feel?" I went in prepared to learn about and schedule chemotherapy, hormone suppression, and potentially, future radiation. I come out convinced I could drop dead or be killed by him at any second and spend three hours in bed sobbing while castigating myself for jeopardizing my immune functioning with all this fear and sadness. While I huddle in a miserable ball, Nancy gets online and finds a breast cancer specialist at a teaching hospital a couple of hours away. I have an appointment tomorrow.

I begin to have a paradoxical response to the lorazepam, which is prescribed for muscle spasms in the chest and pain management. I cut back and space them out rather than having them space *me* out. I feel much more like myself, less fearful, hopeless, and inadequate. I manage the pain, much of which is secondary to the binder, with ibuprofen. I still can't concentrate enough to read, but walk slowly every day. Yesterday I drove to the store. Other than discovering that I couldn't close my hatchback once it was open, and must like a little scamper monkey pull it down carefully with the handle of my umbrella, all went well. I can't stand music. It all seems discordant. The one piece I can manage is Brian Eno's *Music for Airports,* which is calming. Before I even listened to it, I thought: I need *Music for Airports,* which I had never heard. I have no idea why.

Cancer becomes more interesting than horrifying, so pain is just pain, divorced from warning.

We schlep to the cancer center two hours away. We are impressed by the facility, personnel, and medical oncologist, none of which can be said of the previous clinic. My new oncologist, Dr. Luz, makes a reasonable case for chemo. I wouldn't need chemo if the right-side tumor had stayed put since it was slow-growing, but because this cancer yearned to clamber up my lymph nodes and out to the periphery, it must be destroyed, not unlike a lion that has developed a taste for human flesh. Despite the drive time, the need for overnight stays for follow-up, and required check-ups between the visits, I am happy to schedule my chemotherapy here.

I go to the university and spend a little over an hour with one of my graduate classes, saying hello, using a cane to signify that people should stay at a distance and not hug me, sitting in the back and listening to my guest instructor. It's exhausting, but meaningful to me. On the approach home, a flock of wild turkeys keeps me from garaging the car.

Some days I fear the treatment more than the cancer, but this is misplaced, displaced. I find a better cancer message board and join two groups for people about to have chemo in March and April. We are still friends.

Long ago, my psychotherapist said that I have a strong libido. She clarified: "In the 'life force' sense." This is what is so frightening in this post-treatment time. I feel diminished in so many ways.

> I miss that old man from Nantucket,
> But I have no libido, so fuck it.
> My past promiscuity's
> A sort of annuity.
> I guess only up's how I'll suck it.

Since my hair stylist is leaving town, she does my pre-chemo buzz as my farewell cut. Think Sigourney Weaver in *Alien 3,* but much hotter.

The compression binder is gone, hallelujah! While I understand its utility, it itched, rubbed, numbed, compressed, and hurt terribly in my armpits, especially on the right. Without the binder, I feel vulnerable, my skin raw and over-sensitive, contracted into the incision lines and throbbing from armpit to armpit across the top of my chest, tight in the armpits, a phenomenon we (I am now part of this post-surgical "we") refer to as "the iron bra." It hurts, but I might actually sleep tonight, and the ride home from the chemo clinic wasn't nearly as difficult without the binder. I have been cleared to begin range of motion exercises, lifting within reason (still no 20-pound cats, alas), to use moisturizer, coconut oil, vitamin E and aloe, and to take a bath, hallelujah, hallelujah.

Flat as a pancake, mammal sans mammaries.

Years ago, when Nancy and I visited Athens at the start of the Lesbian Cruise to the Holy Land, we toured the Acropolis and admired the caryatids. She started laughing. "What?" "I'll bet you could find a decent bra in Greece." She points to a caryatid's rectangular torso, her high, large, widely-spaced breasts. It's true, I could probably find a well-fitting bra anywhere in the Mediterranean region. Later, I discussed this with Ellen, one of the psychologists interviewing me for a temporary job at the university. I commented, "A mighty fortress is our bra." This may have clinched the deal. Now it is just a story with no further utility in my life.

From diagnostic to die agnostic.

I have medical activities the rest of the week, including blood work tomorrow. I am now allowed to have draws from my left arm. A thoracic echocardiogram and PET/CT scan on Friday. Medical oncology appointments next week will probably be followed by having a chemo port installed in the cup of my left shoulder the following Monday. We will talk with the medical and radiation oncologists about my numbers. Will it be chemo, radiation, or both? I exclude "neither" from this chi square. Radiation may not make a huge difference given the invasive cancer's size and slow proliferation rate, but, as the surgeon said, even with that it got out to a node, so despite being indolent in other respects, it may be an opportunistic varmint (my paraphrase).

Dr. Luz calls to say I'm anemic and need five iron infusions immediately in order to begin chemo on schedule.

About a quarter of the time that I'm standing or lying down, the skin of my chest feels over-sensitized, painful, and crawly when anything touches it, and I still feel like I'm wearing the iron bra, hoisted up tight into my armpits. I can now do several of the range of motion stretches to their fullest extent, though they pull. I'm almost at the starting point for one that requires holding my straight arms over my head—after I master that, I'll be able to add a bending-from-side-to-side component. Zebulon would report that the most important gain is that I can reach up with a bent arm far enough to pet him as he sleeps on the bolster behind my pillow.

> Men burn to ashes
> when girls have hot flashes

Anecdote is singular for data, not a gospel, not a hospital checklist. Not everything fits in a regression equation.

I have one of the worst experiences of my life. At the regional infusion center, the nurse can place the IV but it won't function. She also can't get a blood draw. While she keeps pushing and jiggling to no avail, and I cry in pain, she keeps saying that I have "tough veins" (which is news to me) and "too many valves." I don't know what the problem is—I had an easy blood draw on Wednesday and an easy IV yesterday, and it's never taken more than two tries to get an IV or draw to work in that arm. Another nurse manages to get an IV running in the back of my arm and a bag of iron sucrose into me despite the first nurse's six unsuccessful IVs and blood draw attempts that have flattened one vein and caused multiple hand, crook of arm, front of arm, and back of arm bruises, and still resulted in no draw. Although I thank the personnel after they get the IV running, don't say anything rude or unpleasant to them, they stop interacting with me, don't say "of course," "you're welcome," "sorry it was so hard," don't offer me a pillow or show me where the TV remote is. It is like suddenly acquiring a terrible back story: *I was just a child, helpless, relying on these adults, but they abused me, neglected me, hurt me again!* And I'm trapped; I can't escape, can't free myself, can't fight back. This place is like a Gothic orphanage because _____. This place is like a charnel house because _____.

I barely get aftercare instructions for the weekend. At that, they are only brief answers to my questions, no information volunteered. "This treatment has an anaphylaxis warning. If I have flushing or shortness of breath, what should I do? Should I take a Benadryl?" "Call your doctor for instructions." On a Saturday? And shouldn't 911 or an ED triage nurse be called for anaphylactic shock? I ask if there is anything I can do to try to make the next treatment easier. She replies that I should be really hydrated. I agreed I can do that and ask how much

I should drink, since right now I'm drinking at least a gallon of water a day. She simply doesn't answer me. She tells me I needed to relax more, though I was relaxed until the third failed insertion. I should "take more Xanax than I did." So I will do this again on Monday, though I am bruised and sore, and I fear they're going to cause lymphedema in my dominant arm. I've never had such tight tourniquets. They get three tries. If that doesn't work, I will need to delay the rest of the infusions, and chemo, until I can get a port installed, and then they can use the port. I've had a root canal without any anesthetic. I cut my hand badly in Israel without crying. I have a high pain threshold. I'm not sure I've cried during any medical procedure as an adult. It was awful and I feel limited in my options. The iron itself was fine—a little burning and aching now and then as it infused, and apparently no side effects. It's a damned shame they're having trouble getting it into me, but I have little control over the problem. I will skip some of my stretches because my arm is painful and I'm afraid to stress it. I think I preferred surgery.

Iron infusion #2 is completely different. The charge nurse, who has "a passion for IVs," looks at the remaining non-bruised sites remaining after Saturday's massacre, gets the IV in on her first try with minimal discomfort, draws blood, and runs the infusion, also releasing the tourniquet when she isn't using it. A CNA offers me water (with ice; we had asked for an ice pack for the back of my neck on Saturday because I was afraid I was about to faint, but instead Nancy was told to just wet some hand towels), shows me where the call button is, takes a manual blood pressure instead of using the machine, talks to me, offers me a pillow, and takes my vitals again after the infusion. I wouldn't have thought it was the same procedure.

The first time we go back to the ponds to look for birds, I don't even have the stamina or pectoral strength to raise my binoculars for more than a minute. Pied grebe, double-crested cormorant, northern shoveler. I'm a sitting duck.

Me being dramatic: Not just one cancer, but two! In two breasts, with two mastectomies! And chemo, and radiation, and hormone suppression! I must really want attention!

The radiation oncologist at the distant facility says the treatment she recommends for me is pretty standard, so she encourages me to work with a local radiation oncologist since it's a 6-week, 5-day-a-week treatment. She says, as does my mother, "Say goodbye to the hair in that armpit." She is not quite as casual in her expression as my mother. For the rest of my life, my armpit hair will grow asymmetrically.

It's Uncle Shmuli! Not my uncle—me in the night hunched up like someone else's grandpa, a hermit crab scuttling to the toilet, the topography of scars, bulging abdomen, broken mattress torso lumpy under myself. Goofy grin, blinking in the light, still off-balance from anesthesia, where are Shmuli's glasses? I need glasses for the bathroom! Oy, my *kishkes.* Maybe a nice piece of fish will settle my stomach?

Humor is my best consistent defense, to be sure. I am also good at intellectualizing, though when I'm on the other side of the couch, I call it "successful cognitive restructuring of negative schemata."

My medical oncologist, Dr. Luz, looks at my arm, still bruised and sore, a few days after the infusion and directs me only to give anyone two tries for a blood draw or IV from now on. I will gladly adhere.

I'll have a chemo port installed on Monday. I say this as if it doesn't flip me out, but it does, though I understand the process and I want the port. I will have the last iron infusion Tuesday or Wednesday and begin chemo on Thursday. I also say that as if it doesn't alarm me, but I hope after the first round it will be boring rather than frightening. At least my Sigourney-in-the-penal-colony buzz cut will be utilitarian, not just a bold fashion statement. After several rounds of chemo I'll have a break, then move on to radiation.

Dr. Luz agrees that flax is okay, though her disparaging comments about it suggest that she herself does not enjoy flax.

Dr. Luz wants me dressed, out of bed, and out of the house, preferably socializing in sparsely-populated locales away from sick people. "Don't go to nursery schools," she says, which is fine except that a great many of my students work in early childhood settings, so I will need to be explicit about people not coming to class when they're sick. I'm also not to climb ladders, play contact sports, or bang into my spleen with anything large during chemo. I can not-do all of these.

I've read *The Emperor of All Maladies* and have no desire to read it again, nor the desire to watch the documentary right now, considering that I can't even watch the hospital's here's-how-radiation-works video without crying and becoming agitated. I am only just recovering my ability to read for more than a few minutes. It's been a long stretch since January.

The chemo port is in. The surgical nurse is disgusted by the 6 still-bruised sites from Infusion Nurse #1's unsuccessful digging around and calls in other nurses to view my arm. They are gratifyingly upset on my behalf. She asks the anesthesiologist to put in my IV as she isn't sure she can work with the available damaged sites. He does so and offers to cap and wrap the IV afterward so the infusion center can use it tomorrow morning. I have monitored anesthesia rather than general, but still go from "Take a breath" to "Are you ready to wake up?" with nothing in between.

Diving into the wreckage, the body's *naufragium,* shipwreck is everywhere. "There are heroes in the seaweed," says Leonard Cohen, so I eat the seaweed.

There is a packing list for chemo days, later a good model for pilgrimage: Pack a snack. Pack your glasses. Will you meditate, read, or talk with the others while you wait? Don't forget warm socks. Will they have potable water?

Taxotere is one of my chemo potions. Taxotere and taxol are derived from species of yew trees, European and Pacific respectively. The yew holds poison and immortality. As I sit in meditation on suffering beneath the evergreen branches, among the taut crimson yew berries, serpents beckon me to partake of death, life, both, in careful balance. Post-Cleopatra, I bare my absent breast. Apoptosis dominocus.

My first chemo day goes well. I receive a handful of glucocorticosteroid pills to match those for yesterday and tomorrow. This and the Claritin and Benadryl I'm taking for four days are intended to reduce side effects. The center needs an order for the numbing cream and has none, so I get a spray of lidocaine on the port instead. I develop terrible itching from their skin cleanser, add it to my contact dermatitis list. Even though I'm still quite sore from Monday's surgery, the insertion of the special port needle is very easy and comfortable compared to even a good IV insertion.

First labs are drawn and we wait about an hour for them to come back. I receive a pretreatment infusion bag. Then drug number one, which floods my mouth with a Band-Aid and salt taste not unlike Ardbeg, a single malt Scotch I enjoy because it tastes like Band-Aids, salt, and smoke. Perhaps I could swig a little liquid smoke to enhance the flavor. Then drug number two, no particular taste. I have a great nurse who goes over the highlights of the entire patient manual with us during the infusion. Really? No aged cheese? Is the chemo an MAO inhibitor? And it is done. We check in to the hotel, then eat dinner at a nice Thai place and take a brief trip to Powell's Books. You're not supposed to eat anything you enjoy or that might cause stomach upset or nausea during chemo on the principle that neurons that fire together, wire together, potentially causing Cashew Gai to make you vomit for the rest of your life. And yet this may be my last chance to eat Thai for months, so *carpe diem.* Tomorrow I will get a white cell booster shot in the abdomen. I clean the hotel's treadmill with disinfectant wipes, walk a slow hour. A short bath, then I fall asleep. An hour later I'm up, wired from steroids. I sit up, don't write, don't read, don't meditate, try not to think. Just sit, for hours.

Even if I have lousy side effects, I've now received 25% of my chemo treatments. Three days out from chemo and two from Neulasta, I feel all right, though worse than when I was taking the steroids. I'm still tender in my left shoulder and neck as well as the port insertion incision and the area of my chest around the port itself. The port was installed only three days before it was used, and the iron infusion and chemo made me swell. It is hard to type. My mastectomy scars, armpits, drain tube scars, shoulders, and neck are sore and puffy. I am not allowed heat, cold, aspirin, ibuprofen, or naproxen. I am supposed to use Tylenol, which does nothing for my pain anyway, only sparingly since my oncologist doesn't want to depress a post-chemo fever unless I reach 100.4° Fahrenheit.

I don't have a lot of sense of what "healed enough to exercise" means, or how much is enough. I'm trying to pay close attention to what my body says.

Lost! Ability to withstand the sun.
Found! The art of the eyebrow pencil.

Lost! Sleeping on my side.
Found! The art of over-moisturizing.

Lost! Toenail integrity.
Found! Swollen, pop-out veins.

Lost! Capacity to chop meat or vegetables without hyperconsciousness.

As a tool-using primate who hasn't had to think much about my immune function, I do generally eat dry food that's fallen to a more or less clean surface, and I do use my mouth to hold or manipulate objects, such as pen or a shirt hanger. I accede to Nancy's request that I not kiss cats on their faces in order to decrease the possibility of zoonotic hantavirus transmission. Now I'm immunosuppressed from treatment. To stop using my mouth in potentially germ-sucking ways, I pretend I'm on one of my trips to Southeast Asia, where I'm scrupulous about filth, germs, handwashing, and putting things in my head. I channel my past work lives in medical-psychiatric settings, where I acted on the assumption that my attention to cleansing and barrier precautions allowed me to interact with patients without acquiring their Hepatitis B. It's odd to do this at home.

My pareidolia, the perception of random visual stimuli as meaningful, has been higher than normal—faces in the trees, words in the popcorn ceiling finish. I always see some, which, not being psychotic, I can simply enjoy, but it's a lot more evident during this non-reading time. This makes me think about brain areas and functions, and how and with which parts of our cognition we make meaning under stress. I feel calmer as time goes on and I incorporate new ideas about myself and my life.

The first chemo treatment's acute side effects last about a week, and I continue to have slightly lower energy, a little transient neuropathy in my fingers and toes, somewhat tender mucosa, a runny nose, and a lightly upset digestive system, all of which is on the mild side. Some of my nail beds ache off and on, and my scalp has an unpleasant tingle that hasn't yet translated to hair loss. This is manageable and shows me the shape of my post-chemo week. Dr. Luz says that the effects of the first chemo are reasonably predictive of future chemos, with the addition of increasing fatigue. On the bright side, my assiduous moisturizing has my skin looking just fabulous.

My form, transmuted, embodies the Star of David, the mystical Seal of Solomon. I begin in water, a triangle arrowed down, the feminine principle. After surgery my shape is the masculine, the triangle of fire pointed up from the hips. Their conjunction reveals the crossed triangles of earth and air. I hold every elemental sign.

Instructions for the EMLA numbing cream: An hour before the appointment, apply to the port, then cover with a piece of Press'n Seal kitchen wrap to hold the goop in place. On some treatment days, this sometimes happens in a parking lot between home and the clinic because our drive doesn't quite get us to the waiting room on time.

Breakage is an opportunity, repair is the next developmental phenomenon. Accidents happen, shit happens, something takes the place of something else. This is normal if sometimes also tragic. Change, mutation, transformation. The image arising from the scars on my chest: A face emerges, aged, scowling, an indignant tree spirit. I am cocooned in the wizened tree, not looking out, guarded by this wrathful apparition.

Make meaning, shift meaning, give up meaning. I search for and acquire a tiny silver breast *milagro*.

I try to align myself with the belief that the surgery took care of the cancer and the chemo and radiation are just the house-to-house mop-up for stragglers. I'm still conflicted about "surgical strike" imagery. I keep picturing the napalming of Vietnam. At the same time, I find I don't have as much trouble with the "killing" metaphor as Frederic did. I want to be as active and agentive as I can in a process where I only control some parts. I need to gracefully acknowledge that there are others I can't do much about. Perhaps a Passover metaphor is better: I have done the mass cleaning of *chametz*, the grains forbidden for Passover, from the house, and chemo and radiation serve the purposes of the next step in cleaning, which is called *Bedikat Chametz.* This is a search for stray chametz using a candle, feather, and spoon to be sure every bit is removed and the house is kosher. Did my family do this? No, but I feel free to appropriate my own cultural/religious traditions in service to symbolism.

I can try to convince myself that cancer is just mutated cells, but the word itself holds that metaphor, *karkinos*, that hard, clacking crab. The Latin word refers only to the crab's leg, says Galen, to the tumor's visible extension, but I have evidence of the whole thing crawling.

Since I was in my early 20's, even before my first trip to Egypt, I've made it part of my Passover practice to ask, *In what ways am I still a slave in Egypt? In what ways can I help liberate others and myself, actually or metaphorically? How am I participating in or colluding with my own oppression and the oppression of others?* These questions feel especially pertinent this year as I balance my focus between health and disease, helping myself and helping others, and how I accept and express my gratitude for the support and kindness my friends, families, coworkers, and internet support group members give me.

I light a *yahrzeit* for my father. *Yitga*-this, *v'yitka*-that.

Such modesty as I had (N.B.: Not a lot) is gone. There is much rearranging of clothing in this treatment, much looking and palpating and sliding around of hands while one is in nonprivate areas. I actually like this, and the pragmatism of the medical professionals. With most I have asked, "Do you need me to put this robe on? If it's for my comfort, I don't care," and most have replied, "I don't care, either." This saves time and the fiction implicit in the covering-up that they are not immediately going to uncover you. If they use the interval to check with another concurrent patient, fine, but I don't need anyone leaving the room out of delicacy about my shirt being off before they take off the top they just had me put on. It seems Victorian. Like pointing to the relevant spot on an ivory Chinese Doctor's Lady. Show me on the doll where the oncologist saved your life.

I can wear a shirt for about three hours, then my upper chest becomes too sensitive and I have to claw it off. This requires some strategy around workplace meetings. Fortunately I'm teaching online this term, making my limited shirt-wearing much easier to manage. I had to go back in the chest binder for a night when I called about an abscessed stitch, and didn't sleep more than two hours because it was so irritating. Like the port, I recognize the utility of, and am grateful for, the binder, without liking it whatsoever.

Cancer is like a library, and I am the reference librarian agonizing about the best organizational structure.

I'm now able to read for about an hour a day, but in that magical way of the universe, everything I randomly pick up has cancer or medical disasters as a focus. Therefore, I've chosen Sir Richard Burton's thousandish-page *Personal Narrative of a Pilgrimage to Al-Medinah and Mecca*, which has little to do with my life at present. So far, there is only one incidental character who dies of cancer. I have also found a good metaphor for the chemo port. Speaking of how to carry money safely, Burton offers, "Others, again, in very critical situations, open with a lancet the shoulder... and inset a precious stone, which does not show in its novel purse." So there you have it: The port is a gem hidden below my shoulder, necessary for my pilgrimage.

When I sleep on my back, which was infrequent until my first biopsy, I normally keep one leg cocked in a "figure 4" position, the Tarot's Hanged Man. In India I attended a lecture at Sri Aurobindo Society about the meaning of this posture, upright, in Hindi religious iconography. It represents having a metaphoric foot in both the secular and the sacred realms. Now that I can only sleep on my back, I think of the stance this way, or like the Buddha's *mudra* Earth Touching, which signifies his moment of enlightenment. I would rather have a foot in both aspects of existence than be the hanged woman.

I think a lot about "body *wabi-sabi*." Wabi-sabi is a Japanese aesthetic and philosophical term that accepts and values transience, impermanence, and imperfection. I have 7 new scars on my torso, two of them quite large. I expect to acquire another when the port is removed. I hope to look at my body in its acquired and changing state as beautiful, interesting, poignant. I hope it provides a fresh perspective, one that is different, not damaged; in the way of *kintsugi, kintsukuroi,* Japanese gold lacquer repair, that it has become better than it was before the breakage and utilitarian ornamentation.

The port has yet to settle into comfort or fade into the background of my daily experience. I can tolerate a lot if I know it's not signaling a physical emergency, but the pain medication and the discomfort associated with typing keep me from getting my work done. It is hard to prepare food, eat, brush my teeth with my left hand. These secondary phenomena are not only their own annoyance but easily become attached to fears related to primary issues: *What if there's something really wrong and they have to remove the port and this interferes with my chemo?* It's good practice in mindfulness, but I would prefer to increase my attentiveness and intentionality in other ways. It also makes it hard to be cheerful, a light unto the nations, a role model for brave little girls everywhere, etc.

The nurses love my "Hi My Name Is" sticker on which I have written "No ChloraPrep!" They've seen how it bubbles my flesh.

The pharmacy and Dr. Luz have a dispute about how much steroid to give me at the start of chemo. The pharmacy initially prevails, but when I begin to have facial flushing and numb lips, Dr. Luz wins and I get the additional steroid dose as a drip before continuing. On my electronic visit report, the reason given for the make-up dose is "error," which amuses me. I like that my oncologist was right about my needs.

Of course, one of the books I picked up, *Wild,* by Cheryl Strayed, turns out to start with her mother's swift death from cancer, but it is the way of the world to throw these at me right now. Two memoirs I was reading in India while waiting for my first biopsy, *Dreaming in Hindi: Coming Awake in Another Language* and *In a Rocket Made of Ice: Among the Children of Wat Opot,* feature the authors' surprise breast cancer disclosures.

Chemo plus Neulasta plus about 120 ounces of fluid equals weighing 8 pounds more when I get home from treatment than when I went in. Yikes! No wonder my incisions feel tight! I lose about four pounds by morning while remaining hydrated, but Uncle Shmuli makes many nighttime trips.

Yesterday was the first time I had trouble walking on even a slow treadmill. My sleep is shallow with repetitive, muddled dreams that seem important at the time but aren't very interesting. I'm hungrier. My eyes, nails, and scalp ache. My tongue is swollen. My eyes and mouth are dry. My scars and the areas where I had surgical drains hurt. This is acceptable as long as I can still manage to eat Thai food after each treatment. Patients are asked to avoid eating foods with strong smells in the chemo area in order not to increase other patients' nausea. No kimchi bento box for me.

My port can be removed at about four weeks after my last round of chemo, assuming all is well and there isn't a reason to retain it. My surgeon says that 98% of his patients do it as a 30-minute in-office procedure with just an anesthetic injection. That sounds disgusting to me, but it's what I'm going to do. I hear and read that it's not as much of a big deal coming out as when it goes in. I can't wait. The port is still uncomfortable at best and painful at worst, though I'm grateful not to have my arm in use for chemo or blood draws. I schedule my radiation pre-treatment positioning appointment, the next awful and desirable thing. *Odi et amo.*

No hair to comb. I've lost my crown of snakes to cancer. Sweating while functionally bald is not at all like sweating with hair. Schmutzy reading glasses from using this much moisturizer are logarithmically filthier than glasses worn with a normal amount of lotion. My eyebrows and eyelashes fall out. I'm on an elevator in a hotel and a woman stage whispers, "Do you have cancer? I did, too." Suddenly nobody thinks I'm queer. I'm not a dyke with short hair, I'm a person in chemo.

The body's assemblage, parts unsumming, setting itself equal to zero. Collect the sparkle, magpie-like, aggregate and view it right, see if patterns emerge, old and new, transformed.

Rules are helpful as guidelines, but they're also too rigid. Therefore, how much should I question my doctors? How not to fall into automatic and perhaps dangerous obedience to authority? What should I do next? What are the consequences of doing and not doing? I can hardly do anything but trace my way through complex decision trees. I see the branches, but what about underground? What of the world-serpent, coiled, tangled into the roots, snarled up with miles of undetected fungi?

We spend a weekend in Yachats on the Oregon coast, with a window facing the ocean. Fortunately it is overcast and not too windy, which means I can walk on the beach with heavy sunblock, sunglasses, and a floppy hat without being burned or getting sand in my chemo-raw eyes. From the hotel and nearby foot path, we see whales, including calves, a lone sea lion, flights of brown pelicans, two to three types of cormorant, two types of scoter, and a variety of shore birds and peeps. Black oystercatchers, "our" bird, so they are a romantic sighting. What, doesn't every couple have a bird? It is relaxing and a pleasure to spend this quiet, unstructured time with Nancy and reading Oliver Saks's autobiography (N.B.: Cancer).

We go to the aquarium gift shop, where I buy a stuffed otter to stick between my shoulder and the seat belt, which rubs and presses excruciatingly on my port. Frederic once had a record player with a needle that skipped unless it was weighted, which was accomplished by means of a small plastic dinosaur referred to as "the anti-skid dinosaur." This phrase generalized over time to include anything with a remotely similar function. Thus, I now have an anti-skid otter.

My job between yesterday and chemo today has been not to fall, like a friend who tripped the day before her last chemo, broke her shoulder, and couldn't use her port for the last infusion. Learning from her unhappy experience, I grip hand rails, watch for obstacles on the floor, and have been deliberate when getting up at night.

My echocardiogram is normal, and the last drug of the last chemo infuses as I write. I've looked forward to my chemo treatments because doing something for my future makes me feel more powerful. I'm sure if I were experiencing a lot of

SHOSHANA D. KEREWSKY

queasiness, I'd have the nausea-conditioned aversion to the building and room that affects so many of the women with whom I share experiences online. I had some nausea in the last cycle, but I'm also a little more off-kilter. I speculate that both are because of losing stereocilia, the hairs in the inner ear that affect balance.

My left shoulder still cups soreness, jewel in the lotus flower, om. I hope removing the chemo port will help. I still have several post-chemo weeks of side effects before I'm closer to whatever normal may turn out to be. A taste of equilibrium, then radiation, then years of hormone suppression. My side effects continue to include a variety pack of discomforts and low-grade pain. Feeling agentive, understanding that I chose this treatment, and being curious about it makes a positive difference in how my pain registers, just like psychology and Buddhism said it would. Although my short-term memory is worse for the wear, and my word-finding is off, I am, as we psychologists say, grossly cognitively intact. I could count backward by 7s if necessary, and remember the named objects at the end of a mental state evaluation. I'm not sure I can name the last four presidents, since I think of them as "Obama, Obama, Rat Bastard, Rat Bastard."

I had heard from friends that the local radiation service is good, and so far that's been true. The lobby is terribly depressing, though, and the facility sends "fun run" and other event spam on their patient portal. When I get an email that there's a message for me on a medical portal, I prioritize opening it. When it's essentially an ad for the center or its affiliates' events, I think, "Really? Are you missing the part where the patients you're spamming are in cancer treatment, that they might be alarmed that there's a message, have finite energy?"

I'm past the two-week post-chemo mark, so I'm beyond most

of the digestive and GI effects, most of the bone pain, and most of the edema. The whole port area, including my neck and jaw, continues to hurt. My toenails are cold, sore, and yellow and red, with chemo ridging. However, they're not infected and are still attached to my toes, which I like in a nail. Sleeping on my right side, despite still feeling like I'm on a lumpy mattress, is an unalloyed pleasure. Soon I'll have my left side back as well. I haven't slept on my left but once since the first biopsy, half a year ago. I will also soon be allowed to drink alcohol again. I haven't had a drink since December, before India, with the exception of a single sip of champagne at a family wedding.

I've missed only five days of work, and at that I was on email every day, corresponding, grading, posting. I teach three intensive summer classes. Sometimes I lie down exhausted on the dirty and cold linoleum classroom floor while the students are at lunch.

When I was young, I would snivel and tense up about medical procedures. I've been forced to get over that. When the dermatology physician's assistant offers to zap a couple of benign but annoying spots on my face with liquid nitrogen, I don't think my pulse even increases. Yeah, fine, kill them with ice, whatever. Cynical Buddhism: *Yup, the current moment blows; oh, well. Whatever.*

As soon as the port is removed, before Dr. Corbin had even sewn the stitches, I feel immediate relief in my neck and jaw. I have kept the port itself as a souvenir of this delightful odyssey. I may turn it into a steampunk medallion, a homemade talisman of St. Peregrine, patron saint of cancer and AIDS, the Catholic Babalú Ayé.

Drinking unsweetened chai in a tea house, honeybush, cacao, carob, cinnamon, ginger, nutmeg, red clover, rosemary, roasted chicory. A woman lingers at my table and flirts with me, saying what a great head shape I have. There's no sense that she is fishing for a response about chemo. I am thinking about bodhisattva vows. One vows to attain enlightenment for the benefit of all sentient creatures, but to delay this until all have been liberated. This looks like compassion and altruism, and I've been drawn to it for this reason. However, in my current state of heightened awareness of my mortality, it starts to seem like a hedge. In my consciousness I don't believe in reincarnation, but my unconscious and symbolic mind believe in something after death. If the argument goes that agreeing to stick around in multiple lifetimes secretly means having a get-out-of-jail card in case there *is* something after, then it's just a hidden insurance policy. I will die, but I will, if I return, return as something with a noble purpose. It seems like a covert pact with the universe—give me life, give me purpose—but also a tremendous attachment to the ego, the idea that some aspect of myself will transcend my death. Would I be so eager to continue my existence if I were a poor, abused woman in Delhi or Cape Town? A Syrian child in the tumbled destruction of war? Would I want to sign up for more lives of pain, or is the desire to return really an attachment to my easy and privileged circumstances? I like to think that my curiosity and pleasure in existing are related to the aspects of myself that are drawn to the bodhisattva vow, but I don't know. My libido, in the broad sense of "life force" is, I believe, positive for the people around me, an exuberance for life without a longing for what I'm already experiencing. I'm sure there's a German word for that, or maybe it's a form of poignancy, of wabi-sabi. In the context of such pleasure-in-being, is the bodhisattva vow an enactment of attachment? A future orientation that clings to existence? A triumph of wish over my best understanding of the nature of transience? Nothing wrong with reverting to carbon, to hydrogen. But I don't want to get off the wheel. I do not want to go gentle, et cetera.

Let's fry the mutants! I finish reading Peter

Trachtenberg's *Seven Tattoos: A Memoir in the Flesh.* After I'm allowed more sun exposure, I want to go on a women's-only vacation somewhere with a topless beach so everyone can say, "Oooh, you're so brave and beautiful! I'm so sorry you're in a committed monogamous marriage!" while Nancy and I hold hands.

Radiation treatment starts with a simulation that marks the body, my body, to create alignment points for radiation targeting. The high-tech part is CT scans; the low-tech part is Sharpie crosses. Transparent adhesive stickers cover the dashes and dots all over my torso for 8 days between simulation and the first treatment, which is why by five days out I sport multiple round, octopus-sucker welts that may be baked into scars by the radiation. While this could seem like an amusing hentai or tentacle porn thing, it is not.

My first radiation treatment is cancelled two hours beforehand because the machine is broken. I insist on having the stickers removed whether or not I can have treatment. Three are replaced with positioning tattoos. The tattooing sounds more interesting than it is. The tattoos are dots made by squirting a drop of India ink on the skin, poking it with a needle, and jiggling. They are supposed to look like "freckles," but what they look like is prison tattoos. The next day, I get three more and receive my first dose. I can't wait until the next time a student asks if I have any tattoos. "Yeahhhh," I'll say, leaning back in my chair, "I have [counting on my fingers] six." If I ever decide to be buried in a Jewish cemetery, I will need a rabbinical dispensation. I should map the dots and hold a constellation-drawing contest. I want to know what image pareidolia finds on me.

The medical building where I receive radiation has breast-shaped wall sconces. They are an uneven, blotchy yellow with dark, irregular lines running around them. It's terrible imagery. Another patient in the waiting area confides that she asked the surgeon if he were Christian, because she would never allow a non-Christian to operate on her. As for me, I watched the same surgeon's hands at our first meeting to make sure they didn't tremble.

I don't mind the linear accelerator. It's more like being in the Death Star than the Borg Collective, which was my association for the chemo port. The entire front assembly rotates. One of the appurtenances swings closer to the face and gives me a "No, Mr. Bond, I expect you to die" vibe, especially since my feet are banded together for the treatment. Or it could be a KitchenAid. Someone has drawn a smiley face on a scrap of medical tape and stuck it on a part of the machine that I can focus on. I smile the Buddha's smile, breathe and hold my breath as directed. The metaphor is "cultivating the mind," but my gardens all have beetles and chaff, disgusting slime, so that's got to be acceptable as well.

Some days while Nancy is at work, I still scream into a pillow, walking slowly around the house moaning. It's easier on her and a relief for me. Some days nothing works but *Music for Airports.* Why? Why?

I count countries to try to sleep. Can I name them all? Sometimes I forget which I've been to and which I've only visited in books. If this results in dreams, they are confused as to action, narrator. I gain no insights.

I like Dr. Anton, my radiation oncologist. She's kind and informative. The techs are also very nice. They play the radio during zaps, rock music full of unintentional hilarity like "We Didn't Start the Fire," a fine cancer-burning song, though they don't want me to sing along, even to Imagine Dragons' "Radioactive." They greet me and let me know what they're doing, since different activities happen on different days. They take x-rays every five treatments to check the positioning, and every other day a form not unlike a rubbery plastic shower mat is draped over and taped to the radiation field for bolus treatments, which increase the dose. I've had 9 of 33 treatments and so far, my skin is holding up well. I am to "slather" myself with aloe and moisturizers. "Slather," interestingly, has an unknown etymology. I always thought it was a back formation from "lather," but apparently it isn't. Over and over I think, *"It rubs the lotion on its skin...."*

I'm starting to get "Cute hair!" rather than tragic glances from strangers. This is good, I joke, because my self-esteem is entirely wrapped up in whether strangers find me sufficiently feminine. As a new online friend said, "I told the doctor, "I want to look like a 10-year-old boy!" I am still mostly-bald Uncle Shmuli, up in the night, *again.* "Oy, my prostate!"

Uses for calendula: A) Tomato hornworm; B) Radiation hornworm?

The linear accelerator rotates to roast my flesh. Rotisserie chicken, dark meat only. Someday, I will leap up and dance.

I don't presume that I have a right not to die, though I'm aware of a strong substrate of this underlying assumption.

The two post-"active" treatment medications, melatonin and tamoxifen, tire me badly but make it no easier to sleep. I continue to have bouts of vertigo. At 7 weeks post-radiation, I'm finally getting a chance to heal.

I fear tamoxifen's long list of side effects. I had learned a medicine-taking strategy from a video about AIDS and psychology: Associate the pills with prayer or thanks, so every morning I meet its blank white gaze, an eye in my palm to ward off danger, and address it, "Thank you, Tamoxifen" before I swallow.

Am I a double Amazon, or Tiresias? An undouble-breasted cormorant?

Cancer untruths I have encountered:

- Cancer will kill you.
- If you eat right, you won't get cancer.
- This treatment cures cancer.
- This unattested, anecdotally-reported treatment is better than those poisons.
- Big Pharma just wants to steal your money.
- If you're good with God, you won't get cancer.
- Thinking negatively makes the cancer kill you.
- If you got cancer, you haven't worked through your anger issues.
- You did something bad, and cancer is the punishment.
- If you say the word "cancer," cancer will sniff you out and hunt you down.
- If you skip medical visits, they won't find cancer so you won't have cancer.
- You're better off dying than having your body change in gendered ways.
- Biopsies don't hurt.
- You'll be up and around in no time!
- This will only be slightly uncomfortable.
- If you have a good cancer, it won't kill you.

The myths are signs, encapsulated guideposts. They hold a story but aren't the only story, or the experience.

Nancy and I take an experimental short flight at over 30,000 feet. I do not develop any immediately evident lymphedema. I will need to wear sleeves and gauntlets on flights of four and half hours or over as a preventive measure. Why four and a half hours? Is it statistically significant? No, the major research study was performed on domestic flights in Australia, which are about that long coast to coast. I've begun a low-impact, low-cardio, senior Zumba class once a week, which is just about my speed. The songs, both in English and Spanish, arouse my feminist antipathy and make me weep for humanity. Good beats are their redeeming quality. My instructor, a former colleague at the university, is the wonderful bonus.

I dreamed in the early morning that I looked down at my body and had had my mastectomies. I was wearing a cravat or kerchief but my torso was otherwise bare. I had some feeling of loss or diminution, but this was secondary. I was focused on the dream's action. This was the first dream in which I saw my chest; surgery was 10 months ago.

I dreamed I was in the pleasant waiting room of a medical practice talking with a woman, a fellow patient but with different issues. She put both hands on my breasts to see what they were like, then became flustered. I was startled but took my shirt off so she could see. I had nipples and small breast swellings, which concerned me. I made a mental note to discuss this at my oncology appointment. The woman then pulled on a crepey-ropy veil of flesh hanging from my right chest and axilla to about my knee. She commented that "It's supposed to snap?" I felt the skin to assess it. I had some pain and sensation closer to my chest, but wondered if I could trim it back without bleeding too much. I wasn't too upset; my response was, "Oh, *another* goddamn thing."

I dreamed I was lying on a gurney in a hospital corridor, all of my clothes off and other people walking around. The sheet was pulled down, showing my mastectomy scars. I wasn't there for a procedure or action that had anything to do with mastectomy.

I have achieved a hard-core punk look with my drastic and emblematic hair, my body mod, my tattoos, my sunken eyes and cheeks. Or else clergy: My tonsure, my mortification of the flesh, every shirt a hair shirt, skin formicating with imaginary insects.

It's not turtles all the way down. I am going to die, and I don't like that. Bury me with terra cotta, my warriors of Xi'an.

My body still looks like a portrait by Egon Schiele, proportions distorted, puffy, skin the color of old bruises, hollowed orbits, lumps. My armpits and chest are asymmetrical. I am shaded yellow-green beneath the skin. I chose this; I am still my body.

A year ago, I was in pre-op. I count today as my cancerversary because rather than inscribe the distressing diagnostic events in memory, I want to celebrate the surgery that is what I believe eradicated the cancer. Chemo and radiation were the frosting on the cake, and tamoxifen, I guess, the sprinkles or something. The metaphor really breaks down here. Itemizing my medical visits for the last year highlights how much work this has been, and continues to be.

I've been on tamoxifen since September. It has its side effects, hot flashes, leg cramps, and more delicate muscles, and its scary rare-but-possible side effects, like increased risk of endometrial cancer, but it's the post-surgical treatment most likely to prevent a recurrence. I had chemo-curls until my most recent cut; my hair returns from the deviation to the mean, though thinner, greyer. I now own more than one pair of sweat pants and I'm conversant on contemporary hip-hop and Spanglish pop.

Nancy and I fly to the Caribbean for a rescheduled vacation. It is wonderful to be back to birding and seeing different countries, and as a bonus, my now-constant vertigo and my motion sickness cancel each other out so I have no nausea at sea. In Cuba we visit Fusterlandia, a Havana neighborhood rendered psychedelic, hallucinatory, encrusted with mosaic and bricolage. I feel sympathy for the raw edges, the crude joins that do not try to disguise or beautify the transitions.

Frederic died 22 years ago. That bastard. He skipped out on

all of this. I light a yahrzeit candle a day early since I need to leave at 4:00 AM for my annual test item engineering gig. On the flight I try a set of Juzo compression sleeves and gauntlets. The set I first got itch and leave a waffle pattern on my arms. People smile at me in the Salt Lake airport, perhaps because my shirt is pink, perhaps because of the sleeves, perhaps because I am walking with a cane, or perhaps because there was a memo to all Saints to smile at visitors. The state I'm flying to has just passed an anti-trans bathroom bill, increasing instances of less-feminine women being harassed and pursued when they try to use the restroom. I have short hair and no breasts. Nancy exacts a promise that when my team eats at a restaurant, I won't try to pee unaccompanied.

When I can't sleep, strung up by tamoxifen and flapping in the wind, disbelieving that I will ever sleep again, I review the interesting places where I've ever managed to. On the landing of a dormitory stairwell. In a large cardboard box in the sweltering Swarthmore Alumni Office because I was working the alumni weekend and needed a hidden nest, safe from patrolling Security officers. On a bench in Victoria Station, arms locked around my backpack, waiting for the early train to the early ferry so I could cross the Channel to meet Laura and Frederic in France, then drive for hot hours past undulating fields of sunflowers under the white sky. Atop the White Cliffs of Dover, blaring horns and searingly bright beacons through the night, which, at that, didn't truly fall until about 11:00 PM and lasted only five hours. On a staff psychologist's musty hospital couch, many times, because the break between my Saturday evening and Sunday morning shifts was too short for me to drive from Boston to Providence and back. In the back seat of my Tercel on a residential side street in Vermont after no one answered the door at the bed and breakfast. In a padded medical chair of unknown function in the bowels of a Virginia hospital after driving all night from Rhode Island, my father in surgery to remove and replace his liver. At an unused and mildewed Sea-Tac gate, travel alarm clock propped beside me, to sleep through the last layover between Cambodia and Portland. On the concrete floor of an abandoned house in a *batey* in the Dominican Republic, my students restless beside me, acrid smoke in the hot air, electricity off, my mosquito net collapsed onto my sticky face. Several of the students had brought paperback copies of *Fifty Shades of Grey*, which made me wonder, *Of all the books you could take to an international spring break service-learning project to do construction work with local people, why choose boring porn? And why not at least share one copy and bring other books to share as well?* Exhausted on a different cool cement floor while the women of the batey blast music from a boom box and teach my undergraduates to twerk. In a CT/PET machine. In an MRI, banging out its arrhythmic lullaby.

I have a uterine biopsy to be sure tamoxifen hasn't given me endometrial cancer. The doctor has to biopsy twice, unable to get a good sample. She says this usually means that there isn't cancer, but because of the endometrial thickening, even a clear result is likely to mean I will still need to have a D & C. It is painful, then crampy in a food poisoning, innards-twisting way, then densely painful as if something heavy is stepping on me, an alien animal whose feet sink into my abdomen. It isn't the worst thing I've experienced.

In the strange hospital I automatically follow the cancer center signs, but I'm here as a psychologist for a professional meeting, not as a cancer patient.

I keep my toes flexed to decrease terrible muscle cramps in my calves from the tamoxifen. I do not cross or stack my legs, instead sleeping in an awkward sideways swastika. This is to ward off blood clots. Since the biopsy, I have had uterine cramps most of the night. Most of the day as well, but I notice them less frequently. My eyes are very dry.

Up in the night, hot flashes, insomnia, melatonin rebound.

Gripping my pen kicks up aching tamoxifen tendonitis. What if tamoxifen causes me to have a stroke? I should practice writing with my right hand to lateralize my language centers. If I have a blood clot from tamoxifen and become aphasic, how will I let anyone know I'm having excruciating muscle cramps in unexpected, atypical muscles like my shins?

In short increments, and with a floppy hat, sunglasses, mask, long sleeves and pants, socks, gloves, and 50 SPF sunblock, I do a little yard work and gardening in the shade. No digging, no playing in the dirt, no lifting, no planting. I've helped set up the water for the season, weeded a few small areas very thoroughly. Since I look like a Buddhist nun, I might as well weed mindfully and with as much of my attention as I can give it.

In our home office is a shelf I think of as The Little Shrine of Significant Loss. It includes only two framed photos, Nancy and her now-gone brother, and me on vacation with bleached blonde hair, wearing a dress with a plunging neckline. On that trip, men talked to my breasts. What would they do now if I were blonde? Would they meet my eyes?

Some people have said stupid stuff to me about cancer, but I've had much more stupid stuff said to me in any year of lesbianism.

I take my melatonin and fall into an impoverished sleep. The iPod under the covers, *Music for Airports.* I sleep poorly and dream imperfectly. My dreams are still superficial, unsatisfied. I dream about thinking about tasks I need to do for work. I dream about thinking about being awake. I dream a rehearsed dream of walking through an airport looking for a place to sleep between flights in my doctoral psychology internship interview outfit, eventually discovering, for the first time, the Alaska Airlines waiting area in SFO. There are seats here in 1996 that have no arms as barriers to stop me from stretching out while I wait for a morning flight. The cat walks across me and I drag my arms up to cover my scars. There is no sensation from my short ribs to the incisions, on my back behind my right shoulder, in my right armpit. I am awake with a sense of urgency, a painful ache, not like the instant of an automobile crash but the instant after, when the muscles alert, alarm with deep, aching pain. Still half-dreaming. I massage my arms and side in what has become the automatic gesture of manual lymphatic drainage. I can't feel my own hands on much of my chest. I have little sensation in the surgical areas, and what I do have is misguided and misleading: Zaps, fizzes, pains not associated with my skin and yet unpleasant. That is the right side. The left is simply empty.

Tomorrow marks the two-year surgical anniversary. This is a particularly good one because for estrogen-receptive tumors, the rate of recurrence drops into a lower statistical group.

The Grail may or may not be a breast, missed and missing.

Again, spotting. This means I need a hysteroscopy with D & C. I'd rather not have a hysterectomy. Martha refers to my uterus as a "chaos demon," but I'm still using it to keep the rest of my insides from sloshing around.

> Thank you, tiny white-
> flowered weed, for holding soil
> through this long winter.

I'm out in the sun, the now-dangerous sun, with no hat, with no sleeves, with no sunblock. I am comparatively naked under the sun. Now I will get lymphedema. I should have paid more attention. I should have been more intentional. I should knock off harvesting this coriander, go inside and cover myself with sunblock. I don't want to get sunblock on the coriander. And put a hat on, for God's sake. Is this what a mindfulness retreat will be like? Probably it will be a hell of a lot worse.

Picking coriander is like my surgeon feeling my lymph nodes

while I'm split open. It is a story about turning the experience into fiction, but what is fear, and what is art? Can I, as Jung suggests, move from the *negredo,* rolling in psychic and alchemical shit, through the *albedo* and *rubedo* to *citrinitas,* a goldenness of consciousness, reclaim my creativity? I tell myself little stories about the cilantro: What does it smell like when you're picking it? It doesn't smell like anything. Rolling the tight seeds off the stem, not knowing if they are ripe or will ripen. If I were a child in India, I might know. This is the opposite of mutation, it is normative cellular change. Is it cellular? Lack of mindfulness leads to spilling the container. Bad dog. Put it down.

Also, spiders on the cilantro. And rescuing spiders from the cilantro. I used to be the spider wrangler, the digger of holes, the shoveler of bark mulch. Tiny spiders. Spider, crustacean, crab, cancer. If I create fiction about cellulitis, does it answer a fair question, is it interesting to anyone else? Does it serve me to turn it into art? Or am I just appropriating someone else's story?

Dropping the coriander in the bark mulch. Picking it up, swearing at myself, telling myself not to swear at myself. Be in the moment. In the moment, I am pissed off. Collecting the coriander. Picking through it, devising a plan to sift it through various measures and colanders to separate out the mulch. Is it worth it? No. But it's a metaphor. No, it's not a metaphor. It's a fear. But it's a fear crouching in a metaphor. Shut up. Don't be unrealistic. Realism is not thinking in metaphors. Drop it, doggie. Drop it.

Coriander, something about mustard seed, that's not in the Jewish part of the Bible. I wonder if it was actually mustard. I don't think of mustard in Middle Eastern foods very much. I will need to research this.

So many scars hold the story, and so many ways to tell it. I was a relatively unblemished child. Just a few chicken pox scars, nothing important. I continued as a mostly-cicatrixless adult, acquiring a few dings and bumps but hardly even any freckles. Now I look like I've been caught in the cogs of the universe's machinery, which I have, welted and chopped at.

It's a dangerous time to be a woman without breasts in America. Am I now a monster, with acquired monster disability? Am I morally suspect, hideous, because I didn't reconstruct, pretend I still had breasts?

> Song of the golem:
> I colonize this lumpy wad of flesh,
> Midas-touching, self becomes gold.
> My own palm burns my skin,
> handprint in the dark.

[Long draw on well-worn pipe, apple-scented smoke, gazing into the distant swell, cabin girls at my feet, transfixed]: *It was a knife fight with a mermaid. She slashed me once or twice, and her octopus tangled me up—see here? You can still make out the marks from its horrible suckers. Then her shark came after me, a big one, bit me up good, and just when I escaped, that damned swordfish stabbed me again and again! Well. You can see the burn from the explosive decompression, though it hurled me right onto a few of those spiny sea urchins!* [Reflective pause and pull on the pipe.] *Good thing I eat those creeps for breakfast!* [Cackle.] This version might require prosthetic wooden breasts, peg-breasts, perhaps a woodpecker familiar rather than a parrot.

Or I could start it this way: *If I ever get scurvy, I'll unzip at my seams.*

Is cancer like a journey?

Is the memoir like cancer?

Is the journey like cancer?

Am I a cancer survivor? The term is a temporal lie, since

I may yet die of it, the same mutated cells in hibernation, in stasis, zombie apocalypse in waiting. I don't know if I've really survived cancer or just temporarily suppressed it. Am I a diabetes survivor? This isn't the language that's used. My diabetes is "well-managed." It's true that its expression isn't squelched, waxes and wanes in measurable waves. Perhaps the distinction is that this breast cancer was a tumor, that cancer is like a distinct thing, a count noun, whereas diabetes is like a verb. It's ultimately a false distinction. Both are the signs of metabolically-mediated dysfunction, disruption of the body's homeostasis. Am I a chaos survivor?

I don't believe in omens. Symbols and patterns are compelling, and useful as organizational schematics. And yet, I read memoirs of breast cancer, and I notice: Author X: Dead. Author Y: Also dead. Author Z: Yup, dead. I have to dispute my superstitious fear that writing about cancer will kill me.

How can the idol rise, regain her footing? The body deconstructed by surgery, made into something else is still the same, changed, scarred, but not disassembled, not random. This is true of stories also.

Don't ask how I managed to get those Mardi Gras beads.

THE SLOW FWMMP, FWMMP OF ENORMOUS WINGS

Airports in sleep

Which airports are these
that organize my dreams?
Grooved silver walls,
texture of a mackerel evening sky.
Citizens overhead, photographs
of unremarkable waves,
a row of rocking chairs.
An ear of corn improbably in flight.
Necklaces depict tortoises
too common to identify.
A different row of rocking chairs,
wafts of competing crab cakes.
Portland, standing on the old carpet?
Demons churning the sea of milk—
this must be Bangkok, where I bought
three tins of lime leaves.
This must be Inchon where I visited
a temple crusted in thick snow,
kimchi fermenting in covered barrels,
magpies squawking challenges in cold trees,
then back at the airport
ate *bibimbap* from a cardboard bowl.
Where was that high-vaulted passage,
ill-lit and damp, smelling of cigarettes?
Where I walked and walked, upward
of five miles between my flights.

Atlanta, San Francisco, spiral, ascend,
descend, return to the same dream.

I'm not sorry

I no longer sweat on the right, my armpit slightly lumpy and hairless, a naked mole rat, a Sphynx cat of an axilla. Zebulon avoids it. Perhaps my cells still slowly ooze Taxotere and Cytoxan.

Leah mouths, "I'm sorry!" as I toss back a handful of colorful medications, vitamins, and supplements. I'm not sorry, though. Thank you, Tamoxifen.

My cells are dying; I am reborn. My healing chest looks less like a huge pissed-off guardian, more like a sleepy Buddha, as the swelling slowly reduces, the red wounds lighten so slowly, nominally, over the years.

The baby that kicked me

The first time after surgery that I flew a lengthy flight, frightened in my seat, swaddled up in compression garments, I was kicked by a baby. The baby didn't mean to kick me. It was little and held in its father's arms, gently jostled to lull it to sleep in the aisle of the dark plane. It kicked like a little animal, balance reflex to the swaying, or maybe the baby dreamed.

I was vulnerable as well. To lymphedema from air pressure changes and stretching for my bag in the overhead bin. To damage to my healing tissues, still zipping themselves up, settling into place. My flesh unpuffing, deflating, re-elasticizing, a process of several years. Receptors resetting, phantom breast pain becoming ectoplasmic and fading, incisions shaping my new form. Zap and fizz and tingle and burn becoming familiar, boring, gradually decreasing. The baby, dandled on daddy's chest, slept and kicked. This type of baby gear is called a "soft structured carrier," a pleasingly ambiguous name that could refer to every part of the action: Carrier, baby, father. I am also a soft structure, a soft structured carrier of something, perhaps. *Bap! bap!* The baby kicked my arm.

When I explain to the daddy that I've recently had surgery that affected my arms and ask if he'd mind moving a foot forward or back, he says nothing, does nothing, just looks at me. He is focused on the baby, I tell myself. He's probably a lovely person. *Bap!* I'm tired of being hurt or injured in relation to this cancer. Nancy nudges me *Don't tough it out.* We get up and exchange seats. This requires the daddy to move slightly forward in the aisle, which is good, and it's also fortunate that the plane is dark because Nancy has a horrifying Look of Death that I wouldn't want to see unleashed on a stranger. The most frightening quality of her Look of Death is that it is not a look that wishes death upon one, but a flat, disinterested gaze that says, *You are already dead.* It is the look of the serpent who proceeds the gods. She has already eaten you and shat you out. It is not liminal. You are far beyond the gate.

I recognize nothing

I walk across a campus where I once taught for a semester, non-credit classes informally referred to as So You Failed the Test of Standard Written English. There have been changes, new buildings and paths. I recognize nothing on campus. No one says hello. I want to sit with a cup of coffee, but since I have no university identification, I can't enter the cafeteria. No one I ask knows where a visitor can sit, look at the bay, warm her hands on this drizzly day. So I walk 11 miles, 16 miles. Cancer has made me more introverted and restless, untalkative and walkative.

Incidental redemption

At some point the emergency abates enough for me to wonder, *And what now?* I need to shift the imagery that haunts me. We are metaphor monkeys, clashing cymbals and symbols.

 I eat a chicken salad sandwich in the regional airport, waiting for my flight. I write in my journal. A man at the next table strikes up a conversation about my writing. He introduces himself. He is an author whose work I know. I reply that I am making notes for a memoir about cancer. He is encouraging, remarking that redemptive travel memoirs are very popular now. We chat a little more, leave for our flights.

Narratives in genres are often formulaic, featuring obligatory elements and tropes. Boy meets girl, boy loses girl, girl dies. Until the mid-1970s, the real-lesbian protagonist tended to lose her only-sort-of-lesbian beloved to a man, or to morality. She was either wild with sorrow, regretted her deviance, or killed herself. Sometimes all three. That's what could find a publisher. Then came the era of the coming out story. A positive acceptance of self, or symbolic enactment by one kiss, dot dot dot, formed the climactic moment. *Finito.* Finally there arose books where lesbians just worried about the electric bill and hitchhiked across Brazil with their German Shepherd or argued with their partner as they drove a VW van full of goats to Oregon, occasionally doing some lesbian thing, but primarily existing, not becoming but being lesbians. *Man on the land!* I know why a cabinet stuffed with a huge variety of teas is a cultural lesbian joke in the era of my young adulthood. Do you?

It's good to have coming out stories, positive accounts of self-realization. I was never in the closet, so these memoirs tell me about the people around me more than about myself. I do occasionally do some lesbian thing, so I'm attracted to the latter sub-genre.

I don't need or want to be redeemed, do I? Can't change be measured in raindrops and mist rather than lightning strikes? Am I broken and in need of fixing, or am I enacting kintsugi, decaying, remaking, revealing even more beauty through slow change? *These rocks are not so sad. Gold lives inside of them.*

I know what to say at an AA meeting, how to tell my story, even though I'm not alcoholic. *Hi, Shoshana.* Long ago in Providence, a continent away, I had a cup of Wickenden Street Blend at Coffee Exchange with an acquaintance. She told me I should go to 12-Step groups to find people to date. She wouldn't believe that I had no reason to attend. No addictions? No eating disorder? No emotional dysregulation? No history of abusive, violent, or neglectful relationships? Surely I was in denial, because the story didn't allow for other options. I finally asked, pointing to the church across the street where a regular meeting took place at that hour, "Are you suggesting that I should lurk outside the Love and Sex Addicts Anonymous meeting and try to get somebody to slip?"

There is a redemptive travel plot, often enjoyable and interesting to read, sometimes predictable. I, probably female, am dissatisfied at work, betrayed by my love, searching for more meaning. Or my job and/or love dumps me. Therefore, impetuously, I travel the world, looking for healing, a new spirituality, a new boyfriend who is an exotic mystical fellow. I describe the ashrams, the colorful, inscrutable guru with the beautiful black hair in a beaded braid down to his waist, the peacocks squawking all through the night, my disenchantment when I discover, shockingly, the guru and someone much prettier or much uglier than I am fucking in a storage closet. Really, I wasn't trying to spy, I just needed more lentils. *I was on kitchen duty!* Sticky buses, always with chickens clucking in the children's laps, careen around hairpin Peruvian mountain curves. Inches from the edge! I am A) Terrified, which knocks me out of my rut, and I vow that if I escape alive, I will X, Y, and Z. Or B) Too miserable to care. Being dead in a tangle of flaming wreckage far below sounds peaceful. After a series of adventures (camels, assaults, shamanistic beggars who grab my hand and scowl at my lifeline), I find, by accident, my meaning, my lover, my healing. I was in Kansas all along!

There is nothing wrong with this story, but it isn't how I see myself. It embodies a stage theory of emotional development, asserts the myth of progress, that dramatic and sudden ascent is the goal and the end. It is the spiritual story that ends with coming out, kissing the goddess on the lips.

A mosaic is fragmentary yet not broken. Change isn't always evidence of a flaw. Whatever and wherever I am, I am whole, wholly myself, in that instant. When have I been anything but composite, kaleidoscopic, linsey-woolsey, still life, still, life, with mixed fibers.

Breast cancer stories tends to include finding the tumor (a lump, or no lump but a worrisome mammogram), shock and disbelief. Existential threat. Consultations, biopsies, radioactive injections, whirring and clunking machinery. The tumor's characteristics, sometimes discovered to be different over time. Size, spread, stage, type, hormone receptivity, a march of acronyms. Treatment may include nothing, surgery, more surgery, chemotherapy, radiation, immunotherapy, hormone suppression. Or IV Vitamin C and a bewildering number of supplements and herbs, depending on how you approach the problem. The fall of all hair, clumps of leg hair, armpit hair, pubic hair as well as head hair, clogging the shower drain. The eyebrows, eyelashes. Puffy from steroids. Nails discoloring, peeling off. Dry eyes, dry mouth, dry gut, runny nose. An intermediate period of "normal." Reconstruction, another odyssey, or the decision to leave flat alone. The re-emergence of the self. I am a person, not a medicalized object.

I relate to this story. I tell aspects of this story. But not as a story of return, of trying to get back to how I was before.

Instead it is a story of joinery, enhancement, of being changed by living a life, making golden connections, treasuring the passage of time despite its obstacles and horrors. Kintsugi to rebuke the chop-her-up murder of the story. The collaged text is not broken but is itself.

Pilgrimage's story is frequently similar to redemptive travel, though often more intentional. I made a choice to go. I articulated what I hoped to learn, to earn, to receive by grace. Sometimes pilgrimage is by accident. I thought I'd go on a hike with my mates for a lark, then I was accidentally enlightened, smacked by circumstance into *satori*. I staggered under my heavy bag. I packed so many items that seemed essential but then when I fell asleep by the path at the river, the fay stole my rucksack, stripped me bare, crushed my iPhone with all my apps and maps, and crapped in my water bottle. I awakened alone and afraid, in a chestnut gloaming, my unwashed technical underpants pulled over my head, wet Merino socks hanging limply from each leg-hole like an ass's ears. Then my journey truly began. My Beatrice, an unlikely Lithuanian woman who barely spoke my language but was an angel in disguise, found me naked and shivering behind an eccentric glacial boulder, covering my privates with a torn page of vegan restaurant recommendations. She assessed me, saw that I did not yet know who or what or where I was. She gave me a pair of running shorts, too large, and a tee shirt with an unrecognizable cartoon character from her pack. A Lithuanian chocolate bar, the flip flops garnished with yellow plastic daisies off her own feet. She motioned me to follow, led me to a bar at the edge of Aldea Nada, and when I came back from the restroom to thank her, twigs scrumbled out of my hair, she was gone. I never saw my mates again, but a kind Scandinavian monk took me under his wing, helped me re-outfit with the things I truly needed, which was almost nothing, and onward we walked together. The people I met, the cold, cold beer, the entertaining or grubby hostels, my blisters, my blisters, my infernal and desperate experiments related to my blisters. After long labors and many insights, sometimes falling physically and symbolically, encountering ferocious dogs and threatening ghosts, my feet growing tough and admirable, I reach the shining city, where, initially elated, then deflated, I understand that the journey itself is the answer, and is ongoing. This is when my peripeteia kicks in. Oh, and an update on my blisters. I treated them like this; a Korean lady showed me how. I wish I could find that Korean blister cream in the U.K., but it was an object symbolic of the heightened state, the rarified other world, and cannot be found on Amazon.

This is also partially my story. I was not seeking. I was celebrating, expanding. Each step was a new step, no less or no more a goal than Santiago de Compostela. I didn't think I'd write a redemptive travel account. I recognize, though, that my story can be read in this light, and could be told from that perspective. That's not my intention, but it's all right, too. I see my life as ongoing practice, ongoing kintsugi, is and isn't, yin and yang; not always balanced, ultimately asymmetrical, sometimes punctuated by more emphatic events, despair, elation, times with crisper definition, increased self-scrutiny, more universal awareness and connection to all things and beings, extant and fantastic. I don't think of it as self-actualization or self-repair, but as ongoing sameness and difference, a thing that is sometimes its own thing without comparisons. Realistically, though, it's probably both, so I suppose this is a kind of redemptive travel memoir after all, despite my initial protestations, the question, *Redeemed by what or who?*

Sage overtaking

The fall garden is wabi-sabi, so many leaves and stems in soft decay. I uproot the aphid-infected kale, deadhead the tiger lilies. Later I will strip them of their axillary bulbils, poke them into pots to overwinter and redistribute the new plants in spring. The garden is kintsugi, mending the pots, dividing cluttered rhizomes so they have more room, don't trip over themselves. I leave the tiny flagstone patio unscrubbed. It is more poignant in the winter light, creeping thyme and Corsican mint self-seeding between the flat blue pavers, sage overtaking a sprinkle of clear marbles, Arctic and Marian blue pebbles.

The slow fwmmp, fwmmp of enormous wings

I step out of my daily life and into a silent retreat, a Buddhist adventure in the California mountains. Tamoxifen makes me easily emotional and overwhelmed. That plus almost two years of cancer fears and cancer-driven action has me deeply tired and easily depleted.

I have questions in mind about what makes a retreat "silent." Is this to be a time of limited social discourse in order to be intentional rather than automatic? To decrease monkey mind distractions? To attempt to remain in meditation? To notice the world more vividly and acutely? The retreat center suggests bringing journals and books, so it's not about being non-linguistic. Arguably I would benefit from a non-linguistic week, but I need language in order to grieve.

A winding road leads to a turn-off at a store. Initially it's paved, then there is a long and very dusty gravel rise. I imagine walking it with my backpack. Maybe next time. After miles through quiet trees, the taxi drops me at a small, attractive main building with a *gompa,* library, office, dining area for group retreats, and an assortment of teas and coffee. The Ridge Cabin area is silent, centered on the founder's cremation site. Adirondack chairs face the Santa Cruz mountains. A small bathhouse also overlooks the peaks and sky. A communal refrigerator holds breakfast foods; lunch and dinner will be dropped off at about noon, signaled by a bell. All vegetarian. A note tacked to the message board warns of possible mountain lions, suggests that if one is encountered, I should raise my arms and try to look big. That it would be appropriate to shout my wish that it be reincarnated in a higher form in its next life. What could be a better incarnation than a cat, except perhaps being *my* cat?

I walk down to the main hall and back, then around the Peace Trail loop. The trail smells wonderfully of redwoods and loam.

Unpacking, I find gifts from Nancy tucked into my bag: A necklace with a *hai* pendant, a candle, Imodium, tiny prayer flags. I've brought a quilted throw made for me by one of my chemo support group friends; I put it on the single bed. For dinner there is a potato soup. I add an apple from my bag, mint tea. I like my cabin. It's spare but cheerful, with a deck and non-potable wash-up sink, a shrine, a table big enough for a few books, a chair, the bed, a cupboard with hangers, a little kitchenware, a 2-burner gas stove, faded carpet, a broom. Prayer flags on the deck. I add the string from Nancy.

- Wild turkey
- Black-tailed deer
- Steller's jay
- Blackbird
- Dark-eyed junco (Oregon race)
- Dragonflies

Continuing with the question of what "silent" means, one is invited to write a note to staff if anything is needed. I've read that some monastics use sign language. What is silence? What is its purpose? A Jewish prayer begins, "Lord, open my lips, and my mouth will declare your praise." When I taught English at the yeshiva after returning from Israel, the girls informed me that men should sing this aloud during prayer services, but since women's singing is distractingly sexy (my paraphrase), they should not vocalize but mouth the words silently. Is that what I should do as I walk in the quiet woods? Roll in my mouth the unspoken syllables of the *nembutsu, Namu Amida Butsu,* save me?

Things I know about my mind: There is always music. At this time, it is all Zumba songs, annoying because they're trite. However, I realize that they're also rhythmic, and remind me of the commitment I've made to exercise hard and strive to be healthy, to be in my body, to be in the moment and in community, not to curl up like a hermit crab in fear.

A young black-tailed deer browses in the undergrowth behind the *stupas.* No, there's more than one. It's getting chilly. What a pleasure. Crows caw. No smoke—the Loma wildfire is 14 miles off and downwind. I relax in my cabin in a tee shirt and my black and white *krama* worn as a *longyi.* I read that prayer flags predate Buddhism in Tibet, as do the symbolic animals: Snow lion, thunder dragon, *garuda,* and tiger. Wind horse. Syncretism. Four Dignitaries, Eight Symbols of Good Fortune. Mahakala was formerly a demon; he has a fierce expression. The medicine Buddha holds in his right hand a healing plant. We must kill the Buddha we meet on the way; we must find the light within. Vajrapani is a bodhisattva. One of his functions is to inspire fear in order to shake you loose, make you less rigid, make you challenge your unexamined assumptions. He holds a diamond lightning bolt and sometimes, when he's feeling jaunty perhaps, a crown of skulls. His Tibetan form is elaborate, with symbolic elements. Third eye, check; necklace of snakes, good to know. He protects bodhisattvas from ghosts as well as people, which seems helpful. The phrase *Om mani padme hum,* often translated as "The jewel is in the lotus flower," may actually be an invocation of Vajrapani, rendering it problematic from a Jewish perspective if I'm worried about having other gods before [Him]. Fortunately, the obstacle is the path.

Om and *hum* are referent-free interjections, instants of emphasis and breath. In haiku, a cutting-word, *kireji,* a voiced non-semantic particle can be used to indicate an emphasis or shift, punctuation or pause, the end. They include *kana, ka, ya,* and several suffixes, each with a slightly different import. I am fond of *ya,* which creates an emphatic focus or highlights the juxtaposition of the haiku's elements.

What is missing from this experience is *sangha.* To say it another way, it is like being a psychotherapist in private practice, doing good work without ready engagement with a community of peers. Though usually people won't meditate next to me. My silence is too noisy, whir of cognition. People get up and move away. Now I'm not supposed to sit still for too long or cross my limbs because tamoxifen puts me at risk for blood clots. "I want you to fidget," instructs my physical therapist. Okay, try to stop me.

Awakened by insect shrill and animals scuffling in the leaves behind my cabin. I sweep the floor, make my bed, tidy the books. Monastic life light, no call to prayer. In the cool morning sun, I hike to Castle Rock State Park to walk off some rumination. A three-mile uphill climb through oak and redwood, the newly taxonomically split-off California scrub jays, California towhees, a magpie, little warblers, shiny juncos. Small grey lizards, grasshoppers, squirrels. Bright, blue sky, rocky, the smell of dry Western mountains. Smoke at the ridgeline, a glimpse of Monterey Bay in the distance, beyond ranked ridges. Baked stone, madrone.

> The opposite of petrichor.
> At the fuzzed conjunction
> of rods and cones,
> a Steller's jay flashes,
> liquid blue. Did you
> see it, too?

The hike is good practice. It ends not at a scenic overview with a bench or rock to sit on, but a chain gate with the declaration that one may go no further. Just a reminder that being present in the moment is the goal, and that what looks like a goal or reward may not be anything special. Maybe I should take off my watch. The bell lets me know my meal is available, so what purpose does it serve?

Skunk scent blossoms on the air. Prayer flags snap, wasps stalk my orange peel. Acorns thump to the ground, as if they had an intention.

- Excitingly larger lizards, a pair, tan with black

markings radiating from the spine
- Spotted towhee
- Chestnut-backed chickadee
- Brown creeper
- Northern flicker

I try to let go of the idea of a particular practice as the correct practice, instead asking, *What is useful now? What holds me in the present, what decreases suffering now?* Challenging some fears that make me tentative, make me feel held back. Yesterday I went outside without wearing a medical alert bracelet for only the second time since surgery. I didn't go into the woods, or away from Lama's Ridge, without it. That seems like bravado, not bravery—a blustery gesture. But even on this reasonably isolated mountain among generally unseen and silent strangers, I can sit and look at the valley for an hour without it. This helps me transform the bracelet from a badge of incipient danger, a declaration of dread, to a matter-of-fact amulet, simply information, a talisman, room to breathe rather than a gate clanging shut. A declaration of how to help me rather than a shackle constraining me.

My chemo port scars itch and burn. My right chest constricts and my arm below my armpit throbs deep in its meat. I notice, I massage myself gently, I move on. I resist fear's invitation to interpret every painful sensation as pernicious. A difficult balance between vigilance and letting it rest.

I commit to tasting the zucchini soup with an open mind.

"Silence" seems to refer only to verbal communication, and at that, silence is requested outside but not inside the cabins. I assume this is to allow chanting, mantras, prayer. It's hard for me to sit contemplatively while people are working. I want to chop vegetables, organize the library, sweep, untangle prayer flags snagged by the wind. Not today. Today I am silent even in my cabin, meditate, read, and write without enacting any verbs of mutual relationship.

Cold zucchini soup.
Better than expected, but
still zucchini soup.

Eyes everywhere! Knots
on a tree trunk, pebbles,
the Lama's stupa.

Wrapped in my krama,
I recall bathing in
another hot country.

It is cooler this evening, a great pleasure. Prayer flags flapping, horizontal, blue, on wooden poles at the edge of the shelter; I hear them as I meditate. Friedman suggests the affirmation, "I am making it through with flying colors!" I like this, with its invocation of prayer flags, blessings in the wind, but I like "I am flying colors!" better, or even, "Flying colors!"

An overcast morning, and I may go without sunscreen, Bringer of Hot Flashes, while the cloud cover is heavy. Jeans, jacket, cap, heavy socks. Good practice for cold days at the bottom of the world when I travel to Antarctica next year. Bird chirp, squirrel chirp. I don't want to stay in the cabin all day; it's too soporific. Periods of meditation, a little reading, food preparation. I spend most of my time outside, sitting, as now, in an Adirondack facing the next ridge west, or walking. The walking options are: In clockwise circles, around the stupa. Also: The big stupa down the hill. They hold all the directions, so walking means walking around a pole of the world, wherever on the globe I stand. This is circle magic. Toward Castle Rock State Park, uphill to the chain gate and downhill back. To the Mountain Store at the junction of the main road, miles away, a store with surprising lacunae—no dried fruit, not even raisins, no miso. Fruit juice, at least. Downhill several miles through the woods, quite a pleasant grade and attractive curving walk, even back uphill. To the gompa for coffee or to borrow a book from the library. To find and sit by a fountain. To find and sit by a depiction of fearsome Vajrapani. The Peace Trail, with one steep descent and one or two ascents depending on route variations. I like the road to the Mountain Store best despite dust and an increased feeling of vulnerability. Yesterday I circumambulated a stupa for about 4 miles.

A little sitting practice, a little qigong with minimal vocalizations, a little crying, a little stretching. Reading Buddhist philosophy about death while sitting at the altar. Fragrant wax from the candle drips on my clothes.

A staffer tells me she saw mountain lion tracks on the ridge this morning. She reminds me of the sign posted by the refrigerator, says they're most active at dawn and dusk, liminal lion. "Be careful at night!" I silently congratulate myself for bringing a jar to use as a chamber pot. I had already picked up and peeled a 2' stick to make myself look bigger and fend off bandits. For similar reasons, Bashō disguised himself as a Buddhist monk when he walked the pilgrimage around Japan.

At Vajrapani

My new red shirt, hung
by the prayer flags overnight,
smells of wood smoke now.

Dark-eyed juncos fly,
emissaries from the sun-
lit side of the hill.

Cold October light.
Trees shaggy as animals,
moss, bark, twigs, more moss.

The end of the day.
What did I do? Walked the sun
up, walked the sun down.

What I do each morning: Rise. Watch the sun. Open the windows, sliding door, blinds. Sweep. Make my bed. Straighten the room. Boil water for tea, or pour sun tea. Take a handful of pills. Dress, stretch. Prepare breakfast, which I eat outside, facing the ridge. Wash my dishes, return yesterday's food bag and compost. I am disguised as Bashō.

I read, write, walk, or sit. Work on sorting out useful constructs (as, Dalai Lama XIV, *How to See Yourself as You Really Are*) versus strangely self-referential religious injunctions, knotted up with themselves (parts of Dalai Lama XIV, *Advice on Dying: And Living a Better Life*).

Afternoon is like morning, like yesterday and tomorrow. I also walk in the afternoon. Sunset, shower, dinner. Close up the cabin. Wash dishes. Read, write, cry, sleep, dream. Soften, become less vigilant.

This would be more relaxing if I didn't feel a host of external pressures. Though I suppose the point is not relaxation but noticing, detaching, breathing through. Impermanence notwithstanding, we more or less exist and my kindness to and utility for others seem more important than engaging deeply in spiritual practice, which isn't what I think I'm doing anyway. I'll reply to one email later today, because doing so and letting it go is more important than stewing while maintaining radio silence. This is the lesson of the monk and novice on the way. They meet a woman at a flooded river. Though the order forbids them from touching a woman, the monk picks her up and carries her across. She thanks them; they go their ways. After some time, the novice bursts out in frustrated criticism: *How could you do such a thing?* The monk replies, *I set her down at the river, but you're still carrying her.*

Another lovely 10- or 11-mile walk down to the road and back. Nice elevations, a mix of sun and shade. Plenty of birds, including a covey of California quail, a huge, almost scary colony of acorn woodpeckers, a Bewick's wren, lusciouslyfledged and colored Steller's jays and California scrub jays, many chestnut-backed chickadees, California towhees, dark-eyed juncos, and one Cooper's hawk. Rustling leaves behind me in the underbrush make me break my silence, the only time this week, "Namaste!" I croak, raising my arms to be big, then seeing that it is not the mountain lion, "—Squirrel."

Friedman, citing someone else, suggests that it's good to do something with your hands while meditating or saying a mantra. She explains that the reason is the proportion of the mind given over to the fingers and thumb. Ah, the motor homunculus. It makes sense as a way to focus and reduce monkey mind resources to chant or vocalize, plus use the hands to count beads. This morning I read about *mala,* then tried today's walk with and without playing with an acorn while meditating. It was easier to focus with, and there is that medical injunction to fidget for post-treatment circulatory and lymphatic reasons. When I returned to the retreat office, I bought a clear quartz mala-ish bracelet. It has 22 beads, which I don't think is standard, and yet since I don't believe in magic numbers, so what?

> A white plane overhead,
> small as an ant, large as
> the rest of my life.

> Dirt road, five miles up.
> The shadow of erratics,
> dust of mica grit.

> Paired dark-eyed juncos
> tumble to the ground like brown
> leaves, then spring to life.

I read the Dalai Lama XIV's translation of the Diamond Cutter Sutra, which differs from most others in the specifics. The text generally says something like, "That all things which admit of definition are as a dream, a phantom, a bubble, a shadow, as

the dew and lightning flash. They ought to be regarded thus."
The Dalai Lama's examples are looser, including "figments seen
with an eye disease," a startling and evocative phrase that stays
with me as a rhythmic walking chant.

Laughing at myself because I didn't put my earbuds in my
pocket before walking 22 miles today—if I'd wanted to listen, I
couldn't have. But I didn't want to listen, so I didn't know, and
was happy. Buddhist fun!

Demons and hungry ghosts. Butter lamps, dreams. I have
monkey mind privilege, enjoyable distractions turning into
rhythm. Two pileated woodpeckers swoop past from behind
me, pterodactyls in the wood, silent but for the slow *fwmmp,
fwmmp* of enormous wings.

I return to the acorn woodpecker colony, stand and listen to
the syncopated drumming in the trees. Woodpecker wabi-sabi.
Should I hope to fill those holes with gold? What is right in my
body?

Evening at Vajrapani

To air is human.
Or in this case, pants: Sweaty,
smoked, clean on the line.

Two cups of cold rice!
Later, I will cook congee,
eggs, seaweed, coarse salt.

Sharp, hot, redwood scent.
Pileated woodpeckers
alight, peck, glide on.

Mountain lion prints
on Lama's Ridge. Be mindful,
be calm as a cat.

It begins to drizzle in the night. A light but steady rain, a bright grey sky. Now different scents arise from the wet ground and trees, damp and spicy. I cried less than I thought I might. Next time, more sitting, sangha. I will walk in the airport until it is time to fly home.

An orange-red line on the horizon

When I have the time, I like to walk the entire airport. I enjoy noticing the similarities to other airports, and also the differences, displays of local and regional art, how prominently hot sauce is featured on menus, whether there is a dedicated bookstore. I like the stretch and exertion. I like noticing how far apart the gates seem when I'm not in a hurry. Today I'm not in a hurry through Salt Lake. Bees are well-represented. My compression stockings are bunching and the sleeves are hot and itchy. Still, when I see myself reflected in a glass display cabinet or clothing store mirror, I'm pleased that I look more or less the way I hoped I would in middle age— competent, interested, sturdy, with a faint smile. Not fast, not angst-ridden, not poor, not drunk, not outraged, not sobbing, not lonely, not unfulfilled. Not extreme. Not a perfect balance, but balanced enough, in my comfortable travel clothes, sipping a cup of tea. No drama, no flirty business, no trying to see me in the shower, unless you want to, in which case, go ahead. You're in for a surprise.

You wouldn't know how dizzy I am or how precarious my balance. You wouldn't know that I'm not just rubbing a sore spot on my neck or abdomen, but that I'm performing a reasonably extensive manual lymphatic drainage. You wouldn't know that I'm surreptitiously monitoring the straps of my backpack, shifting their position every quarter-hour to be sure I'm not blocking those lymphatic pathways.

I am called "sir" by a flight attendant, twice. Earrings and a big ass aren't strong enough to counter my short hair and direct eye contact. Walking to the restroom at the back of the plane, I spot an older woman seated on the aisle. I can see the edge of a chemo port, dressing and capped cannula, protruding from the collar of her shirt. I stop, ask, "How are you doing?" She looks at me, but we don't share a language. I nod to the port, then pull aside the neckline of my blouse, showing her the scars in the hollow of my collarbone. Her face clears, she nods once, holds out her arms. We hug; I kiss her cheek.

Overheard: "She died of metastasized breast cancer—what a terrible disease."

I am on a journey, onboard in my solo cabin with its big round window. Cancer isn't like a journey, but maybe journeys are like diseases—not always anticipated, not always predictable, they may separate you from loved ones, require new vocabulary, make you rely on professionals, disrupt your routine. They may include unpleasant surprises, are expensive, dislocate you. As, Puerto Williams is close at hand, visible from the window. We were supposed to stop there, but the schedule has changed due to weather predictions. We are here, but not the way we thought we'd be. We move on; the captain has decided to run ahead of the storm.

We traverse the Drake Passage in hurricane winds, Beaufort Force 12. I lie supine on my cabin floor, a glass of water and a couple of hard rolls on a plate beside me. For two days I listen to Apsley Cherry-Garrard's memoir, *The Worst Journey in the World,* to remind myself that while I'm just severely seasick, the Antarctic explorers had an infinitely worse time: Frostbite, death, ships crushed in the ice, stranding on icy desert islands. I do not eat reindeer. I do not eat cold herring in glistening aspic, trays of other fish exuding nauseating odors. I think about the Andean condor we saw in the Chilean fjords. I haul myself up for tea in the early morning and a briefing on plants and birds in the afternoon, but not for a film documenting a voyage around Cape Horn, which seems like the opposite of settling my stomach. When the captain announces wandering albatross following the ship, I stagger up, stuff my feet into boots and grab my optics, stumble in the pitch and yaw to the stern where the three huge birds glide, grey against the churning grey sea and cloud-heavy sky. I return to my cabin and vomit four times, which is four more times than when

I was in chemotherapy. As long as I can keep my tamoxifen down, I'm content. The floor of the head is heated; how soothing. I doze at the toilet, my hand-washed underwear and wool socks drying on a towel beside me. Small pleasures that are my whole universe. The known longevity record for an albatross is about 60 years. I aspire to outlive that old bird.

Our approach to land reveals rocky hills backed by barely-broken higher snow fields—steel sea, dark brown, white, grey-white, glacial blue, blue sky. Glaciers, icebergs, a group or two of Adélies or Gentoos porpoising and bobbing. *Pintados* glide past. The water is calm. The vista allows a good perspective on variable weather, with small areas of precipitation or fog, then sun.

At our first port of call, I pick my way between snow and rocks, Gentoo and Adélie penguins. At the water's edge, I peel off my fleece headband, remove the ship's waterproof jacket, my long-sleeved undershirt, wind pants, trousers, two pairs of wool socks, and my landing boots, stand in a light Antarctic breeze in flip-flops, swimming trunks, and an athletic tee. I wade into the Southern Ocean, submerge myself, float with big sky, big snow, and penguins all around. This is a terrible stunt for avoiding lymphedema, which may or may not be exacerbated by extreme temperature changes. The research is unclear, though, and I wouldn't want to miss my opportunity for a polar plunge. If I develop lymphedema, I will at least have a good origin story.

I am trying to stretch back into my image of myself, confident, inquisitive, attentive to but not preoccupied with the body's minutiae to the exclusion of engagement with the world. Knowing with immediacy and clarity that as well as my life, my death circulates in my cells, held in balance only by other cells that chew it up, tear apart mutations, unpatterned errors. Why not immerse myself in the ocean at the end of the earth?

We have beautiful, clear weather. The staff at the Polish research station sell earrings and lanyards, offer tea and dried fruit in their warm, snug wooden cabin. In theory, our passports are being stamped *Antarctica,* although this is not a country. The landscape is complex but at first appears austere. Those rocks are penguins, motionless. I am happy with my gear. I am happy to be here.

Icebergs, humpback whales, skuas, continuous penguin clusters. Luminous blue sky, high cirrus cloud wisps, shores and peaks of many-shaded whites, greys, blues, blacks, sparkle and shadow. A snowy sheathbill perches on the ship's rail. I spot a Wilson's storm-petrel, clipping dark grey at the surface of dark grey waves.

At dinner, Jin expresses his regret at not having seen a whale yet. As I always do, I scan the sea through dinner and spot a pod of whales blowing on the horizon. "You wanted whales, Jin?" He borrows my binoculars. From the shape of the spout and the tail color I'll guess humpbacks, but they are literally at the far-off edge of water and sky. A few minutes later, there is an announcement that humpbacks have been spotted by an iceberg near at hand, and we will pause there. Three humpbacks swim close together, snuggle toward our hull, stay with us awhile, spouting. Penguins and skuas dot the ice.

The directionality of metaphors matters. "Cancer is a journey" tends to emphasize positives and adventure. It's a useful reframe, except that it may be too different, allowing a person to lapse in fear back into "cancer is death." "Journey is disease" emphasizes the negative but captures the anxiety in a way that may be useful because it holds the prospect that it may be finite.

I mail postcards today, which means I buy postcards and British Antarctic Territory stamps at the desk, then return my completed cards to the same place. One is to Ursula Le Guin to say that I've been re-reading *The Left Hand of Darkness* here among blue glaciers, how much I appreciate her. Our mailbag will be given to "the Ladies of Port Lockroy" if they come aboard at their port, or may be transferred to the M.S. Fram, with which we will rendezvous this evening, or it could be carried by this ship, M.S. Midnatsol, until its next voyage and another chance to intersect with the Ladies. It's a procedure both precise and approximate, like mail hand-carried from the post barrel on Floreana in the Galápagos, personally delivered around the world. The ship provides a decorative stamp, but the Ladies of Port Lockroy will formally frank each piece "Antarctica," then send them onward on a cruise, research, or commercial ship to the Falklands, possibly this ship, where they will be transferred into the actual mail system at Port Stanley. I've been to Port Stanley. I can picture the post office, the streets shifting to bogs and tussock grass just outside town, the beach with King and Gentoo penguins, Falkland steamer-ducks, kelp geese, upland geese, and *Cinclodes antarcticus;* the farther beach with Magellanic penguins and hourglass dolphins, far downhill and separated from us by rusting signs warning DANGER—MINES!

I snowshoe. I've never done it before, so why not? I make it to the top of the hill. I have never tried contemporary snowshoes and they work well despite my outturned feet. It was foggy with light windy snow when we disembarked, but the sky has cleared. As we reach the rise, we have a crisp view across the water to Half Moon Island. Through binoculars I can see my shipmates recording evidence of breeding and noting species sighted for a citizen-scientist project. I'll be over there this afternoon, holding my journal in my gloved hands.

The ship has a large exhibit about Thor Heyerdahl. I read *Aku-Aku* when I was 7 but still haven't made it to Rapa Nui. It's how I first learned about archeology, anthropology, and what a virgin is.

We sail into the only volcanic caldera navigable by a ship this size. Pintados and chinstraps settled on the cliffs. Evening lectures, plumage of the Arctic and Antarctic terns.

I take a rather strenuous hike around a cinder cone with lovely views in black and white, punctuated by small blue-green glacial ponds. The rocks are grey, pumice, black, green, red, yellow. Is that a fumarole? On one hill, the sand is steaming. It's hard on the toenails to hike in the ship's landing boots, worn to protect the environment from pathogens, disinfected upon re-embarkation. I photograph myself with my jacket unzipped to show my Swarthmore tee shirt. Down at the shore I'm tempted to take another polar dip since I'm hot and the beach is gravelly sand rather than rocks, but I don't have swimming clothes on. Fur seals laze around the minimal pier. I keep my distance; they bite. I couldn't have walked this a year ago.

After the evening briefing, Mary, Diana, and I go up on deck to enjoy drinking wine in a hot tub on a ship at sea, cruising by icebergs dotted with penguins in the snow in Antarctica. The breeze blows pintados past us as we chat. Mary is garbed in a bathing suit and thick fur earmuffs, while Diana's attire includes an enormous fur-brimmed Finnish hat.

I kayak between twisted ice floes, sometimes skimming just a foot or two over their submerged surfaces. Looking up at the ship, a waterline perspective. It's another beautiful blue and white day in Antarctica, a blue willow china scene with no willows.

Penguins stand like *moai* on a frigid Rapa Nui. Hard sun, glittering water, crumpled white and grey mountains. Sea spray; salt on my lenses. It's the yaw, not the pitch. As I plant my feet on the rolling deck, I recall a lecture by a neuropsychologist who advised, "We evolved in the trees. The forehead is protected by thicker bone. The sides and back are thin. If you must take a blow to the head, try for the front of the cranium."

A foggy evening provides a few hours' respite from the sun, though at midnight, it's an orange-red line on the horizon, bright-blurred. I can sleep in that light, but I keep hopping up to stare at the blocky mountains and whale-pocked waters.

We visit a Chilean research station on a pungent islet thick with penguin guano. The Gentoos are nesting, thieving each other's pebbles. The skuas perch at the edges, sharp-eyed for untended eggs to eat. One Gentoo is leucistic and sits with its normally-colored mate on a stone pile overlooking the water. There are penguins at every step. If they were crows, this could be *The Birds,* though the penguins seem happy to walk around us without pecking. They are a waddle, not a murder. I buy Nancy a mug featuring the pale penguin. When I compare it to my photos, though, it's a different bird, so perhaps there is a genetic component to leucism.

It's strange not to know our itinerary until the night before. It is a good exercise in having no expectations.

Today is the anniversary of Amundsen's successful run to the South Pole, a different side of Cherry-Garrard's story and the fatal Scott expedition.

The Ladies of Port Lockroy come aboard. They have an opportunity to eat and shower as well as give a talk, manage the mail, and sell tchotchkes. Part of the U.K. Antarctic Heritage Trust, the islet where they live is "the size of a football pitch." Around 3,500 people applied in this round for a handful of Antarctic summer positions here, monitoring penguin breeding, cleaning the bucket toilet, and franking postcards. Upon request, one of the Ladies imitates penguin calls. I wouldn't enjoy the bucket toilet duty, but the idea of being on a tiny island for several months is appealing. Some of my tablemates say they would be too lonely, but I think I'd enjoy a few months with a couple of other people and a lot of penguins. Because I've had cancer, I'm not eligible for U.S. jobs in Antarctica until I have lived five years without recurrence. Two years, two months to go.

Cancer and journey are similar because sometimes you're bored and self-critical for not leaping up to do something necessary or interesting, for wishing you were home again. These are not exclusive characteristics. They are shared with every venture and adventure. Travel is like cancer because there are parts where you don't get to stop once you're underway. Because the more privilege you have, the more opportunities you get. For example, this trip cost more than I earned in a year of working in Israel. Because knowledge and curiosity can improve your access to services. Because sometimes your circumstances cause unexpected diarrhea.

There are humpbacks aplenty, some swimming in tight circles, bubble-netting for their breakfast. I hear them breathing by the side of the hull.

- Southern lapwing
- Spectacled tyrant
- Austral thrush
- Rufous-collared sparrow
- Andean condor
- Southern giant petrel
- Cape petrel
- Snowy petrel?
- Black-browned albatross
- Light-mantled albatross
- Wandering albatross
- Kelp gull
- Rock cormorant
- Antarctic shag
- South American skua

- Chilean skua (may be same species as above)
- Brown skua
- South American tern
- Prion (probably Antarctic)
- Magellanic penguin
- Gentoo penguin
- Adélie penguin
- Chinstrap penguin
- Snowy sheathbill
- Wilson's storm-petrel
- Southern fulmar

- Dusky dolphin
- Humpback whale
- Right whale (spout)
- Weddell seal
- Fur seal
- Elephant seal
- South American sea lion

- Hair grass
- Lichen
- Kelp
- Pearlwort?

We re-cross the Drake Passage, still turbulent but relatively calmer. At Cape Horn, we trek up the steep wooden stairs to visit the monument to the thousands of sailors lost rounding the horn, a large metal sculpture framing an absent albatross in flight. The small Stella Maris chapel, the lighthouse.

- Kelp geese (male and female)
- Striated caracara
- Bar-winged cinclodes
- Upland goose
- Imperial cormorant

Trip summary by expedition leader: "White, white, white,

blue, blue, blue, and penguins." It was indeed shocking to see green at Cape Horn.

To say that cancer is a journey is to emphasize the more romantic aspects. The encounter with the mysterious unknown rather than the vomiting. "Travel" implies that the experience is voluntary and not coerced. Travel is not like cancer because putting oneself in danger differs from being put in danger. Cancer is like being kidnapped; it's not a dream date with destiny.

A brief time on open water before we return to the channels. In the fjords, hill upon hill upon mountain, layered like construction paper cutouts of Chile, dark birds lofting overhead, too high and distant to identify.

A map of the known world

At the end of my Memoirs of Mental Illness class, a student comments on the readings. She says she's learned that a memoir humanizes the subject. Can you know me, identify with me impressionistically, in collage, in bricolage, kaleidoscopically? Or more formally, Cornell box-style, evocative assemblages? Stepping forward, tesserae distinct; back and back, to see them blur to a heron with a snake in its beak, a shark gobbling a disorganized blotch that may once have depicted an ordinary crab, now disarrayed and distorted; outward and upward, meanders, a map of the known world, centered on Jerusalem? My world, this world.

Am I visible with fewer of the standard narrative signifiers?

> Can you see me without
> "and then, and then"?
> Without coming out,
> with and without eyelashes,
> on the earth's dusty roads
> without itinerary, lacking
> detailed accounts
> of blisters and routes?

Without the names of hospitals and hostels, without commentary about the others in treatment or on a Way, people who might prefer to tell their own stories rather than be an embellishment to mine.

My body is not

"Our body is not a static thing—it changes all the time." (Thích Nhất Hạnh)

My body is not a static thing. It
changes all the time. Heap of percepts, I;
heap of feelings, I; heap of constructs, I.

My body is not a metastatic thing, includes
something, the form's mutations,
overgrowth and growth.

My body is an ecstatic thing,
consciousness, everything,
wonder unremarkable and gone.

Next

Cracked to tesserae,
smalti, Antarctic blue, is
what becomes of you.

Nothing from something,
my body is a gold web—
kintsukuroi ya.

ROAST CHICKENS RE-FEATHER

In a dark wood

Nel mezzo del cammin di nostra vita, I screamed a lot but didn't lose my way. Eventually, I walked the Way.

I have always been an atheist, and I'm going to die. Not right away if I have my druthers, but sooner rather than later, I hope without too much pain. We all live and die on the Way.

Recently I've read a lot of books about walking. There are many reasons to walk. Fluent walking and awkward walking. Walking to an end, such as buying a book. Walking for meditation, walking for exercise, walking to take the air, walking for pilgrimage. I have done all of these.

Miracle play

Each day is a piece of the miracle play

I hoped to be myself when I grew up
and here I am, trying to remember
messages I sent from the future

Chill and my losses burn my empty chest
undergraduates in inadequate jackets
scurry past in February fog

A good long walk
I want to meditate while having a hot flash

I want to meditate while people snore
I want to meditate while drunk people have a
good time without me
I want to meditate as my feet blister and
　peel
to meditate under hot sun
to meditate across the top of Spain, not for
pleasure, not for pain

I want to walk across the top of Spain
walk in the rain
to breathe like Caligula, "alive!"
at the end of that play by Camus

In the heat, under the scary trees
in closed-in rooms to meditate
while Spaniards giggle and grope two beds
　from mine
not to drink wine
to stay this course

To meditate in the heart of Christianity
Auto-da-fé, limpieza de sangre
Quemadero, burn the Jews
Auto de los Reyes Magos

The wind through the cork oaks also sounds
　like Lorca
seda rasgada por diez cuchillos

I'd walk a million mysteries for one of your
　similes

Permission to walk

I have wanted to walk the Camino since my friend Krista
asked if I knew about the St. James Way, saying she hoped to
walk a section with her family someday. Although I didn't, an
image immediately came to mind: A line of sweaty Europeans

with backpacks cresting a sun-glazed hill, lipping over the rise, headed my way. Dusty yellow, light green, light brown predominate. A crumbly soil path with rocks transecting a grassy passage, humped up to either side. The pilgrims reach down a steadying hand to help the next ascending. Bleached dry grass and crumbling white stones, a yellow valley with tree-lined roads behind. Turning, looking forward, an indistinct impression of tall pines with vaguely Japanese huts beneath, probably influenced by reading Bashō. In and around the huts, curls of smoke intimating food and warmth. Pilgrims negotiate for bunks, step outside for food cooked over a fire. An exciting vision, a compelling image.

To even consider peregrinating, I have to be medically released to carry a larger backpack. Why do so much work to heal and avoid lymphedema, reduce the risk of cellulitis, only to compress the lymphatic vessels and do damage? It takes four years and the permission comes with specific instructions about hip straps, sternum straps, weight allowance, weight distribution, injurious arm postures, manual lymphatic drainage, sunscreen, hydration, frequent checking, a medical alert card. The Camino Francés is a good experiment with its shorter daily distances, lighter packs, trekking poles to keep the arms moving.

Tamoxifen destroys my equilibrium. Before: Air traffic control strike, no plane, arrive late at Heathrow, no hotel, sleep on a bench at Victoria Station? No sweat. After: I can't open a jar of peanut butter because my pectorals are weak from surgery? I cry for 15 minutes in angry frustration. I still can barely prepare or eat a chicken breast, knife shuddering into thick meat. I want the Camino's challenges; I want to cry if I must cry in the vast open Meseta, pull myself together. I want to push the edge of caution, stretch back into however I can be now, reinscribe myself in the book of my life.

I begin the Camino long before beginning. Whenever some

unpleasant interaction or distressing thought arises, I turn my attention to my packing list—bedroll or sleeping bag? Comfort or weight? Swiss Army knife or steak knife plus can opener? And later, how many kilometers on this part of the route? If there is no room at this *albergue,* will I sleep on that church porch or spring for a *pensión?* I picture the Way, its contours and rises, its asphalt and pebbles and mud. I imagine walking and breathing, conversation and silence, sleeplessness and sleep. Wherever I am at these moments, I am neither here nor there. The brush with mortality raises questions such as what should I do, and why should I do something?

Pilgrimage is like a quest. Pilgrimage is like a garden. Pilgrimage is like cancer. I map my intended journey like a mural of a hajj, blue airplane, blue bus, blue train, blue boots. Yellow shells across a map of Northern Spain, blue city of destination, blue Atlantic.

> Four winters ago,
> after my last mammogram:
> Hope for growth, not growth.
> Hope for no efflorescence.

Getting ready

When I lived in Israel, only two brands of toothpaste were widely available, one option for each: Zebra and Colgate. I used Zebra because it was cheaper. When I returned to the U.S. after that year, I was paralyzed by the cartoon-like toothpaste aisle at Super Giant, stunned by the ranked shelves of minutely differing formulations by brand, the garish colors, the exclamation points, the new technology of shiny reflective and holographic letters, bang! pow! bursts and bubbles, solrads and squeans, so I left, emanata trembling above my head, a mighty briffit in my wake. Now I must again choose toothpaste, utilitarian yet versatile, lightweight, with an acceptable taste.

Gear is a topic of consuming interest for *peregrinxs*, including weight, shape, specific and general utility, ease of use, ease of washing and drying, durability, versatility, physical comfort, emotional and psychological comfort, necessity, ability to fit in a carry-on luggage compartment, and availability in Spain. I choose a red backpack because it will be more visible to searchers if I'm lost in a field or murdered and lying in a drainage ditch. Some bear their prayer book, rosary, or cross. I carry electrons, Karen Armstrong, the New Testament read by Johnny Cash, Friday night songs in *Ladino.*

Packing for the Camino is like packing for a visit to the chemotherapy infusion center. Do I have my paperwork? Have I reviewed the manual of instructions? What will I eat, what do I need to pack? Do I want music or a book? Where am I sleeping? Do I need my own pillow? Who will be there, loquacious or self-absorbed? Which medications should I bring? What should I do if I feel sick? Who will answer my questions? Will everything be okay?

More than a kilogram of my initial pack weight is medications and supplements. Helpful people assure me that Spain has pharmacies. Yes, but does Spain have my particular generic tamoxifen, the only one that gives me mild rather than excruciating muscle cramps, that only causes a dull ache, not shooting pain, in my ankles and knees? Will I easily find the specific combinations and brands suggested by my oncologist and naturopathic doctor? For that matter, is the shampoo free from phthalates and parabens? It is less stressful to trade out a pair of sneakers and a book. As I walk, my pack will become lighter in increments measured in dekagrams.

When I look for post-chemo nail care instructions online, a search returns a photo of my own toes a year after, poached from the cancer message board where I posted it. I recognize them immediately as mine.

Not going all religious on us

We have friends over for dinner. When I mention my plan to walk the Camino de Santiago, one exclaims, "Don't go all religious on us!" In the moment I wave this aside, but I do have to wonder what it would be like to have a spiritual or religious experience. I don't know if I'd want to, but I might. My left temporal lobe seems to dole out the correct dollop of numinousness from time to time, but the wonder funnels into meaning and symbols, not an entity. I'm pretty sure that if I were blinded by a bolt and dumped from my donkey, this would signify not enlightenment but an aneurism, a tumor, a seizure, a failure of the wetware. Should I ride a donkey to Santiago just in case? The accounts I've read portray this option as unappealing, and chances are I weigh more than St. Paul. It would be cruel to the donkey. Is a cancer diagnosis like being struck off your donkey?

I do love to read about religion, learn about people's experiences of faith and doubt, hear how systems of meaning and belief arise, combine, diverge and dissolve. If I were at all religious, I would have had to become a rabbi or meditation teacher. I discuss their spirituality with some of my psychotherapy clients, existential considerations with others. On inpatient psychiatric units, we don't document that "the patient is hallucinating." This is a guess about subjective phenomena, unmeasurable except by self-report. Instead, we write, "The patient is responding to no known person or stimulus." When I teach classes on diagnosis and psychopathology, I point out that even if we can pinpoint the locus of the brain from which atypical electrical impulses arise and the explanatory role of physiology in visions and prophecy, this doesn't subvert the possibility that the divine speaks to and through us by these means. It hasn't happened to me, but it might. I will be satisfied to feel more like myself, incrementally less tentative, less cautious, less dubious, less afraid. I want to learn what I am like now, my abilities and limitations. I want to walk in gratitude directed to no known person or Person, in *gracias a la vida.* I want to peregrinate on the Camino to see if I can, to meditate and walk all day, my life stripped down to basics. I don't want to make a lot of rules for myself, or take detailed notes, or shoot a lot of photos. I would like to participate in non-denominational pilgrimage sangha. I would like to hurl Frederic's angel pendant into the abyss. I would like to walk in the spirit of pilgrimage, abstemious, moderate, desires noticed and let go rather than dictating my acts.

I want to gain more balance in my relationship to European Christian history, which is also European Jewish history. Call it kintsugi for my understanding of my people's story there, a remaking that still holds the chronicle of the damage.

The mote in my eye

I have outlived my best friend. I'm still trying to outlive my father.

Nancy and I finally return to Europe for the multi-country train trip that we had to cancel because I needed cancer treatment. She spots a scallop shell ring for me in Bruges. We visit Germanic countries. Did the Nazis kill people with cancer? Will I resist the Erlkönig's blandishments, wrested from my father's grasp, *"In seinen Armen das Kind war tot!"* My father recited this to me sometimes in a macaronic polyglot rendition, as he sang to me of the Turkish drink, as he sang *"Mit Rosen bedacht."*

My travel has to be simultaneously adapted and normalized. I recall that I didn't like people running carts and bicycles over my toes before cancer, either. There is no need for me to give in to reductive explanatory conclusions in which everything orbits a knot of horror.

We visit Switzerland, take the train to the hamlet and visit the Ecole where my parents taught, more than half a century since I'd been there last. I can't say if the landscape is familiar, though it is a green that I remember, only green, *que te quiero.* And *heimlich,* a canny valley. What's largely missing when we ride the Glacier Express is glaciers. The bright, hot sun smacks through the south-facing picture windows. At first I think I held it for too long in my peripheral vision, dark spidery afterimage a monster clutching the mountains. When it doesn't abate, no visual purple shading out, it becomes clear that I've burst a blood vessel in my eye or something similar. Is it the altitude? I assess the leggy blot. It's not flashing the semaphore of retinal detachment. In the future I will learn that I have pulled my vitreous humor, though I don't really know what "I" means in this sentence. "I" think "I" was a bystander while my body did its thing, though my body is "I" as well. I spot a raven on a gravel mound that ought to be iced over. *Quoth the raven,* "Metaphor!" We arrive in Zurich. The heat wave has intensified, which makes me worry about Spain. To stay cooler, we take a short cruise around the lake, seeing black-headed gulls, great-crested grebes, coots, mallards, and other waterfowl, a red kite soaring overhead, the huge bronze eagle that is also a god.

> Good advice for Zeus:
> Catamite and catamount—don't
> get them confused!

I dream I need another operation, so it seems as if I've had a recurrence. I wonder what my chest will look like afterward. I am led into a room where I am to sleep. I am surprised not to be going right into surgery or back home, but surmise that the plan is to keep a sterile field while waiting for test results. The aide says she'll be back soon. I try to look at my chest, but the mirror folds and baffles itself, and I can't figure out how to reset it. The cot is like a tanning bed, a recessed blue-lit plastic cradle without pillows, blankets, or mattress, situated in the center of a small room. I hear human noise from the mall outside but assume it will stop after everything closes. I take off my clothes. There is no hook, no robe. I grow increasingly annoyed, wondering about breakfast, when the aide will return, what I am supposed to do, fret irritably about whether my insurance will cover this.

Ultreia

I dream that we find a different church in Dublin, with a model of the Church of St. James in front. I go in to see if they can stamp my *credencial*. They are very excited and ink the *sello*, give me a slip of paper with a blessing, a pilgrim's meal.

We fly to Ireland, the start of my Camino at the non-dream Church of St. James in Dublin. I visit a chapel for the Camino, I guess—I don't know the architecture of churches, only that a "narthex" is to the west—and place my feet on either side of an inlaid golden scallop shell. Now I am on the Way. St. James is the patron of lepers. That seems hopeful should I begin to disintegrate. I light candles for myself and Nancy. Since the sacristy is closed, my credencial is stamped with its first sello at the Guinness Storehouse around the corner.

After we view the Book of Kells and the Long Room at Trinity College's Old Library, I buy myself a triquetra pendant, navy blue and teal enamel on silver. The three-looped knot is syncretically Trinitarian, but in its origins it is elemental, temporal, holding a symbolic woman's phases of life, maiden, mother, crone. I wear it with Frederic's angel.

I send my merino shirt back home with Nancy. I like its weight, how it catches faint breezes, but it's rough on my scars, too much like a hair shirt. Scratching doesn't quiet the itch; the nerves of my chest are mis-wired and the sensation is divorced from any action I can take to stop it. The scars of medicine are often tidier than the scars of torture, but sometimes not by much. I breathe, I smile the Buddha's smile.

The true miracle will be if this scallop shell, bestowed on me by the Portlandia pilgrim's group, doesn't break before I get to Biarritz and fix it to my pack. I mouth the pilgrim's rallying cry, *Ultreia!*

A good sign

The Ryanair flight to Biarritz is a circle of hell in which a family with 6 or 7 children demonstrates coercion theory in action, the imps screaming until the parents give in. Its mystical purpose is to render the albergues' snoring and the rustling of plastic bags in the early morning more benign.

In St.-Jean-Pied-de-Port, a road sign directs traffic to the Zona Artisanale Frédéric. A good sign. I buy raisins, a banana, a sausage for tomorrow, trekking poles and a small knife. The forecast for tomorrow is "very hot." I hope for a dry Middle Eastern heat. I set my phone wallpaper to a Fahrenheit-Celsius conversion chart.

I awaken at about 5:00 AM, if I've slept at all. Better to say that I arise. I dress as quietly as I can in the dark *gîte,* careful of the creaky floorboards. Someone has liberated the toilet paper roll from the restroom during the night, but I am prepared with my own supplies. Quietly I step down the wooden stairs, following a dim light from the unoccupied kitchen, then I begin to walk toward Santiago de Compostela on the cool cobblestones in the grey early light. Five minutes later, I'm back. Fortunately and unusually the door isn't locked so I creep inside, locate my trekking poles, marked with a bit of rainbow tape, and again walk west.

A stone to lay down

I begin my Camino with a few symbolic items—a small black Japanese river stone that sat on the corner of my desk at work, my scallop shell ring, which I wear as my wedding ring while walking. My triqueta from Dublin, Frederic's angel medal. A pair of silver hoop earrings that have no meaning at the time but will acquire it by virtue of my Camino. A red 28L Gregory backpack distinguished from all the other red 28L Gregory backpacks by a patch of a penguin with the legend "Port Lockroy, Antarctica." I expect to find nothing, or Nothing, its numinous big sister.

Frog in a new pond

I am immediately calm and happy as I wend my poky way over the Pyrenees on a beautiful and terribly hot summer day. I notice my muscles, my breath, my posture. I take the steep inclines and declivities slowly, rhythmically, evenly. I've spent a lot of my life being told I talk too much, I'm strange, I'm intimidating, I'm incomprehensible. On the Camino, no one knows me. It is a relief. Being in a meditative trance is a relief, angling uphill past cowbells and sheep, deep valleys, green peaks, running low on water.

Is all travel pilgrimage? Clearly not. Are all journeys? Does it matter if the destination is sacred or secular, exterior or interior, motion-full or still? What about disease? Is disease a journey, is a journey a disease? Is cancer a pilgrimage? What about cancer treatment? Do mutant cells call their proliferation through the lymph a peregrination?

> Frog in a new pond.
> *Ya* Bashō Banana-Boy,
> Leap into my Way!

La Chanson de Roland

I pass the Fountain of Roland and listen to *The Song of Roland* as I walk: "*He worships Mahomet and calls upon Apollo.*" I am not Orlando Furioso, though I am the Orlando of Virginia Woolf, striding through time more or less ambiguously gendered. I cross a cattle grate into Spain, descend a long, rocky distance through the woods. After a very hot day, over 38°C, I limp into the Roncesvalles monastery much later than I expected and I think, *Next time I'll know how to do this.* I want to sleep but instead I shower, wash my sweaty clothes, and eat a communal pilgrim dinner: Red wine, potato soup, pork in red sauce, potatoes, ginger cake.

> I wash today's clothes
> but don't attend Mass, bloody
> socks for stigmata.

Las flechas

I like to read personal narratives about cancer and the Camino. They often tell a story step by step, incorporate guidebook-style information, maps, impressions, emotions, complications, and then, and then, and then resolution. I sense that my experience will be more discontinuous. But can't we understand postmodern texts as leaping, alighting, entwined at a distance, arcing over the missing transitions, drawing attention to the synaptic cleft as a divide that joins, a separation that renders good-enough wholeness? Doesn't postmodernism in fact demonstrate the contention that although there is narrative artifice, though conventions and forms may be recognizable, the story triumphs as a mosaic, a gestalt, a pieced-together and unnatural thing? The story is blurs of movement, not lumps of corpselike text.

Is this a journey? That implies endpoint. Is it an endless journey? Perhaps not, for an atheist. The heart of the mystery is unknown, unknowable.

A bottle of red wine

I walk on fist-sized stones. No boot-lacing technique will save me. I feel blisters coming on, the tops of my toes banging the toe box. Sometimes it happens even when you set up everything right. At the albergue there's a run on beds, but eventually something is arranged for everyone. I bring a bottle of red wine back from the corner grocery, uncork and hand it to the pilgrims in their 20's with whom I don't share a language. I don't want any wine, I just want to sit in the yard and be washed in the cascade of multilingual words, stare at the flutter of unidentified birds.

> Learning to follow
> las flechas amarillas,
> Marias watchful.

Peregrina in Pamplona

I pick my way down a long downhill path made difficult by diagonal slate outcroppings.

As I thread my way through the San Fermín throng, my strategy in the crush of revelers is to follow on the heels of a woman pushing a baby carriage, for which the crowd makes way. As I press through, several people point and exclaim *"Peregrina!"* to their children, with a wave to me. I like this intersection of our purposes, that we are all present at this time and day. I see no peregrines, but I have become one, *Falco peregrinus shoshanae.*

In red paint on the Camino west of Pamplona: *ESTO NO ES ESPAÑA/ HAU/ EUSKAL HERRIA DA!*

Some pilgrims I met yesterday had planned to run with the bulls. I see them later today, still in their red wine-spattered white shirts. What risks will we take; what does the tale require us to sacrifice? Will I soon turn St. Sebastian, shot through with these yellow arrows?

The Camino is like cancer

It's very useful to have lived through cancer. The Camino is like cancer because I'm not surprised to find that my body can be damaged in service to a positive goal. I already know to attend to my tolerances, take care of myself. I am already disabused of the fantasy that everything will go well, already in touch with existential considerations, knowing the ebb and flow of challenges, physical, psychological, interpersonal. What are my new abilities and limits? Which fears are reasonable, *cave cancrem?* How best can I focus my attention inside and out, explore, let go, breathe in?

> *Gora San Fermín!*
> Black bulls and *mozos* stampede.
> <<¡Ai, Peregrina!>>

Hiring a donkey

In Cizur Menor, the *hospitalera* treats my toe with Betadine, drains it with a sterile insulin syringe, bandages it up. She shows me how she wants me to tie my bootlaces, which is the way I'm already doing it. She wraps sanitary pads on my insoles. She says the Italian men simply refuse to consider this, but my buddy Scott from Nova Scotia boasts about needing extra-long pads. I decide to send my backpack on ahead. I ask if the hospitalero at the receiving albergue will criticize me for using a transport service, and she replies, "Don't be guilty. In the Middle Ages, pilgrims hired a donkey to carry their bags." I offer to hire a donkey, but she says they're too much trouble.

Cancer, of course

> Cancer, of course. *Az-zubana,* the claws.
> Everything likes to go walking.

> Pleiades. Seven sisters, seven seas,
> mastectomies. The irregular limb,
> music of dissonant spheres.

> Farewell to the moon rabbit,
> *vale* her companion, also rabbit,
> also moon. It is your auspicious year!

> To be no more than a moving mote

of the *Vía Láctea, ser compuesta por miles de millones de estrellas.*

Hidrógeno, algo, nada, caminar.

The long straw gets pounded down

I once participated in a professional training group focused on diversity. I mistook the invitation to speak about our lives for a real invitation. I shared that I feared Christianity, that I and my Venn diagram of minority groups had been tormented and reviled in its name. That anti-Semitism was on the rise and I was scared. Now I'm less naïve, now I know what comes next: Now I am told that in telling the context of my life, a bigger story well-documented and historically attested, I have offended and affronted. My autobiography, my cultural histories must not be spoken because this is painful to others, because it makes them defensive and angry, though I expressed it as a subjective emotion, not an accusation. I am wrong because some of them have found comfort and succor in Jesus. The long straw gets pounded down. I should have remembered this from my early days as a feminist: The victim is blamed if she speaks up. The object, the conquered barbarian is some kind of nut job. If I were to have this conversation now, I would say: My problem is not with Jesus. If you don't like the story I've just told you, please hear it, live with it as I do. I acknowledge that Jewish history is blemished as well, that sexual minority communities bicker and exclude their members. How can each of us, right now, reject being lulled into atrocities, how can we stand up to the violence that power makes so easy? Can we commit together to be *Homo sapiens sapiens,* to resist the primate urge to smash at difference, to destroy the other? How can we find each other in the murk of our vulnerability? I want to hear and hold the story of your salvation.

St. James is a Jekyll-and-Hyde saint, both peregrino and Moor-slayer, Frankenstein and the monster. Christianity poses the same dualistic dilemma for me, a religion of peace and love that periodically herds my people into a building and lights it on fire. May James's Janus nature, looking both ways at the threshold, help me accept these opposites, see them both, feel them both in their right measure.

Sunflowers

After a night of thunderstorms, the morning is clear. I eat breakfast at a bar in Zariquiegui while watching a report on the day's bull-running injuries on television. A joyous morning walking through undulating rows of sunflowers, evoking my time in France with Frederic and Laura. I climb toward an attenuated line of wind turbines, stretching to the distance. I look at today's map page, realize I'll be walking all the way out there, on beyond the last churning arms atop the mountains at the horizon. In the delicious breeze on Alto del Perdón, my hair ruffles and sticks out. I, too, am a sunflower.

Although I don't see myself as spiritual, I am willing to participate, push the envelope of relationships with foreign gods. At times, I do experience awe, wonder, oneness, oceanic connectedness, appreciation, and peace in not knowing. I stop in Obanos to light candles. I had offered to my friends and colleagues that I'd do this if they wished, and I am making good on it now for the first time in Spain.

Walking with philosophers

The hero usually finds a guide. Shirley MacLaine had Charlemagne, Paulo Coelho his reluctant spiritual peer. Even the hanged boy of Santo Domingo de la Calzada had St. Dominic, or maybe St. James himself, as have so many others, including the entire regional army of defense, James *Matamoros* on his white charger, chopping off the heads of my Hamite and Shemite brothers. Oops. Maybe the Other doesn't rate a guide. The noble savage, not world-weary, not effete, has just a magical Brierley map book, pages torn out and recycled along the journey, the past shredded, the future progressively crumpled and shortened, stained with sweat.

Am I John Ruskin's scary wife? "But though her face was beautiful, her person was not formed to excite passion." The Platonic ideal goes down the drain again. Maybe he was distressed by her menstruation, maybe her pubic hair, maybe some other fleshly flaw to which we aren't privy. John, want to see my mastectomy scars? I shall tell you the tale of the Jewess who fought a mermaid and her unsavory sea-dwelling friends, *el pulpo* and the sea urchin, *erizo de mar,* spiky hedgehog of the deep. If you prefer, Mr. Ruskin, your shade can visit me during chemo, when body hair would not threaten to disrupt your manly sensibilities. Smooth as a clamshell I was, Venus arising, puffed up on steroids, roly-poly as the Laughing Buddha, and now committing the pathetic fallacy by attributing sentiments to the endless sunflowers, the circling turbines, the very air.

"Sir, a woman's preaching is like a dog's walking on his hind legs. It's not done well; but you are surprised to find it done at all." Well, Mr. Johnson, I'm not quite preaching, but I like to think I can engage in rhetorically sound exegetical disquisition, as I thump bipedally along this ley line, *mirabile dictu,* though it's true that balancing precariously way up here in Manland is rubbing holes in the bottoms of my feet.

The Y-shaped cross

I cross the bridge. There used to be a tower here, and a statue of the Virgin. A little *txori,* "bird" in Euskara, would clean Mary's face, dipping its wings in the river to wash her, a tender gesture.

Overhead in a hot blue sky, storks bomb the infrastructure, brake to land with deep-cupped wings, looking just like the Y-shaped *crucifixus dolorosus* in the Iglesia del Crucifijo of Puente la Reina. I light more candles in the church. Five flames, five intentions for the good of those who are loved.

I light more candles. Please St. James, Thank you St. James. Try it on. *Swisser Swatter. Batter my heart.*

I can't write about cancer without writing about travel, nor the reverse. I can't say what my Camino is without it. I walk in order to walk. Does gratitude require a recipient, or is it broadcast like seed? Tamoxifen cramps my calves. Thank you, anyway.

At the albergue I find a copy of Paulo Coelho's *Diario de un Mago* in Hebrew and skim it for a while as the sun sets.

> Tattoo in the form
> of a Japanese sword guard,
> crane shapes its circle.

The cross I bear

I wake at about 5:30 AM in an open cubicle with two bunk beds, many similar cubicles a labyrinth around it. I wash my face and brush my teeth while wrapped in a cotton shawl and carrying my waist pack of valuables: Passport, phone, euros, tamoxifen, medical information. I carefully lift my clothes from a hook, dress and pack up in the dark, quietly, no crinkling plastic, check my legs for bedbug bites. I tiptoe out of the dormitory, locate my boots and trekking poles in the boot room, drink a glass of water, fill my bottles, hoist up and strap into my pack. Then I begin to walk. I follow yellow arrows, stylized blue and yellow shells, and street signs though towns, beside fields and farms, vineyards and orchards, through scrub and forest, listening to a Camino-related book on my iPod when I tire on the ascents. I'm nearing the end of *The Canterbury Tales.* I am more the Wife of Bath than any of the tiresome clergy. *Y-thonked be God!* Rome, Jerusalem, now on my way to *Galice at Seint-Jame.* I chat with pilgrims, some whom I already know and some I don't, both on the path and when I rest. I walk alone because I walk slowly. Perhaps I am the slowest pilgrim on the Camino. I pass no one, but then, there are those who are behind me, also slow, or starting late. I am happy with my pace, the swing of my hips, the sun on the back of my neck.

At midday I stop at a café to eat a dish of olives and a bowl of creamy gazpacho, sharing an outside table with a woman I met last night at the albergue dinner. We talk. She reaches into her bag, perhaps a little hesitantly, and pulls out a small cross of brown metal. She hands it to me. I have learned from the red string bracelets of Siem Reap and Rajasthan, accept the gift without hesitation. Thanking her, I loop its cord around the zipper pull of my waist pack. I want to be flexible, I want not to cling to automatic behaviors rooted in beliefs I do not hold. Yes, the cross communicates an assumption, though like a man wearing a pretty skirt, the message is more ambiguous than it may seem, not so reductively interpretable. If I do not believe in supernatural beings, I will not offend them by loosening up.

I pass as something or whoever. I don't claim to be or not to be anything. I don't announce myself as a Jew, a philosophical Buddhist, an atheist, a lesbian, a pink ribbon-wearing cancer something. What the hell, I pray as I stagger and glide and fall across Spain, and not just the songs of Friday night, not just the assertion of the *Shema, Hear, O Israel.* I pray to a Jewish god whose sobriquets include "Lord," to St. James for intercession, God help me if there is indeed a God and it is indeed the God of the Jews, to a diffuse and squirmy numinous something shiny, om. Whoever I am is my body, unremarkable and unidentified, my qualities unnamable, blurring in the boundaries, melting and congealing with the heat, Achilles and the tortoise getting somewhere but never quite arriving, prayer doing something but who can say what? Something rhythmic, something kerthumping in the basal ganglia, a chant against too much disarray. The sun smacks my roasting bones and blood, my dehiscing integument. The East burns the base of my skull, seat of my autonomic self; the West incinerates the whole homunculus through my stinging eyes. Interpenetrated, not here nor there, I become more of the Way, its sparkling dirt and crumbling stars.

Distress, elation, mostly the pleasure of the pulse of the world, the *abecedario,* thump of the feet, roar of trucks grinding uphill in low gear, tinnitus in the chestnut forests, alive, thump thump, alive. I cry. No despair in the wilderness, just the misery of tamoxifen and feet.

Breathing in

I breathe in the om
I breathe out the om
in the ether 5000 miles from home,
into and out of
the rarified air.
Into the air, into
the sunset glare
5000 miles from home.

Shall I wrestle death?
Why? We die,
by flaming sword,
by burning bush,
by flood.
I throw an angel
off the world's
wet edge.

So, my love, we create
mythology,
signs and numinous
eschatology

in our instant of glitter,
neuron spark to dark.

Music for Airports

I continue walking. A pilgrim, passing me, comments that he likes how I stay on pace, don't race. Some of the young gazelles are starting to have huge weeping blisters on their heels, hip or knee pain. Some who are staying up late drinking *vino tinto* are rising later, though many still pass me when we walk. I pass by blue wooden doors crusted with dull metal ornaments, reliefs that may be family crests high up on walls.

My toes are better for the hospitalera's interventions but by the time I reach the albergue, the combination of streets, rocks, old Roman cobbles, gravel, dirt, and mud has worn me down. I leave my boots in the atrium and claim a bed, dress in tomorrow's clothes, hand-wash the clothes I wore today, hang them to dry. I rest with my damaged feet up on a chair, charge my iPod so I can listen to *Music for Airports* on repeat when it's too hot to sleep. So far, it's always too hot to sleep.

At dinner, I try to engage a Franciscan cleric who teaches textual rhetoric in Luxembourg, but his answers to my questions are brief, so I leave him be. A Chinese mainframe programmer on a tour, a Bolivian, and a bicigrino round out the table, all male. No one else is sleeping in the separate women's dorm room. In the brutal heat at about midnight, I borrow an unused fan from the hallway. In the morning I have blotchy rashes on both legs, but they don't seem to be bedbug bites. They are vasculitis, but I don't yet know about vasculitis. The blood spider in my right eye is sad; it is hungry; it would eat those absent *chinches* right up.

The ferry man won't kill you mid-river, dump your body overboard. We are already dead. No need to steal our pilgrims' coins.

My sister Becca once said her friend told her that our dead father was in a better place; *Yeah,* she thought, *in a cardboard canister in the downstairs cupboard, next to a flat of Costco green beans.*

Call it secure attachment. As a baby participant in frustration experiments, I missed my mother but didn't squeal, dropping quickly back to emotional and physiological baselines. I miss my father, I grieve my father, but I don't think he is somewhere where he can hear me. As far as I know, anything left of him has gone with the ebb and flow. And yet I mutter "Oh my God!" at the next steep incline.

Adding amulets

At the Ayegui Forge I buy an iron feather for my mother, dark grey iron scallop shell pendants for myself and Nancy, and another for Laura, who intends to fly in for a few days and meet me somewhere near León. My new shell clinks against my triquetra and Frederic's angel as I dip my pilgrim's scallop shell at Fuente de Irache, catching a spoonful of wine. Wearing my mess of amulets, do I evoke ancient enchantments? Do I pass as Christian or does the pre-Christian world poke its snout through, sniff the Catholic air of the Camino? It is interesting to wear Christian symbols and be perceived as Christian, being in the moment and environment in which I've placed myself.

My back to the Taj Mahal

I am terrible at travel writing. I would rather explore the texture of a glaze on tile than recount the history of the church in which it's found. I am more interested in a particular view of ducks on a river than the architecture of the bridge from which I spot them. Though sometimes, I can wax enthusiastic about a catacomb, archways constructed of Capuchin bones. Still, my back to the Taj Mahal as I scan the Yamuna River for riparian birds; still, I pass on the opera house and Eva Perón's mausoleum at La Recoleta to sit on a low wall behind the Hilton, watching a mixed flock of waterfowl in Laguna de las Gaviotas. As I spot a different hornbill landing behind the Jeep, my back to the giraffe in Botswana. But I had already walked through the Taj; I didn't want to goggle at a grave; I had marveled at the Mokolodi giraffes the week before.

I am a rock in the river

A flood of children in matching tee shirts belt out songs and chants in Euskara. I am a rock in the river.

The hero clumps through the Other Place, in transcendent ecstasy and worried about a blister under her toenail. It is exquisite to walk; it is torture to walk. I walked through cancer and its helpful, horrible treatments. I pick my way down a scree-covered hillside in Spain, intensely aware of my body, every balancing shift. *Odi, amo.*

> That castle? Ruins
> warp in hot air, no closer.
> Mirage? Miracle?

Pain is inevitable

I limp into town. Pain is inevitable yet as blisters engorge under two of my toenails, I worry that I am doing my feet irreparable damage. I lost no nails to chemotherapy; will I lose them now? In fact, I've never lost a toenail at all so I am at a loss to evaluate the risk. I confirm that the farmacia in Villa Algo de Algo Algo cannot meet my needs. Will my arms swell with sun-induced cellulitis, my frangible ribs snap? I still carry my kilo of medications and recommended supplements, lug my non-phthalate, non-paraben toiletries across Spain. I am superheated, melting like a wicked witch, dislocated, dysregulated, itchy. I empathize with the idol with feet of clay, toes crumbling. Shall I crawl on my knees to the sea? I've seen skinny cows, too, in Cambodia, like Nebuchadnezzar's dream of the lean cow years. I know what it is like to fall.

The hospitalero is frazzled and chastises me for not somehow alerting him beforehand that I would like a bottom bunk. He criticizes me for being too late for dinner, which is startling since I haven't asked about dinner and plan to eat in the square with other pilgrims. The albergue has many rules, including an interdiction on hand washing clothes. This is a good opportunity to practice letting go of my emotional response, I suppose, but I am in throbbing pain and it's difficult to remain as placid as I'd like, neutral, whimsically detached. I eat dinner in the plaza with 12 other pilgrims, then wear my clothes into the shower for a rinse, hang them discreetly behind a towel to dry. This is the only time I violate a rule on the Camino. In the morning, the hospitalero is still huffy. I don't know why. It's a well-reviewed albergue and people love him. I'm trying not to take it personally. Sometimes we never unravel the mystery.

The joke in Frederic's medal

It's not intended to be a joke, nor would it be a joke for anyone else, but I discovered it, lovely synchronicity. On the obverse of the angel is a bit of Psalm 91:11-12, *For he shall give his angels charge over thee, to keep thee in all thy ways. They shall bear thee up in their hands, lest thou dash thy foot against a stone.* In Hebrew, stone is *even*, and Frederic's surname was Evans. For added Camino serendipity, there is the reference to "ways."

I don't really want to fling Frederic's angel medal into the ocean at Finisterre. I'm doing it for him, because he would find it meaningful, moving, hilarious. Even though he's dead and, as far as I know, beyond appreciating my efforts to please him. *You flew to Europe and walked over 500 miles for that? You couldn't have just dropped it in the Willamette?* I'm doing it to loosen up that tangle of grief: For him, for him not knowing what my life has been, to let go of some fraction of sorrow on my own behalf.

Crunching gravel

Scott from Nova Scotia and I, both footsore, shop for shoes. I buy a pair of oversized sandals, men's sandals. The women's are decorative, pinched, slick-soled, not made for walking. Ultimately the blisters don't alarm me. They are so easy in contrast to the unseen, unknown cancer. I have a blister: I feel it, see it. I had cancer: I have only someone else's word on it, no tangible evidence of its reality.

When I walk, *cuando camino,* I understand in my body how much cancer has made me tentative, fearful, unbalanced. This surprises me. I'd thought I had regained more of my confidence. When I walk, I have repeated disturbing or painful fantasies about people I might meet, dangers I'll encounter, the menacing chestnut forests. Despite my painful, damaged toes, I need to stride, plant my bruised feet on the dirt of the world like a modern dancer with taped-up toes. Not to be an invalid poking for the floor beside her bed. Open my ribcage, roll back my shoulders, smile, crunch the gravel, smell the hot, dry stone of villages at rest. Sometimes I cry, not because walking is so hard but because walking makes me remember that walking used to be easy.

Camino alba

I walk away from the new day,
toward the dark western ocean.

Toward the dark western ocean,
against the revolution of the earth.

I pass vending machines stocked with chocolate, yogurt, cans of olives. What a marvelous country. However, it appears that this region of Spain has an overabundant bunny problem.

The hills, the sky, fragmented like stained glass into a luminous mosaic whole. The bricolage of cognition, shiny bits, junk, repetitions that may circumscribe a theme; memories collide with immediate perception. I do not know the name of that flower. I do not recognize this charcoal feather, white-stippled, but later will know it as cast off by a great spotted woodpecker. I listen for cuckoos but never hear one. The haiku masters invoked the cuckoo, *hototogisu,* as an emblem of the countryside and rural life, and also of poignant longing. Hototogisu flies between the worlds of life and death. What is the meaning of an absent cuckoo?

Darwin describes the *vizcacha,* a South American rodent that collects hard objects, stones, bones, a dropped pocket-watch, arrays them at the entrance of its den. The Gentoo penguin snaps up pebbles in its beak, builds its nest of their mineral comfort. I collect shine and sparkle, words, images, facts, like a magpie, a crow, jackdaws and jays, a burrowing owl. Sometimes I dare the fire, walk as if on coals. Peripheral neuropathy is like stepping on a lit cigarette butt, on a bumble bee, static electricity, a spiky pebble, a Chiquita banana label stuck to your sole.

The crux of it

I once took a job at a Catholic hospital. At orientation, the new staff crowded around a conference table and received the welcome gift of a hospital-branded coffee mug. We were asked to describe how we felt about working in a Catholic organization. After a half-circle of "Oh, I feel fine," I said I, too, felt fine, though it was somewhat startling to see crosses all around. Several of my new colleagues insisted that there were no crosses. I held up my mug and pointed to the rim, around which was a circumference of white crosses, a religious decorative flourish. Apparently these were invisible crosses, or didn't count, being so small or so normal. The discussion continued, now with comments about how "we all worship the same God, and the Christians have Jesus and the Muslims have Allah, and the Jews have… whoever they have." That would be the crux of it. You don't know who the Jews have, do you? The empty throne, the missing link, the messianic absence that is a meaningful distinction. But I was finally old enough to have learned that no one would be interested in my explanation, my happy cascade of helpful and informative monkey chatter. 1, 2, 3, 4; 1, 2, 3, 4. Everything's a counting song, *How shall I send thee?* Is it passing not to name a difference that others don't perceive?

Meeting it

The longer and farther I walk, the more inevitable it seems, and the more I enjoy it, "enjoy" here meaning that pain is just a part of it, nothing remarkable, a warning noted and set aside. I consider simply walking, not until I reach my destination, not until I am enlightened, not until the messiah arrives. Walking until the end of time, or at least until the end of my time, after which the distinction is irrelevant. What would it be just to walk, relationships attenuated or changed, perhaps exploring, peregrinating, following patterns or the trackless void? What if every day began with the intention, *Today I walk?* Today I am curious and attentive. Today everything I am is pilgrimming. The slow circuit of the turbine blades; I watch for hours as they slice the unseen air. The mountains seem firmly planted, but by walking I inch them closer. When the Buddha meets the immovable object, she moves it by meeting it. Primate walking an old primate path, I am always at the center, the galaxy solid and numinous spinning out around me in all its swoops and tentacles, curlicues and swirls.

Some pilgrim hands me half a can of olives. He's French, they're Spanish. They are delicious. He smokes several unfiltered cigarettes, the tobacco a comforting childhood odor. We drink coffee at our adjacent tables. I scan the heavens, watch the swifts, *Apus apus*, flee from *Milvus milvus*, the red kite.

Twig crosses in the cyclone fence.

> *Juego de la oca,*
> geese step-step,
> play their own goose-game.

If I'm not just a knee-jerk atheist monotheist, I don't want to emphasize Christianity more or less than the nature goddesses. Juno rides her goose.

At night I turn like a bird on a rotisserie, soaked in my own juices.

Ungeziefer

When I awaken this morning I am transformed in my sticky plastic bed, find myself to be both myself and something unsavory, a hideous unkosher bug, all clicking legs and mandibles. I scuttle, climb the walls, rustle like a cellophane baggie in a dark pilgrim hostel. I have become an enormous chinche! I scurry out before anyone screams, *Bedbug! Bedbug!* And if I were wearing a Star of David instead of a cross as I walk this pilgrimage road? This is a real question, not rhetorical.

Ghosts

Rioja is a wine-producing region. It's too bad I drink only a little wine. I walk through Cirueña, a ghost town of sorts following an economic collapse. I see some people, but none return my greetings. It's broiling, sunlight careening off white surfaces. When I ask to refill my water bottle at a bar where I've ordered a sandwich, the woman at the counter jerks her chin in the direction of a fairly unpleasant restroom. Ghost town, ghost rabbits; I continue walking.

> The shuttered village,
> depopulated by sun,
> no shadows but shades.

I consider the difference between motionless and dead. So far I fail the last test. "From the earliest times there have always been some who perished along the road," Bashō begins his *Narrow Road to the Interior,* but aren't we all headed that way, transforming step by step? Wouldn't it be better to acknowledge this, hold the thought glowing within ourselves to illuminate our actions?

The hunged man

A town of miraculous chickens. In the window of a *pastelería,* I see chocolate chickens, *gallinitas del santo,* and pastries in the shape of a man inside a scallop shell, labeled *"hunged man."* He is upright, so the snack must represent the boy post-miracle. I buy and eat one since it seems prudent to gobble up anything relic-like I encounter.

> Silver glitter in the dirty sack.
> The hanged boy, strung up like a Peking duck,
> dances with reanimated chickens.

Did I read a version of this in *The Decameron* or something similar? Boy meets girl, girl accuses boy, boy dies, boy is reborn, mayor's arrogance is checked by symbolic chickens which are also resurrected. Are they re-feathered? I hope so, poor things.

Inside the church, I admire the live chickens on high, the unlabeled reliquaries, windows to desiccated body parts, the smalti-rich tesserae of the Three Wise Men. A mosaic depicts the hunged boy, dangling by the chickens, which stand unconcerned on the mayor's plate, like a representation of a not-dead chicken reliquary or the martyrdom of St. Águeda. The overturned bench beneath the boy's sandaled feet is a nice detail.

> So *mucho* depends
> upon
>
> an undead
> *caballero*

raised by saint
portage

beside the roast
chickens

Elsewhere in the Cathedral, I encounter the startling juxtaposition of a reliquary and a tabletop display of modified Lego figures in a cheerful mixed-use tableau of castles and crops, Christians and Muslims slaughtering each other. I presume the Christians are winning. From on high, perched in a plastic nest, a plastic stork observes. It is not a carrion bird; it is merely interested.

Did the roast chickens
re-feather, or dance in flame
with Abednego?

I know this litany, I know where it has led, where it can lead. Heretic, unnatural, Jew. *Hep, hep.* Nobody likes to think they're Torquemada, but I know who is tortured until they confess to lies; I know the signs of danger. Like the bright light in the house that reveals the mess—not my mess! But it is. Someone is revealed as Grand Inquisitor. Let me tell you what happens when you are told to convert or be killed: You are killed, or forcibly converted, or convert. If you convert under these circumstances, it won't save you or your grandchildren. Across the generations you will always be suspect. Forced conversion; the joke's on you. Who poisoned the wells? You are who gets the thumbscrews, the flail, the rack. Couldn't we find a symbolic interrex, fertilize the soil not with my blood but, oh, I don't know, manure? Spare me your *Reconquista.*

Hep, hep. You say you're taking back Jerusalem, but it isn't yours to take.

Pilgrims on horses stand in a light rain. My most chemo-compromised toenail also has a blister under it. The skin is bright purple, bubbled at the nailbed. The nail itself is a lighter and complementary lavender, its surface slightly lifted. My foot frustrates me. Tonight I'll elevate and smear it with antibiotic and ibuprofen gels. I am a mountaineer stuck at Everest Base Camp.

> Tarsus
> Metatarsus
> hit by a bolt
> status epilepticus
> Saul to Paul
> translated
> transmigrated

Light on the land

I drink black coffee at a bar and watch the run-up to today's *encierro* with several Spaniards. They have emphatic opinions about the injured foreign mozos, who are idiots, unprepared, unknowledgeable about the slippery streets of Pamplona. Strong coffee, cigarettes, newsprint scent wafts from papers waved in gesture and smacked on the table for emphasis.

I'm not surprised that my backpack is sufficient for my Camino. I have volunteered and traveled in Cambodia and Vietnam with a small carry-on and backpack, with even that much only because I was in professional settings, transporting books for donation, and in need of a set of cold-weather clothes for the 11-hour layover in South Korea, which was often more than 33°C colder than Cambodia in the winter. And I had traveled to Antarctica, limiting my bag due to the small plane weight restriction from Santiago to Ushuaia. And I lived out of a small backpack and tiny tent for two weeks in France and England while traveling between festivals with Laura, Frederic, Catherine, and other musician friends. *Mochila, chanclas, saco de dormir de seda*—check!

> Bus with my backpack,
> passing pilgrims. I should still

be out there, walking.

Lists

As I have read in Camino narratives, some peregrinas are anxiously self-conscious about their appearance. *What do the townsfolk see? I look like a bag lady! They must think I'm homeless.* I continue to look like myself, though roasted and not yet re-fledged. I don't lose myself in these experiences. As far as I can tell, nobody is thinking about me—not Spaniards, not Basques, not the other pilgrims, not the truck drivers, bus drivers, baristas, hospitalerxs, pleasant pharmacy personnel except their sympathetic *Ahhh* when I display my toenails.

I try not to judge. Usually it's easy but sometimes I am caught in it. I notice that I'm critical of

- Pilgrims who call loudly to each other in the midnight albergue
- Pilgrims who drop their backpacks on my made-up bunk
- Pilgrims who brag about breaking the rules
- Baristas who won't give me water with my Tortilla Española
- Bicigrinxs hurtling downhill on the primitive paths without calling a warning or ringing their bells

I hear many conversations about who is a real pilgrim. They're identical to arguments about who is a real lesbian.

- I don't care who's a real pilgrim
- I don't think the terms of a real pilgrimage, whatever that is, are the same for everyone
- I don't care if people are religious, read Tarot, commune with ghosts

I don't care if they snore, bike, listen to Gregorian chants or Britney Spears, send their bags ahead, stay in hotels, take a bus to Sarria, sing with 500 Basque teenagers hopping from rock to rock, pass me at a brisk pace with a cheery ¡*Buen Camino!* I'm not fascinated by making rules for other people, delineating who is in and who is out.

What matters to me is the integrity of my own pilgrimage, and to this end I practice

- Moderation
- Cleanliness
- Appreciation
- Abstemiousness
- Engagement in religious and spiritual practices that are not antithetical to my values

Not rules but decisions, personal decisions. Yes, I will do chemotherapy. Yes, I will stay in an albergue rather than a hotel. Yes, I will light these candles on behalf of others because they believe even if I do not, so performing the ritual is meaningful.

> What would it be to
> wait on my own steps? Passing
> pilgrims crest and wave.

My boots feel so heavy. I am short of breath, the air, deceptive as *khamsin*, unviable and dry.

Mío Cid

I rest in Burgos, soak my feet in saltwater, eat vegetables, read La *Poema de Mío Cid*. At intervals I venture out, then return to soak my feet some more. I walk to the Plaza Mayor for a late breakfast of local cheese and *queso-y-jamón* croquettes near the Cathedral. The Cathedral houses the remains of El Cid and his wife, though they were moved there fairly recently. Today's foot experiment is silicone toe cots. They work pretty well for the nails but rub further down the toe. The best strategy may be to shift techniques at midday.

I visit the Museum of Human Evolution. By hanging around the reservations desk and emailing daily as I let my feet catch up with me, I snag a cancellation seat on the tour to Atapuerca.

Mother is not a Neandertal

When I have the wherewithal to consider it, I become curious about whether this cancer has a genetic component. Insurance pays for some testing, but not for every test available. For example, "BRCA mosaic" is excluded. I call a genomic and ancestry testing company. How long would I need to wait after chemotherapy to spit in a sample collection tube? I wait; I spit; I send saliva in the mail.

Results arrive relatively quickly and I transfer them to a site that provides a statistical health report for the underlying data. No increased risk of breast cancer for the genes and constellations tested. It's either an as-yet undiscovered constellation, luck of the draw, or an environmental factor. I lean toward the latter explanation.

On the website, I read about my presumptive ethnic heritage. As I expect, it is not the colorful "mongrel" background so many people joke about with these reports, but a big teal circle for Ashkenazi Jewish with a splinter of related groups. Over time the proportions shift slightly, but I'm always over 85% Ashkenazi and .5% Asian, though the locale for the latter changes from Rumi to Golden Horde territory, sometimes more specifically identified as Korean or Yakut. A different genomic site interprets the same data as overwhelmingly Ashkenazi with 1-2% Middle Eastern, 4-5% West Asian, and 8-10% Sephardic and Mizrahi Jewish. I assume there's a Berber somewhere in my mix. Genghis, meet your African in-law Sakina.

My mother has an even narrower ethnic distribution. "You must have gotten that other stuff from your father's side of the family." My Neandertal gene quotient is low, under 2%. My

245

mother's is lower. She is not a Neandertal.

I don't know what "Atapuerca" means, but whenever I hear it, I picture a sow. I am glad to have gone through the museum first, since the tour is in Spanish. I understand more than half of it, supplemented by a few English signs. There's not a lot to see at the dig other than scaffolding and what appear to be students and archaeologists crouched in the soil across the railway trench, but it is still a very interesting visit. Binoculars help. I learn that by eroding the karst, the Río Arlanzón created the caves at Atapuerca, those of note being Sima del Elefante and Sima de los Huesos, elephant and bones. I couldn't tell whether these oldest-known European people, who might be Neandertal or may have come before the split, chivvied animals over a cliff, or opportunistically took advantage of a precipitous drop. Either way, they ate dead stuff. They may also have been cannibals. Human flesh is not kosher. Whether these humans were *antecessor* or *heidelbergensis*, Neandertal's grandmas, it is thought that they could speak. Perhaps someone has found a hyoid bone to suggest this. If they could speak, they might say, "I am not *your* grandma."

Mosaic and bricolage are kintsugi, building from tesserae and artifacts. Collecting bones, wiring them together makes a skeleton, not the fleshed and breathing animal it was, but something new. Stacking stones and brushing dust from the interstices doesn't make a village but a new thing, a reconstructed new construction. My friend Laurel, a potter, smashes her rejects in the woods, adding to her midden of clay potsherds so future archeologists will have something to do.

The bus drops us at a museum that is not specific to Atapuerca, so after a while I watch birds instead, scoring a pair of Southern grey shrikes.

> At Atapuerca
> students dig, unearth carrion

teeth, bone splinters.

Coming out

I meet for a drink with Scott from Nova Scotia and acquaintances from the Portlandia chapter of American Pilgrims on the Camino in the Plaza Mayor, outside the sprawling heap that is the amazing Cathedral, too large to frame with my phone's camera. We talk a little about what it's like for each of us to be surrounded by so much Christian history, iconography, art, religion. There's more to say, but it's time to part.

Scott and I eat dinner together, *sopa de ajo,* lamb. We talk intimately as the Cathedral's shadow shifts. This is the only time on the Camino that I say I have a wife, in part because Scott asks me about myself. And then he's gone, off to meet his own wife for the rest of their walk.

I listen again to sections of *El Cid.* I soak my foot with its beautifully nacreous nails. I take my turn sitting with coffee and calling out "¡Buen Camino!" to passing pilgrims. I move myself around the Plaza Mayor, pursued by the sun.

> Hototogisu,
> absent dream bird, why do you
> elude me in Spain?

Looking for St. Águeda

I cannot locate a statue of St. Águeda that I thought was in Burgos but might be in Astorga. Her breasts were excised, manageable with general anesthesia but a different proposition all together without it. She is the patron saint of wet nurses, bakers, and breast cancer survivors. She is invoked against eruptions of Mt. Etna, which makes visual sense. Her attributes are shears, tongs, her own breasts on a plate. Unlike the chickens, they do not revive. St. Lucy plucked her own eyes out. St. Águeda was not so autonomous. Both offer their body parts up on a plate, but only the tits become pastries. *Minne di Sant'Agata,* anyone? They're topped with a cherry. In Sicily, green marzipan candies are eaten on the day of the Feast of St. Agatha, a.k.a. Águeda. Because of a story of olive trees feeding her, these are referred to as "little olives of Saint Agatha." Olives, right.

What are my attributes? I am no saint, but I propose an upraised fist in a women's symbol, a yellow star inked with the word *Juif,* a test tube of mutated cells, the bumper of the car that will eventually run me down at a peaceful rally for human rights.

During the Black Death, the Great Mortality, the Pestilence of *Yersinia pestis,* the Patriarch of Catania tried but was not able to secure St. Agatha's relics, bring them to Messina as plague prophylaxis. Which relics? Later, she was cut in five to smuggle her body out of exile, one breast left elsewhere as a gift. The woman's body is a text, so chop her up, boys.

The Grail may or may not be a breast, but many things are tits in Spain, and not just the long-tailed tit, marsh tit and coal tit, crested tit, the blue, penduline, and great tits, but titsy bread and titsy cheese, St. Águeda with her titsy tits yearning heavenward, cupolas and domes. I eat cheese in the shape of a breast. It is not breast-cheese, neither the relic of the Virgin's milk nor heavenly milk slurped from St. Lidwina's breasts. Breast as mother-goddess, breast as mountain, the Grand Tetons and China's Breast Mountain, Maiden Paps, Fort Mamelon, Paps d'Anu, Tetica de Bacares, Mamucium, Khao Nom Sao, Cerro las Tetas. The whole world's landscape is littered with tits.

The gendered geographic distribution is not equivalent. Three Fingered Jack in the Oregon Cascades is not Big Dick Mountain. St. Origen castrated himself; St Augustine had help, but this was not their means of martyrdom. Still, did they serve them up on a saucer, in some way pointing heavenward, regain celestial testicles? In *Codex Calixtinus,* I find the devil disguised as St. James convincing a randy pilgrim to castrate himself. Would you eat teste cheese, ball bread, testicle cookies? The Grail is a Lacanian phallus, a prehistoric breast. The Buddha is the Grail, only symbolically exterior. To be a pilgrim is to tolerate the question, not to find the answer. I will continue to look for St. Águeda. Bonus points for excellent presentation, really striking plating. Perhaps an olive garnish would really pop the presentation.

I did not have surgery on St. Águeda's Day. I was, in theory, cured of cancer later that month, when my surgeon laid me barer than bare, flayed and flensed me with methods that could have been torture in another time and place, but were instead salvation. The rest is anti-cancer frosting.

The manuscript of my body, my own vellum, scraped and re-sewn. Chopping up the body of the text is like hacking at the saints for holographic or fractal relics, but only if you gobble their dust, suck their marrow.

What does a breast reliquary look like?

> I couldn't find St.
> Águeda, and I'd lost my
> own breasts already.

The humors

After three rest days, I can get my foot back into my boot without agony. Even at its worst, this beats working. I am walking by a little after 6:00 AM, through the university and pleasant suburbs, then a pleasant stroll into agriculture.

Something troubles me. Why chickens? Is it that they're convenient, ubiquitous, easily at hand? That every peasant has a chicken? Or is there a humoral explanation? Meat creates blood, blood is air, is hot and wet, moist and warm. Who needed a more sanguine disposition? What is the story below the story, the understory, the underbelly, the lost story that everyone used to know? What is so obvious now that we fail to describe it in telling our tales? Was Joseph Smith really visited by an angel bearing golden plates of the new story? In 500 years, will "Bohemian Rhapsody" be interpreted as a song about AIDS even though it predated our awareness of AIDS, Freddie Mercury's death from AIDS?

An unexpected blessing

On the Way in Rabé de las Calzadas, a religious beckons me from the path to his porch. He—cleric? Reverend? Father? Brother?—crosses me with a swatch of twigs, shakes holy water over me from their leaves, blesses me and my travels. It reminds me of the *lulav* and *etrog,* waved with willow and myrtle at *Sukkot,* during the service and by the *Chabadniks* standing on the sidewalks around urban universities in the fall: "Are you Jewish? Would you like to wave the four species?"

A gradual ascent through more wheat and red poppies, redstarts both black and common, goldfinches, tits, and others not in my bird guide. I miss Nancy. The first view down to the plain of the Meseta is dramatic. A nice breeze makes walking a pleasure. I am still in pain, but my feet and I have reached an understanding.

I sign up for the communal dinner, secure a bunk in a very clean room with two women I met in Scott's company in Burgos, sit in the yard watching the peregrinxs walk by. Maya is from Germany and is impressed that I know that Lübeck was the second Hanseatic city. I know Lübeck primarily as the home of Niederegger Marzipan, but sure, also as it was concerned with the salt trade. This is more like what I anticipated of the Camino—walk, rest, check out the local church for storks and services, light candles, go to Mass, read about tomorrow, drink a San Miguel. I light more candles. The town also has a chicken story. In this case, it's about Napoleon's chicken-thieving soldiers.

We eat paella with chicken, artichoke, pepper, a flat bean I don't recognize, with bread, salad, water, wine, lemon yogurt. And how we talk!

> Impromptu blessings,
> poppies, candle wax, water.
> Crossed, I don't refuse.

I anchor myself in my silk sleep sack like an otter tangling in kelp in order not to float too far away in dreams. Like that lady who floated off, who knows where, unmoored, disentangled from her hmmm, ummmm, Lordy, Lordy, I remember that made-up story....

Noche estrellada

Doré's lithograph depicts a skulking, big-nosed Jew. A wandering Jew, diaspora Jew, not a pilgrimage but a life. Do I err, errant? I would never have denied Jesus a drink of water. Where are the wandering women, remaking Jewishness on the Way? The way to what? Do we wander the places we were exiled from? Iberia, Babylon, Jerusalem. I am walking out of Chelm. I am a Jew who is and is not a Jew, and not just a Jew. My angels are Isaiah's, not this tidy white robed androgyne on a religious medal. My angels are not human-like, not gendered. Fire, wings, eyes, wheels. The gods are mostly gendered because we are mostly gendered, mostly straight because most of us are straight. Yin to yang, Seal of Solomon. Do we continue to explore, our destination unimportant? Demons, I command you out of my body!

Constantine turned Jerusalem the Gold into a garbage dump. She is in good company: Santiago de Compostela, the compost heap, boneyard, that is also the field of stars. As the Church on Spilt Blood holds the memory of its years as a morgue, a refuse tip, a warehouse for vegetables. "Stupa" means heap, but I don't know of what. In Cambodia, pagodas turned to fish sauce factories. Starving, we eat the silkworms plucked from the mulberry trees, destroy the assets of our future because we are hungry now and the future is an illusion. Soldiers fire their soup pots with books from the National Library. Enemies are executed in the garden. Ancient treasures are pulverized. We are worse than the monkeys, more vicious, with better tools and thumbs. At the Royal University of Phnom Penh, a nun relates the history. After the Khmer Rouge time, Year Zero, classes resumed but the empty elevator shaft still gaped open. Finally, she and some other Maryknoll nuns boarded it up, shut that gateway to hell.

I pound across Spain, stamp the ground, form the Way more into itself. I like the step step stepness of walking, the slowly shifting surround, the landscape minutely kaleidoscopic, falling in with a crush of colors. I am passing on the Camino, passing itself with myself, passing *las cruces pequeñas y gigantes, pasandx. Camino el Camino con una cruz,* resting my atomizing toes, my heat rash-spotted legs. I still wear the little bronzy cross on my pack, an angel, a scallop shell, a triquetra at my throat. Me who almost never wears a Magen David, infrequently a tiny om. "You shall not follow other gods, the gods of the peoples all around you," *s'vivotekhem.* The KKK would leave flyers and business cards tacked to my high school bus kiosk: "You have been paid a friendly visit by the Ku Klux Klan. Shall we pay you a real visit?" I once found an unadorned silver cross in the gutter at this stop. I picked it up, gave myself this option for Christian disguise, but I never wore it. Whenever it seemed like it might be useful, I remembered the Jews marched toward the ovens, saying *Kaddish* for themselves and each other. Is it better to die than convert or pretend? Is it better to burn, or to pass by omission or commission, to be passed over? If you don't believe any of it, gods, God, idols, demons? If you are clasped to your identity by outside forces, compressed into yourself? What speaks to you, and do you speak back? Do you listen? Does it listen to you? If Messiah comes, Messiah comes.

Do you have to leave the world to leave the world? Untrackable tracts, untold stories of the liminal spaces, thin spaces. I am in this world. I am grateful for a place to sleep, water, a hunk of bread. I am grateful not to lurch toward Santiago de Compostela in a fever, catarrh-wrecked, bubo-ridden, struck by a plague and falling, no wayside memorial blurred by time to illegibility. I disentangle and re-tangle the narrative strands, like fractals' alternation of simple and complex.

> Camino stories:
> I never saw her again—
> hototogisu.

Earworm

There's always music in my head. The iPod with related books and music is not a distraction but part of the trance of this moment. Every time "Smooth Criminal" arises in my monkey mind, I substitute "Le chant des pèlerins de Compostelle." For now it's just the chorus because I find the scansion a little challenging in terms of where the syllabic stress on *Deus* and *adjuva* should fall linguistically, but I'm getting there. Once the chorus is automatic, I'll move on to the verses. This should serve the dual purposes of substituting more wholesome sentiments for the earworm's narrative and giving myself a Camino-related walking song. The chorus works well for inducing the alert trance state I enjoy while in motion or while sleepless in a hot albergue. In addition, I'd like to start my mornings by exclaiming "Ultreia!" to myself rather than "Up and at 'em, Atom Ant!" which, while expressing a similar sentiment, doesn't quite evoke the mood I'm hoping for.

> I'm just minerals
> taking water for a walk,
> particles of light.

Thump and click

The Camino is not a reset, but the simplification of routine that allows the increased intensity of practice paired with loosening other strictures, yang and yin snuggled-up achromatic kittens. Abstemiousness, early rising, only the walk, the walking, the having walked, the big sky speckled with the drifting ghost bugs in my vitreous humors, the insect shrill that lives in my ears, or maybe the drifting spectral stars, the music of the spheres. The Way colored in, backlit, crosshatched, loops and swirls of breath. I still don't know the constellation tattooed on my chest. Dr. Anton said I could have the distinct inked dots removed, and I think about a cover-up, honey bees for Frederic and Nancy. But *vanity of vanities; all is vanity,* restoration is a fruitless illusion, we cannot go back. Maybe I'm a radioactive crab, *MUL.AL.LUL,* snapping my sparking claws, bigger than the sky. My eye-spider's legs retract and disappear as I find mine. Only a dark spot remains.

I'm sure I'm supposed to have a sidekick, like Jedidiah Jenkins and Bill Bryson do. Or maybe I am the sidekick, Sancho Panza or Dr. John Watson. In the edematous swelter I don my gauntlets and vambraces, or at least my compression garments, my rustic anti-cancer armor. What would Don Quixote make of these three-armed wind turbines? Too tall to tilt at, too slow to suggest a threat, but definitely giants. Is it picaresque? What constitutes an adventure? A woman walking slowly to the west.

This hot wind is a breath of fresh air. I am walking the pilgrimage into being. Slow walking in the rhythm of the organism, of most humans in most human history. The breath is the act and the prize.

We are strung like luminous Murano beads along the thread of the Camino. Imagine I walk town to town, not alone, but with my band of screaming flagellants, my dance to death. I am ignorant, sedentary, metaphoric; I am nominal, vengeful, minimal. I walk in time and through time, through sun and sunflowers. I am peripatetic and discontinuous, a mess of rods and cones, the whole shebang. Most of what surrounds me is sky. I never see Hesperus, only Phosphorus, light-bearer.

To walk is exquisite, reductive, expansive. I look forward to it even as I endure it. The Camino assaults every bodily humor by means of overstimulation of all organ systems. How to cure insomnia, blisters, the range of derangement? I wear a clinking scallop shell, no yellow star, no cross of St. James. What Jewish ritual do I do? Nothing novel or exotic. I know when to shut up, when to sing Kaddish to the wind.

The thump thump, click click of the pilgrims' progress. The rhythm of the pilgrim is not always that of the communities through which we pass. The tumbled towns are melancholic and embody beauty in decay, slow mineral return to the elemental as we churn the sea of milk, labor or amble under the Milky Way, face into our galaxy, edge-on. I walk toward the black hole at the center of universe, nothing ultimately learned at the event horizon. Zeno and calculus approach but do not reach the limit as I fling myself toward everything but dissolve before impact, luminous, voluminous, numinous. I am not lonely. I am evenly suspended, engaged but impersonal, fused to the topography, the wind and dust. I am here in the moment in pain. I am here in the moment in the meditation trance.

> Orpheus's hell
> was a cold thing, not like this
> heat-bleached Meseta.

My mystery is not known, not knowable. Can I enjoy the syncretic symbols, find comfort and relationship in the rites and practices? Sometimes. That's part of the attraction of the Camino or any pilgrimage. Some skip the Meseta. I love it like South Dakota's golden ruffle and warp. I don't need poetry in my hat band; my brain is saturated with glitter, repetition. The serpent aerates the tree of the world, churns the roots, spices the soil. I am content in this beauty and motion.

What is between the stars, the churches, the albergues, the hills? This intention that glows in the mind. Stunned into spiritual synesthesia, I am congealed, a conglomerate, an accretion, an assemblage of bacteria and mitochondria not doing their job, respiring and digesting but not pumping energy to my legs, my brain. Estivating on my feet, I dream in Christian. Aeroglyphs spangle the sky like the Galla Placida, sparkle and swash; I am awash in universal slosh, as close as I'll ever get to the moon.

Not flashbacks. Call them mild intrusive thoughts, slightly unwanted daydreams. Idle recollections randomly stimulated. Specifically, the courtyard in suburban Romania where the Ceaușescus were dragged and executed. Specifically, out the subway line from Mexico City, hard by Frieda Kahlo's house, where Trotsky was murdered with an ice axe.

I pray to St. James. To the ineffable thingie. I pray without belief, a focusing yet expansive chant, to more than one thingie, to masculine or ungendered thingies, tangled in beliefs about monotheism that I don't believe but apparently hold, limbic, basal ganglia under the thin paste of neocortex, the optional add-on of the frontal lobes.

My codex, *Liber Kerewskiensis,* will tell the tale of my pilgrimage to Santiago de Compostela from anaphora to epistrophe, less lascivious than the Wife of Bath, better moored and more Moorish-ish than Shirley MacLaine. The storm of sunlight! The Quixotic windmills, giant arms slowly sweeping over sunflowers and grain. My painful toes; I step in fresh manure. Imagine my historiated initials: I am the hunged woman dangling from the Tau cross of my T, impinging on the next lines of text. T is for Templar, *tortilla* and *toro.* Tiny rats squinch the corners of the page, plague rats, golden marmots for the Golden Horde. Flea in my right eye, resolved to a hopping peripheral speck. Fill in around me, *horror vacui,* wrap me in a carpet page, no space left empty for troubled thoughts. Sing now, welcome the Sabbath Bride.

This is a story of B for *bocadillos,* for breakfast in a bar, another slice of cured ham on a roll, another cup of café latte, watching the same news clip of a bull and a mozo colliding hard on a street in Pamplona. This is a story of P is for *pato,* Muscovy ducks regarding me from the stone edge of an algae-green millrace. *Me gustan los patos, patos almizclados,* with their warty red wattles.

I move westward, as I followed the Equator. I snack on local vegetation. People like to put things in their mouths: Dust, ditchwater, crunchy little bones of the saints. I chew them into sentences and words. I light candles as if. I am everywhere and somewhere specific, *ubi o ubi,* ubificated, hocus naufragium dominocus. I am nothing special. I am safe from Jerusalem Syndrome. I enact my brain privilege in bubbling tangents and associations.

Juego de la Oca: Goose game

Jugo de la Oca: Goose juice

Should I try to win eternal life, or to accept inevitable death? My goose game uses smooth black Japanese river stones, more irregular than Go markers, as its tokens. Perhaps they are also the prize.

> Uncertain journeys.
> Ostraca and knucklebones

foretell a story.

Miraculous sweat

I sweat profusely. Menopause meets chemo hot flashes meets Spanish heat wave meets Meseta meets albergues, no fans, windows shut tight. Maxwell's demon is a slacker. Hey! I smell under both arms! My radiated right sweat glands are improving, returning to some level of function.

> Hot albergue, hot
> flashes. Sleepless with Eno's
> *Music for Airports.*

The pain in my toes is not toe cancer. The pain in my knee is not knee cancer. The sun, though radiant, is not targeted radiation. Particles and waves, I have waited for you for 8 minutes.

I find no local Jewish services on the Camino. I am a little afraid to ask in case people who have never met a Jew press, as some did in Maryland in my youth, to see my horns, a mistranslation of the Hebrew root Q-R-N that led St. Jerome to translate "shone" as "horn" in the Vulgate. In Hebrew, vowels are represented by *nequdot,* marks added to the consonant base. While efficient, this system lends itself to misreading, both on its own and through flyspecks on a manuscript. A rope is not like a camel. My torso bears six diacritical marks, artifacts of the superannuated alphabet of cancer intervention. I fantasize about starting a *minyan*-based prayer group, with discussion, singing, and kosher snacks somewhere on the Way.

The Jewish concept of tikkun olam, the repair of the world, is understood differently in different traditions, but generally includes the idea that we should do something to make the world more perfect, more harmonious, closer to an ideal. A broken world is like cancer because. A broken world is like a garden because.

Pilgrimage highlights the symbolic over the cognitive, a longing for meaning that incorporates rather than restricts. Jews adapt to the cultures around us, learn to live beside foreign gods. It is attested that non-Jews can have divine powers. Discerning how to maintain but making pragmatically permeable the fence around the Torah.

> Hours of sunflowers
> Jerusalem behind and south.
> *Girasol* I turn, face to the sun.

Must travel be sad for those who have experienced pain? I sit on the patio of a Spanish bar in a brown-walled town, my feet aching, drinking an electrolyte soda and running through a manual lymphatic drainage routine to account for many hours already walked with a backpack in the summer sun. The barista juices oranges and sings loud karaoke pop songs, substituting Camino- and pilgrimage-related lyrics. The Australian peregrina complains that he's off-key, but I find his loud, rough atonality delightful. Beyond the patio, linnets flit.

Cats wander around the albergue, lie on the sidewalk. They drink from the outside faucet, and we eat bibimbap. It's fun to talk with the Korean pilgrims and use my one remembered phrase, *"Gam sa ham ni da!"* memorized through its repetition on long Korean Air flights to Cambodia. In the courtyard, a woman sits miserably in her bikini and sandals while her clothes and gear are de-bedbugged by the hospitalero. She leaves before the process can be completed.

Phlogistication: The residue of air left after burning is all there is to breathe at night in the sweltering albergue. I burp. Too many bocadillos, an excess of *ensalada con atún.*

Roget's Thesaurus begins with Abstract Relations, Existence, Inexistence. I remember the reverse, beginning with the void, but that may be the interpolation of *tohu v'vohu,* empty, before the light. The Dalai Lama says, "The nature of the body is to disintegrate." To make a mosaic, start by breaking, unmaking. Or collect the shattered pieces. Aggregating is the opposite of murdering the text. Assemblage makes relationships; mosaics create patterns.

Cancer and the Camino are secret societies: We recognize each other by our symbols and signs.

Cancer is a question with no compelling answers. The Camino is answers without knowing all the questions.

The body of the land is not fractured but continuous, always repairing itself and always in decay.

> Conversations in
> the present indicative,
> the Way is just now.

Not a funny story

Hot flashes. Thank you, Tamoxifen, which slams down on estrogen like this bright blue sky-bowl traps the earth. It's true, though, that after a certain point I can't really get hotter. I've always swung this way. Israel wonderfully bone-dry in summer. Grit-aired Athens in a heat wave, feral cats sacked out in a park's undergrowth. We marvel at the recollection of flat Cycladic faces. Galápagos a vision of hell itself; imagine a ship of missionaries, blown off-course. Hordes of mud-colored marine iguanas surf the roiling waves, slam and stick to the lava rocks, clamber up, spit salt juice from their nostrils, lie on each other in monstrous black piles. There is no water on the island. All is lost.

Penguins in the waters of the Galápagos. Hoopoes on Palatine Hill, wood pigeons at the Atomium, monk parakeets in Buenos Aires. More than 70 species spotted while working construction with my students in the Dominican Republic. Bee-eaters in Cambodia. Now hototogisu, metaphorically. Cancer's post-traumatic hypervigilance is great for birdwatching. I am Adam's boffin sidekick, naming the animals in taxonomical nomenclature, *Xanthocephalus xanthocephalus!* I cry, though not here but in a different desert.

Walking for hours like a machine, but no, I'm not a machine, I am an animal stepping, stepping in thigh-high grasses, wshhh, wshhh. A rough Fibbonacci-ish kilometer beast slouching toward miles to be born.

Cancer stripped my delusion of immortality, lends potential significance to every bump or dull ache. I am tougher than I look. The infinitesimal shift of the mountains and the slow crawl across the plain demonstrate that deep breaths and moving grains of sand do work. The insurmountable takes care of itself. Frustration is boring, not urgent. Thank you, El Shaddai, thank you, St. James, thank you, ineffable floaty thingie, thank you, numinous nothingness, thank you, Tamoxifen.

The Camino provides a kind of immortality, immersing myself in the pilgrim flood, the human tide since before recorded history. Camino kintsugi, the road we walk, the road we make that makes us.

I am walking as a woman in the world. Not a nomad striding purposefully and alone across the desert, bivouacking under a creosote bush; not an adventurer racing my dogs across the ice field to the South Pole; not a man sleeping at the temple, but not girls, of course; not a tourist waking up still drunk in my own filth, my wallet stolen and my face bruised, isn't that a funny story? I am not the Dalai Lama, disguised as a soldier to smuggle himself out of Tibet. I am a tidy woman approaching 60, return of my Chinese zodiac to my element and animal. As I walk, I cultivate serenity, unremarkableness. I am not Paulo Coehlo's solo man, independent man, man stripping himself of relationships in search of an isolated and disconnected truth. Isn't the goal not just finding the wizard and getting your magic artifact, but bringing it back to Kansas as a story about metaphors, a different way to see your life? A story that is relational, more and beyond, not separate from your former self and community, a continuous enlightenment and becoming. Not discontinuous, desert island-like. Though I walk alone, walking to join, not to separate myself. Walking to be the walking, *ha dado la marcha de mis pies cansados.*

On this hot day like the other hot days, my body reliquary a crisped rind for my desiccated attention, I arrive after about 24 kilometers to find that my hotel reservation has been displaced by a wedding party. I'm transferred to a nicer *Casa Rural* at the same rate. Over red wine and fruit with Californians, we discuss the Atapuerca findings and whether *homo sapiens* killed off the Neandertals, as well as aspects of ritual cannibalism. When I go up to bed, I lock my door.

Repetition, silence. I lie on the cool tile floor, the curtains closed. Hope is not the same as being a believer, and I am hopeful.

I listen to Karen Armstrong's *The Case for God.* What I extrapolate is that consciousness and the ability to anticipate the future cause anxiety. A function of spirituality is the re-creation of anxiety through rites plus the assuaging of anxiety through the development of egolessness. Practices of repetition, silence, and compassion decrease existential dread. Existence means something, though we can never know what. I can work with that.

I once was lost, or lost a way of being in myself. What bugs me about this? Maybe the discontinuous corollary jump, the idea that everything can now be found, will be the same. A nostalgia for a past self. Before cancer, I was often joyous, playful, entertaining. I hope to reclaim a confidence in my body, not my old body but this current one.

It helps to have lived in Jerusalem, among my co-religionists with whom I didn't share a religion. We figure out how to live in peace by understanding others' practices as not-idolatry. It helps to have had cancer, learned rituals and rites that hold death's reality front and center. The proliferation of human rituals and icons shows how we yearn toward meaning, and that it is easiest to remember and reinforce when it is repetitive and concrete. Although I wasn't raised with Jewish religion, I was raised in Jewish culture, though often not overtly identified. This makes it hard for me to see symbolic representations of the divine as licit. They appear to be *avoda zara,* false works. I wrestle with this, she-Jacob and dogma-angel. It is the difference between a thing and its representation, a misinterpretation of metaphor, which is, after all, a means of comparing by highlighting shared characteristics. The symbol is mistaken for the object, as much a failure of the rules of metaphor as is attributing the unlike characteristics from one object to another, a shaky syllogism.

> I long for trinkets, amulets, and charms.
> I act as if with and without belief,
> I surround myself in meaningful air,
> austerity of an imageless God.

The bones of St. James

If I don't think it matters if the bones of James the Greater, Ya'aqov son of Z'vadiyah and Salome, lie under the Cathedral, what is the basis for pilgrimage? Is it just an interesting walk, or can it be more? Community, intention; can every walk be a pilgrimage, or must pilgrimage be a visit to something, a walk with a terminus? Can all walks be dedicated? Should some walks just be movement in time and space?

> Altered and altared.
> If St. James isn't here, who
> else could be isn't?

We seek the fractal edges of the waves. *Ubique naufragium est,* but is the opposite also true? Will the stone boat, Santiago's paradox, save you, that koan of a boat, sarcophagus afloat, steered with neither rudder nor sails? I ask on your behalf and not for me. I am not anything, not a disciple, not a cowgirl in the boat of Ra, Semite in the court of a Christian king. I ferry us down unnamed oxbows, we become the liminal, the rotting riparian, the hesitation between neurons and electrons. Here is the soppy creek I played in as a child, damming the flow, now slowed by the clay of my father's ashes, creek to tributary, river to ocean, the muddy banks chewing up themselves, collapsing seaward. *Ferō, ferre, tulī, lātum,* I will tell you stories as we float. We steer into the setting sun. Dawn boat, crepuscular boat, the Spanish moon traverses overhead. Fire boat, air boat, not St. James's boat of earth and wet, stinking with the tide. Didn't Gilgamesh stalk by, desperate for the secrets of the Flood? Didn't Eurydice mark mysterious shadows, check her pace and turn back on her own, leave Orpheus in the dry dust, mouth open, bewildered by himself at the labyrinth's core? Empty at the heart of it, oops, does the quest cough up no object? Do I pass as something, *¿me hago paser por algo o alguien?* I am both Orpheus and Eurydice, of course. Is arrival dispersal, will I deliquesce? Am I whoever drowning or the sea? The sea must be cool, still salty as my sweat. Is there something? Is there something?

In the Chapel of the Invention of the Cross, near the Chapel of St. Helena, a depiction of a boat with an unstepped mast, attributed to an unknown pilgrim. Stone boats abound on the shores of the Celtic world. Saints of Ireland and Brittany, the Galician coast. A *barca de piedra* for Our Lady of Boulogne, more saints than I have fingers in miraculous stone boats, stone boats without a mast, floating millstones tied to their necks to drown them buoy them instead to safety. Are the stone masts prehistoric standing stones, lingams conferring fertility? Everyone has sacred stones, alive or gateways to a deity. Some are meteorites, joining us here from everywhere else. Any rock I sit on becomes unsad, omphalos or not. Is a saint like a baetylus, an *inuksuk*? Is the moon rock in the stained glass window of Washington National Cathedral a sacred stone curled in the golden mean, a science stone, the basalt nipple of a breast in holy bricolage?

These stones are instruments of salvation. But not for Virginia Woolf, pockets full of rocks, not floated to safety on another shore but drowned in the Ouse, back to primordial ooze, lacking a Sea of Trees, ghost-home in which to lose herself. Not for the Bhāgavata Purāṇa which advises, "One who boards a boat made of stone is doomed." It's a metaphor. Lord Ṛṣabhadeva wanders like a lunatic, stones in his mouth, a silenced Demosthenes. In a story from Kemet, the Black Land, Set and Horus race stone boats, but Horus's is painted wood. So is the Marble Boat in the Summer Palace in Beijing.

I prefer not to fuck on the sacred stones. I don't want to F the ineffable, μὴ κίνη χέραδος, screw with the stones, get it on with a swan. Was Pasiphaë pacified? I don't want to draw the lustful gaze of any divinity.

A *barca* is not like BRCA, a gene mutation that increases the risk of certain cancers.

I walk through grain fields, sunflowers, sun. I eat gazpacho and a bocadillo, unmiraculous chickens scratching underfoot, the river of pilgrims visible then gone. The river is always the river, though the pilgrims flood through. The awe of worn pilgrim footsteps in the rocks and steps. Each yellow arrow is a dopaminergic pleasure, a little squirt of joy.

> Sing me a love song in paleo-Hebrew.
> Stone fragments of the Iron Age,
> bone splinters of a killing field.

A stone boat beaches in the surf. There is no one aboard but a statue of Mary, like a plague ship drifting sailorless to port. A virgin blackened by intent or smoke, indigenous, synchronic. Black as the negredo, the primal muck from which, if we're diligent and lucky, we are transmuted, from which a savior rises as gold smoke.

Cryptic coloration

Carrión de los Condes may have been named for the abusive counts to whom the king gave El Cid's daughters. Common swifts mob the statue of Santa Maria.

After vespers we sing with the nuns, attend a mass and pilgrim's blessing, prepare our communal dinner. The bunk beds creak and squeak. Packs and shoes litter the floor. By 2:00 AM, pilgrims arise to beat the heat on the next long stretch, rustling, dropping toothbrushes, blazing the room with their headlamps and flashlights, whispering. They clatter down the stairs, out into the hot night. I am resting here for a day, though, so I doze until 5:40 AM when the nuns snap on the lights.

It's strange to catch sight of myself in a window, all these Christian amulets like cryptic coloration.

I stand on the stone bridge over the river and watch the circumambulations of the ducks, joined by a common kingfisher with electric blue feathers, European robins, wagtails, a treecreeper, and chaffinches. When I'm not walking, or if I stay in a hotel, I feel disconnected from the other pilgrims, separated from pilgrimage.

A little before noon I check into my *hostal*. It has a tiny bathtub, but it's big enough to soak my feet, or sit in with my knees up for a bandana bath like someone's grandmama on the prairie in 1880, crouched in her zinc washtub. I have a beer, then dinner, with convivial pilgrims from South Africa and the U.K.

Sangria, more gazpacho, fried eggs with blood sausage over fries in a sort of Spanish poutine. The pilgrims are covered in mosquito bites, or at least, I hope it was mosquitoes.

Would Susan Sontag have enjoyed the Camino? I think not, but it's difficult to say. In her journal she listed her likes and dislikes; they balance fairly evenly in relation to the experience of the Camino. For myself, I like this overheated walking, the boredom of walking, the fancies of walking, acclimating to Christianity. The Camino is like exposure therapy, cognitive flooding, unwiring, less firing.

Can you say om twice? The overwhelming fear and anxiety about death that comes with consciousness is also the understanding of the meaningless indifferent universe. Meaning inheres locally. That is art.

Dear John

Dear Prester John;

I am in receipt of your letter of circa 1165 of the Common Era. It appears to be derivative of several sources, which I have taken the liberty of identifying below. To avoid accusations of plagiarism, please be sure to provide complete citations.

Dear John Frum;

We are sorry to let you know that we cannot wait any longer for your return. Time marches forward, and we have been obliged to tear down the wooden runway, recycle the wooden airplane. If you should pass this way again, do stop in for *laplap* or *tuluk.* We will always have *kava* for you.

Mixed metaphors

I walk past a wall covered in graffiti, most of it names, one swastika, spray paint kenophobia.

Standing in a stand

of ripe grain, I eat stale bread,
golden in the mouth.

The fields are beautifully serene, and also, are they misted with glyphosate?

Must my story be inspirational, redemptive? Is it sufficient simply to report on what it was for me? On the ultimately unknowable and unreportable, perhaps the untranslatable from my experience to yours? Can we share awe in the heart of the ineffable yet understand it in different ways? This is a use of metaphor, of evocation through image and language, rhythm and implication. It is a door held open that is not a door. It has forward notes of bitter herbs and cherry, aftertaste of smoke and salt. It is delicious with the right *amuse bouche,* but I can't choose what will satisfy your hunger.

Symbols, not my symbols, meaningful in an impersonal way. The dispassionate and unattached collective unconscious. Is there always a bridge? Is Jesus a door? Do I want to move toward naming, toward categorizing, or stick with the sticky recognition of resonance, the unknown whatever slowly grinding diamonds in the earth?

I have outlived the Singing Nun with her *guitare espagnole.* As a child I knew her album phonetically, later studied the meanings of the words. *Dominique, nique, nique,* not a girl song but a saint song. *You look down: Your feet in a ditch. You look up: You breathe the night sky.* Now I sing the parts I remember, belt out *J'allais sur toutes les routes vagabondant,* a good pilgrimage song. Under grave financial threat, she and her partner sedated themselves to death. Jesus is a door, *je t'adore.*

Abaciscus, abaculus, vitreous, ceramic, gold, mirrored, stained, pebbles. Opus vermiculatum. Susan Sontag and I both like listing new words in English and other languages, learning precise names. I acknowledge that I'm not sure how to pronounce them all. Semi-nonsensical words sung to familiar tunes,

Adonai s'fatai tiftach; E sus eia! Deus adjuva nos. Does the sing-song disguise horror vacui, filling every scrap of emptiness with *azulejos,* arabesques, curlicues, an excess of ornament performing apotropaic functions? This visual crowding often populates entheogenic art, but I make my own kaleidoscopic spectacle, even without Hildegard of Bingen's migrainous geometric auras. Is the unseen world so cluttered with sign and symbol, sound and motion?

Is this my Camino hamartia? Too much pleasure in clever words, onomatopoiesis, a glass bead game of mixed metaphors? I refuse to dumb it down, pretend this isn't how my mind makes music atop the percussion of my footfalls, but I acknowledge that these succulent utterances can be an attraction and distraction, crackling flame for my magnificent phantasmagoric moth. What could my anagnorisis be, what can I do to save myself from enticing sirens, the fucking mermaids ready with their knives, when this stone boat has no mast to lash myself to? Do I want to? Do I need to? Should I enter the sea?

> A commonplace, a book of hours.
> my pillow book and vade mecum.

> I divinate with *Codex Calixtinus,*
> check the footnotes, *Ai, my feet!*

> Maps evaporate, sublime,
> evanescent, deliquescent.

> This is a guidebook to this instant,
> stretched like taffy.

An imaginary friend named Xhi-Xhi

In the albergues, privacy is pragmatic. It's Europe, so people are more used to mixed-gender semi-undress. I'm comfortable with my scars, but they may be startling so I'm circumspect. I don't think anyone sees them. I'm doing my part not to scare the chickens.

I should name my eye-speck, fly in a flyspeck, diacritical chinche companion. As a very young child, my imaginary friend was named Xhi-Xhi. This can be my bug friend's name as well. Were any saints overtaken by one or many insects, or could this be my thing? Charles Darwin reports that even from the Beagle at anchor offshore, the men could hear the cacophonous insect screak from land. Catch them, label them, pin them in a curiosity cabinet. Xhi-Xhi is a living thing, rings buzzes in my head, endless cicada tinnitus, whine and ring, tintinnabulation of tones too high to sing. Thank you, Tamoxifen.

Return to Big Dick Mountain

I arrive at the municipal albergue, a spacious and airy dormitory housed in a church. I haven't stayed at many municipal or *donativo* albergues, wanting to leave those beds for pilgrims with fewer means. I drop my backpack by a bunk then walk around town, admiring the stone and wood exteriors of historic buildings that are closed today, no candles. Of the restaurants recommended by the *Moon Travel* guide, I pick the one with the most shade. I choose the pilgrim menu because the à la carte is expensive and the non-pilgrim fixed menu begins with what Google translates as "horse cock." The photo looks like cured meat or jerky, but from which part of the horse? I have already avoided eating pigs' ears. Some saints licked sores, ate scabs and pus, claiming it was delicious. I decline this spotted dick. Instead I order pickled white asparagus with mayonnaise and a red pepper relish, bread, pork fillets, lemon beer, and a lemon cream.

Outlining an itinerary for Laura's upcoming visit is an entertaining game of "you can't get there from here" and "you can get there from here, but not on the day you need to." I believe I can beat the system by adding a taxi to the mix, but on which day? Let us see what reality throws our way.

Later, it is still very hot in the albergue, 32°C outside at 7:00 PM until a sudden pelting rain, hitting hard and bouncing off the pavement, low charcoal clouds, hail. I didn't hang my clothes outside to dry—sloth rewarded!

In early evening as the light fades, I lie on my bunk, try to catch a cool draft, though we have closed the promisingly large windows against the downpour. On two bunks in my cubicle, a family with small children readies for bed. They have suitcases and every night make up the children's beds with their own sheets and stuffed animals. From the other end of the enormous room, I hear Hermann, a young German pilgrim, explaining himself in his booming voice: "I am always depressed except when I am on the Camino!" Loud conversation continues, and so I yield rather than resist. I get up, pull on tomorrow's pants and my shower flip flops, fish a packet of olives from my supply. I walk to the kitchen/dining area where a group of Germans and Danes whom I've more or less paralleled sit at a long table, drinking wine as they prepare a leisurely dinner. I take a plate from the dish rack and sit at the other table, but they wave me over, offer me salad, spaghetti, sliced watermelon. I try to memorize their names and faces so I can return their generosity as a coffee, a slice of pizza when I see each of them again. I feel great affection for Hermann. It's not like the Camino isn't making me happier, too. I want to know what it is about the Camino that soothes him.

I set my sandals and some of my foot care supplies on the donativo table as I leave.

The Camino is like cancer, resulting in sleep disruption, early morning awakening. Preoccupation with body parts, their action and deterioration. The albergue is like a cancer ward, each of us in her own thoughts, sometimes talking, praying, taking notes, asking questions, sometimes just sitting together.

I don't like philosophy and systems of thought that are too self-referential. The glass bead game is pretty, aesthetically engaging, but gets caught up in its own pattern-making, as do philosophically-based models of the body, the humors, the cosmos. I hope for balance and harmony, grace and beauty in symmetry, not the overextension through logic of symmetry onto asymmetrical phenomena, geometry superimposed on our messy accumulation of mitochondria and other organelles. We are handed, we are eyed, we are skewed. Our ears and faces diverge from themselves. We contain salt but are not only salt. The Platonic form is an entertaining idea, good for thought experiments, but why favor it? And why favor symmetry?—so my heart and liver ask you. What does it do for the world, this mirror-imaging, this imposition of rigid analogues? Tekel upharsin. I might prefer the Game of the Goose, but that's fixed, too, randomness the only out. Juego de la Oca: Spiral in. I'd rather step on a goose than Golgotha, place of the skulls. Juego de la Oca: A cul-de-sac labyrinth, curled up in the heart of the nautilus if you win, snack for a minotaur. Juego de la Oca: So spiral out. Algebra spins sudden permutations, flings fractals, hurls hydrogen, red-shifts, tumbles out of bound. Which is more likely as a metaphor for our existence?

The Camino is emotional and has a meaningful relationship to my atheism. It doesn't change me profoundly so much as it brings me back to myself in the present, as I am, as things are.

Up on a distant hill, a billboard of a black bull, bullboard, bulbul, bulbil, *pilpul.*

We keep pulling the god out of the box, but we love the boxes so we stuff it back in. Tombs, graves, Ark of the Covenant, phallus of a gold calf, Holy Grail, reliquary, True Cross, statuette of the Black Virgin. Boxes of words: On this spot; at this time; the correct answer is; you are a heretic.

The graffiti on Camino kilometer markers is like cancer. Cancer and the Camino share the possibility of unexpected growth. Cancer and the Camino can both have deleterious effects on the toenails. The Camino is not like cancer, though both have physical and existential tendrils. I am like a straight, white, Christian without cancer because.

> A smoldering field.
> Helicopters dump buckets.
> Blinded, facing west.

Susurrus of grain, wind in the leaves. I sing a quod libet, made-up invocation over a Sephardic version of *"Ahavat Olam,"* *tikkun olam, tikkun haguf, tikkun shaddaim,* thank you, El Shaddai.

Too many eyes

The imagery of classical narrative therapy is a military metaphor of "fighting recruitment." It's useful, but is fear of recurrence unrealistic? Is cancer a war? Are my thoughts a battle? Is it possible not to externalize the cancer as something outside myself while still rejecting its influence and narration as the only way to tell this story?

I am in an obstinate mood, truculent. My sunblock melts off. What's the point of schmearing myself again? I'm not going to zinc like a white-limbed zombie. Parabens, phthalates. Melanoma risk. Actinic damage, *quelle dommage.*

I rehearse a litany of made-up sins, an if-then list that mirrors my negative thoughts. I lied so the albergue isn't open as advertised. I ate meat on a Friday so there is nothing edible on hand. I didn't replenish my sunblock so I got cancer again.

I hope to be neither overly rational nor too symbolic, caught up in a system of making meaning that forces meaning into tight embraces, locks doors. I want to climb in and out of windows, not to be trapped in self-referential tessellations like an Escher nightmare. I want to remain suspended in the solution, not crystallized, precipitated out.

I must make peace with everything with too many eyes, monsters, seraphim, ophanim, self-scrutiny, the natural and unnatural worlds. I read about the Obama worm, an invasive flatworm accidentally introduced to Spain. It has hundreds of eyes, eats flesh, though only earthworms—well, so far. I must stand still in the glare of the angels' eyes, so many all-seeing eyes tucked in their horrifying wings of flame, spun in fiery orbs. I will not be consumed in the wet earth, burned in heaven's incandescence.

Salt with a whale

The albergue is across from a small marshy lagoon. I opt for a separate *cama baja*, two to a cubicle, with great air circulation. A real bottom sheet, hooray. An outlet and a small locking drawer as well. Light and clean toilets and showers, a large yard with a decent clothesline. I soak my foot in a baggie filled with warm water salted with La Ballena, coarse, brining myself as I eat my dinner of olives, cheese, cucumbers, and bread. In the evening I walk to the lagoon and to the church, storks nested overhead. I pass by wooden doors ornamented with scrolls and scalloped corners.

A peregrino staggers in late and takes the bed in the adjoining cubicle. He keeps his light on until 1:00 AM, then snores and farts until morning. I meditate and breathe, but not too deeply. I resist the urge to turn the light on at 5:00 AM as I leave. This makes me some kind of Camino hero.

On a table under a tree, next to a fenced field, is a bowl of plums and plastic bags. Donativo. I tear up. Someone wishes me well, whoever I may be. Generosity is common and overwhelming on the Camino, a question, blessings, bottom bunks, a cross, a story, plums. I leave a euro for four small plums. They are what

I eat this day.

A chant

Exterior: I am in the world. No one is talking about me.
Interior: I am in myself. I am not talking to myself.
Citerior: I am in the mundane.
Ulterior: I am beyond the evident. Ultreia! Further and higher.

Mostly I walk

I don't enjoy most athletics. Whether tennis, swimming, fencing or self-defensing, archery or bowling, I am lukewarm. Yoga and tai chi make me fidget. I don't have the knees for jogging. It's true that I didn't used to dance, and now I do. Mostly I walk. I don't walk quickly, but I do keep going, camel-like, especially in a dry heat. 23andMe reports in relation to my Neandertal genes, "You have 1 variant associated with having a worse sense of direction." My sense of direction is excellent, *davka.* Circumambulating a Fijian peninsula with Nancy, past the mongooses with their bottlebrush tails and dull eyes, past the enormous fruit bats hanging like zoonotic litter in the trees. I walk beyond the tourist zones, into the villages on red dirt roads marked with incomprehensible signs. I am my own gnomon: I navigate by my shadow and the sun, or the angled solar panels on the roofs, or by luck through the stone alleys of the Christian Quarter, the falafel and carpet vendors of the suq. How easy the Camino is, with its punctuating yellow arrows.

> I miss an arrow
> in undulating wheat. Lost
> again. Ultreia!

Snoring together

This tiny town might as well have a sign that says *"Bienvenido a Villa Cero"* on both sides.

Through interminable nights, the hot plastic mattress covers trap my sweat in the shape of a sprawling woman, sweat angels on my silk sleeping bag liner as I lie awake, taking in the human sounds, no white noise, pilgrims snoring together as we have for eons, communal dreams if not dreams in common. In my earbuds, *Music for Airports*. Breathing in the dark. Bodies, wool socks, cheese, vino tinto, mint toothpaste, cigarettes, the sun captured by drying clothes. Tamoxifen is an antidote to a good night's sleep under the best of circumstances, even more so in a hot dormitory, medieval-style. What a pleasure that my mattress is not a straw tick flopped onto a luxurious sagging rope frame. What a pleasure that I'm not sharing my bed with two other travelers and the descendants of the great-great-great-St. James the Greater's bedbugs. What an infinite pleasure that we aren't sharing this room with the chickens.

> Why not pray?
> Wander the Way, whispering
> to Santiago?

The day begins with crops all around. I walk through a town with hobbit-hole bodegas dug into the ground and the sadly not-yet-open Bar Elvis. The tickle on my ankle is probably sweat, not a chinche, a crusade of chinches, definitely not. There's no reason to think about bedbugs or fleas, ticks from the long grass and thigh-high wheat I walked through this morning, so early, trying to outpace the sun. The iPod with Paul Quenon's *In Praise of the Useless Life: A Monk's Memoir* is not a distraction but part of the trance of this moment.

I dream. Frederic arrives in my dream and I am surprised that his speaking voice sounds different from my memory. His singing voice is the same. We decide to find a pocket of the dream where we can ensconce ourselves, wrap a twist of space-time around ourselves and have an uninterrupted conversation.

The sign

She doesn't know what to do with the sign
significant glyphs arrayed in a line
sparkle and wonder, they number the days,
sort granular data both coarse and fine.

She doesn't know what to do with the sign
if she counted it right, the stars align
dark and indifferent, the moon out of phase
may spell both disaster and everything fine.

You'd think eventually I'd sleep, but I almost never do. I am in the trance of "I'm in a trance and can't be too worried about anti-Semitic history." The Camino opens the door to a different set of rooms.

Reliquaries

I own my father's siddur, his battered pocket copy of *The Prophet,* his *Four Quartets* from teaching English in Switzerland, and two of his rings. I asked to see his liver but was refused. I didn't ask to see my breasts, though I read my pathology report. I have one blue flannel shirt I bought for him, soft for his scarred torso, which later I claimed for my own tender body. I own one shirt of Frederic's, too, with brown and orange stripes, also from the end of his life, too small for me; he was so small by the end. I have his angel pendant.

I had a bracelet the group of us made, we cancer Sisters and Chemosabes, passed hand to hand and by international post, for whoever needed it, for surgery, for bad news visits. I wore it to walk a half-marathon the next year, after active treatment, to see if I could, if I had that kind of walking in me still.

When my surgeon said, "You're tougher than you look!" it was a compliment, I think. I should have asked what he meant. Was he surprised? It is another mystery. That Saint's got backbone, the way he holds up all the north of Spain. Look here: I have the ailerons of Icarus, the flames bursting from the arms of Shadrach, but which did not consume him, behold, a lion that was Daniel's in the den, a nest of vipers for your pretty hair. I hold my lost father in the reliquary of my body, a fine but battered repository, dented, every cell a window to my inheritance. Behold the story of the man walking the story of our people. We come for you, Matamoros, draped in these unclean seashells, we come to view your stone boat, the discarded husk, the split chrysalis empty as the absent Ark.

Who am I when I am walking?

A.) Eaten by the universe.
B.) Chewed up by god.
C.) Lit from within like an evanescent lamp.

St. James's Day. Someone has stolen the hero's binoculars and hardback guide to the birds of Wheresthatistan. She is still a hero. She is still learning.

God on the iPod

I walk between transmission towers dotted with nesting white storks, *Cinconia ciconia* circling above the Camino, the flats and hills.

In conversation, people exoticize the Meseta as natural. It reeks of humans and cultivation. That barley didn't just grow there in moiré-inducing rows. Even Atapuerca, with its happy accident of limestone erosion, was settled by people, bears their imprint as surely as mitochondria colonize my cells.

> God on the iPod,
> *davka.* God, it's hot. Shabbat
> on the Meseta.

I cross a light industrial area, practice the breath and lovely thoughts despite its indifferent appearance, or possibly because of it. Despite the ugly welcome at the commercial edge, I enjoy walking into the city. It's very different from driving and highlights the changes of topography, buildings, and decorative texture.

> What else is living
> in the weeds I just disturbed,
> you jumping spiders?

Not the same as taking Communion

I breakfast near the Cathedral, hailing and joined by Rafael from Brazil. He argues but I buy his coffee anyway. Four Korean peregrinas I know stop to say hello, excitedly summarize their adventures since we ate bibimbap together. A couple I met yesterday wave as they click, click by. Buen Namaste, yo.

In my hotel room, 24°C seems chilly, demonstrating how much I've grown accustomed to the heat. The little wrapped toiletries, big towels, and cotton sheets both thrill and puzzle me. I've acclimated to pilgrimage. The room has a tiny wrought iron French balcony from which the Cathedral is just visible, early Gothic with amazing expanses of stained glass.

I buy a couple of hard rolls, a packet of hand-sliced, air-cured pork, olives for the road. In the Barrio Húmedo I drink a cider and look for a place to eat, not easy as early as 7:00 PM. I exclude the restaurants serving primarily pigs' feet, tongue, octopus, bacalao and trout *raciones.* What I really want is a local dish with leeks, and after several tries, I find a bar where I can order leeks with tomatoes and air-cured beef, a pear and goat cheese salad, and chestnut tiramisu. Delicious. I return to the hotel at 8:30 PM to try to sleep when people are just starting to step out for a few glasses of wine before dinner.

The forecast anticipates several days of rain showers. That should drop the temperature. No rain yet, but it's breezy and cooler. I stop and eat a slice of Torta de Santiago, an almond meal and apricot dessert decorated with the St. James Cross in powdered sugar. It's not the same as taking Communion or ingesting a relic of a saint's body, but eating a cross is closer than I usually get.

Practice

I do what I'm worst at, which is hanging around doing nothing. I grit my teeth and make myself sit still in a hot noisy yard of happy pilgrim chatter, music, cigarettes, beer and laughter. What do I need to do more than this right now? I am seducible by a myth of progress, by a capitalist metaphor in which the coinage of my days hits the jackpot, spills ecstasy and immortality, an avalanche of attainment into my delighted hands. I ungrit my teeth, since this is not conducive to my practice. I have been to India and know that meditation in calm environments is easy, a privilege, and that difficult meditation notices and accepts the noise and squalor, the heat and dust, industrial wastelands, the world not stopping for my ease.

Walking trances

Not Lear, not mad, not on the heath, still stunned by meteorology, in a weather-related dazzle that embodies my daze. I connect deeply to the walking trances, entranced. Walking from Talpiot through the villages of Jabal al Mukabbir, Ras al Amud, north on the Jericho Road. Towns as silent at noon as Basque country. From Talpiot on the Bethlehem Way, the Way of the Bread House, the Meat House. Within Jerusalem's walled Old City, meandering through the suq in a haze, touching dusty carvings, gesturing for an orange, drinking Turkish coffee while perched on a stool. In Cambodia, walking straight out of Siem Reap, destinationless, wandering unpaved towns with no Roman letters. Knowing there are still live landmines on the verge, I keep to the street. I don't want to be chopped like Agatha, poisoned like Buddha, crisped like Joan of Arc.

Walking out of my small hotel near Suvarnabhumi Airport, whose engaging address is "999 Moo 1." Knowing the area was swampy before it was developed, had a reputation for snakes, I avoid the grasses at the edge. I find: A *wat* with crumbling stupas, a Chinese pond heron perched in a tree, a technical college. Roiling, thrashing fish in a muddy, weed-choked waterway. An icon at a stupa has more than enough faces and arms, Buddhist with Hindi sauce. Overhead drift Asian openbilled cranes. In another direction, I find: Gold jewelry sold by the gram, a ladyboy parade whose participants see and recognize me as kin, nod the universal slight dip of acknowledgement. A park with unidentifiable lizards in and out of the water feature, one coppersmith barbet.

The European goldfinch is my most frequent Camino bird exotica. They look dull at a distance but spring into color through my lightweight binoculars, my personal weight allowance like Gus Grissom's Mercury dimes. I hope they don't end up on the ocean floor. Ah, such bright tiny birds! Bite-sized.

One does wonder, will I be so fortunate as to be struck from my donkey on the road? Will a whack from a teacher illuminate me? Does falling over on my own count as enlightenment?

In the clank

I walk with teachers, clergy, people with whom I share no language, engineers, students, Argentines, elders. I'm not actively looking for other queer people, or Jews, or Buddhists, or pilgrims with cancer histories, but I notice that I don't meet them. I also meet neither infants or donkeys, so this observation may not be meaningful.

Counting is sometimes recommended to still thought and improve meditation, but for me it is its own rhythmic distraction: 1, 2, 3, 4, *do sol fa fa fa,* solfège spiral, clank of hand-cranked geocentric orreries, erratic orbits and galaxies. It's not worrying about where I'll sleep tonight; neither is it calm reflection. I stumble from the precipice of thought into a whirlpool of numerals, crystal lattices fracturing along mathematically predictable lines. Counting underlies my mental processes. So do rhyme and meter. Smear them with language, a sudden poem. *Anassa kata, kalo kale, ia ia ia Nike!* Anything with a walking beat, the heart's lub dub pressed into iamb.

Exhausted, I cross Spain in an increasing dreamlike swoon, audiating chants, *pa, vu, ga, di, ke, zo, ni; sa, re, ga, ma, pa, dha, ni; I, ro, ha, ni, ho, he, to; ji, ro, lu, pat, ma, nem, pi;* behold the gamut of the Guidonian hand, *ut, re, mi, fa, sol, la.* A Fatima hand, *khamsa,* raise your right to Ishtar and Inanna. Red thread to edge my garments, guard their apertures from malevolent forces. One, one, two, three, five, eight, thirteen, the golden mean, ultreia!

My monkey mind can count to 4. I return to my breath. Step, step, step. Thank you, St. James, thank you, Adonai, thank you, ineffable flying numinous thingie, thank you, body that is a conduit for om.

> Shell around
> a hollow of air.
> I hold this sky,
> suck it in,
> spit it out,
> barley, poppies;
> malt, opium.

Kenosis, God empties itself out, just for a while, just to see what comes of it.

Sunday

I walk through drizzle all day. I live in Oregon. We don't evade the rain, nor do we ignore it. We join the rain; I join the rain. This albergue has a good write-up in the *Moon Travel* guide; I stop just for a coffee but decide to stay there after I see the hospitalera lend a jacket to a shivering peregrina who has biked in and can't get warm. My phone doesn't find the Wi-Fi, so I walk some more to the municipal albergue for coffee, free plums, and a signal.

My little toenail lifts more and seems likely to detach. I imagine my big toenail will follow shortly on the principle of misery loving company. I keep both coated with antibiotic ointment and, while walking, bandaged up. Note: Flies love the ointment. We eat a pasta dish made in a big paella pan, salad, beef stewed with mushrooms and prunes, and watermelon. With red wine, of course. Rain, rain, cooling rain.

Caminante, No Hay Camino

The Camino is like cancer. Both have multiple roots and routes. Both spread systemically along natural pathways.

The Camino is not like cancer. Cancer's imagery, *slashed, poisoned, burned,* does not correlate to the Camino's symptoms.

Body is not *Bodhi.*

Tumor is not tomb.

"Caminante, No Hay Camino."

> I'm a sphinx without a nose,
> holes where the Elgin Marbles go.
> I've lost my marbles, my Elgin Marbles.

Shhh. I rise slowly from the creaky bunk bed, creep into the restroom to write.

I do better to eat a late lunch in cities because it's hard to find dinner other than the Pilgrim Menu before 8:00 PM. *My my, hey hey, necesito mas café.* I tire of pork lomo, fries, plastic cups of yogurt for dessert. It's Sunday, so nothing much is open in the little towns. I pass a labyrinth constructed of foot-sized stones. I had identified an albergue last night, but when I arrive at 9:30 AM, my options are to sit on the sidewalk for hours until they open or keep walking. I decide to walk. I buy new tips for my trekking poles. My little toenail pulls off; it's the first I've ever lost.

Pendulous breasts

I can't get enough of Gaudí's Palacio Episcopal. I've been to Sagrada Familia, seen his warped Casa Milá, Barcelona bricolage, but this building lifts my heart. Gaudí's red and white framing evokes the *Mudéjar* style, gives me a way to see the *Convivencia* behind the museum's depictions of James slaying the Moors. I am mesmerized by a painting of St. John and St. Bartholomew, in the visual frame of which a cat-sized demon lies on his side looking out at the viewer, a green and rust demon, horned and bearded, claw-footed. He sports a pair of pendulous red breasts. Even the boy demons got titties! I will read that this is Astaroth, though that is probably a masculine appropriation of the old goddess's breast attribute, Ashtoreth, Astarte, Anat, Inanna, Ishtar, Isis. I am so fascinated by the breasted demon, a warped counterpart of El Shaddai, that I forget to look for St. Águeda. Next time, next time.

When I leave the gorgeous, airy structure, I encounter a parade, part of *La Fiesta de Astures y Romanos,* a celebration of the historical city, Astúrica Augusta. Groups dress in togas and furs as their Romanized and Asturian forbearers, another way to see the people behind the counters at shops and hotels.

Classical tales

The paintings and sculptures of testaments both old and new remind me that holy texts are not uniform and continuous. They, too, are collage, bricolage, mosaic, the assemblage of folktales, histories, poetry, almost-parallel versions, letters, visions, prayers, discontinuous fragments, scrolls misordered, images, charts, exegesis. *Alf Laylah Wa Laylah* is a *matryoshka,* egg inside egg with a woman at the core, storyteller and object of the story. *The Decameron* and *The Canterbury Tales* are collections of Cornell boxes, each story foregrounding a set of images and themes. If I owned a printing press, hot type, I would crank out a story as a series of broadsides, text at the heart of each page, nestled in commentary, Talmud style, my wooden box of reversed glyphs and dingbats at my hand.

> Angels in angles.
> Gaudí's bright Gothic. Blue glass
> cools the July light.

I meet Laura's late train from Madrid as she joins me for a scant handful days. Though we have been friends for almost 30 years, this is our longest sustained time together, no other relationships or responsibilities. Laura's first comment: "Oh, good! You're going grey!" *Silver,* I think, but this is defensive. I look down. Indeed, my trousers are rolled. Yet here is a beneficent mermaid, singing of me to me.

Laura and I visit the Cathedral for her first sello. In the Cathedral's museum, I spy with my little eye another well-stacked demon or two, stomping on a saint with some of its demon friends, cudgeling, pulling his hair right out of his halo.

In the Plaza Mayor, we eat a huge plate of *pimientos de padrón.* What pleasure.

Relics

Somewhere there must be
15 or 16 breasts
attributed to Saint Águeda,
gilded and boxed,
glassed chest reliquaries.
Or served up on a silver tray,
pastries hardened skyward,
Saint Lucy's fervent eyes.

Ascent

Laura and I both enjoy packing lightly and cleverly. We've slept atop the White Cliffs of Dover, tent set on grass and chalk. We've meandered in the French countryside, seeing no one but cows. Laura played violin at my commitment ceremony, civil union, and finally legal wedding to Nancy as our nuptial opportunities evolved. We travel well together. Today we walk our long walk west from Astorga. The Camino ascends, acquires scrubby oak and pine, broom, heather, even shade at times. More rocky paths, more towns. Walking, alphabetic repetitions, march to a psalm, *Lo ira ra*, follow the breath line, find my own gasping or natural resting points. My scars itch. Fucking mermaid. Not Laura. The mythic one.

Unseasonable
heat. Danger: Threat of wildfires.
Padróns set red fruit.

These rocks

It is my birthday. We arrive at the Cruz de Ferro, marker of the crossroads, pagan and Christian. A tall wooden pole bears a disproportionately humble cross. The base is piled with stones, an impressive cairn. If this were a Jewish grave, they would signify many visitors. Here they mean that we have put our sorrows in a stone, our worries, our doubts, lay our burden down, a metaphor for intention. I don't know the history of this tradition in this place, what it meant to pagan and pilgrim, but I suspect the meaning has changed over time. This is what it is today. Cruz de Ferro is not the only feature of the Way to accumulate pebbles and rocks, notes and photographs, to become a shrine, aggregate and make visible the walkers of the past minute and century. Though its appearance is massive, weighty, earth-bound as Antaeus, its message is liberation. Not beach rubble; still, as in Sappho's fragment, effluvial pebbles, not to be poked at; to be accreted, added to, joined with. Rocks in a resting place. *Piedras. On this rock I will build my church.* The stones are a source of energy and connection, not repository for negative experience. They remind me that we, too, are carbon. *These rocks are not so sad,* these unsad rocks, their mineral interiors, my rocks, *gold lives inside,* cruz kintsugi. Female redstarts peck at soil around the periphery.

I have two to lay down. One is the small black Japanese river pebble. I drop it with the intention of no longer agonizing about my work. The other is a jagged, unpleasant little stone I picked up between Logroño and Ventoso, early on. I commit not to cling to annoyance about any aspect of the Camino.

We descend, walk the long, rocky downhill. Despite the appeal of Manjarín's clutter of flags, signs, turbines and stacked stone, I'm not up for trips to the outhouse in the dark. *These rocks, these rocks are not, these rocks are not so sad, gold lives, gold lives, gold livivives, inside of them, these rocks,* Neruda deformed by walking. Μὴ κίνη χέραδος, don't disturb the stones.

The terrain shifts as we press into Galicia, greener, cloudier, more damp. Part of the game of Laura's short visit is to be sure we'll arrive in a town with a train, on a day with a train, so she can return to Madrid and then home. We taxi up-mountain to La Faba, breakfast at El Refugio. Laura photographs me and the witch on an Estrella Galicia beer pull regarding each other. The *bruja* sports dashed lines around her breasts, mirroring a meme I made with a photo of myself in the run-up to radiation. The latter shows me post-bilateral mastectomy and post-chemo bald, lying in a hammock with sunglasses askew, clutching a liquor bottle, the proposed radiation alignment area demarcated with an outline of dashed stickers. The caption is "I knew I shouldn't have partied with those oncologists!" I haven't worried about partial nudity in albergue restrooms despite my unreconstructed chest. It probably helps that my surgeon did a fine job with my very large but more or less flat scars. I don't scurry into the shower to undress, but I try to be sensitive to the people around me. I'm pretty sure no one has seen me, though when they have in other places at other times, locker rooms, dressing rooms, we've usually had a good conversation.

Next time I walk here, I will walk this taxied section of the day, not out of a misplaced completionist sentiment but because it is so beautiful. We reach O Cebreiro, its evocation of oak and ash and thorn. *Pallozas* with broom-thatched roofs, a disgruntled-looking pulpo on a restaurant sign, feral cats lying on stone in the afternoon sun, my first hedgehog, *erizo!* We walk out of O Cebreiro above the massing clouds that fill and obscure the river valley to the north.

> Sunlight and bees, bright
> blossoms and bracts, the veil of
> subtle cataracts.

I can't be intimate because I can only conjugate formally. Olive, olive, olive oil …. *huile… aciete de oliva?* Hebrew knocks out huge chunks of Romance vocabulary, *shemen zayit,* olive oil, sure, as well as prepositions and conjunctions, nominal structure collapsing into the construct state, reconstructing the houses of the agents of the verb.

The way has been hilly so we stop at a nondescript little albergue, slightly dirty. Chickens strut and peck under our table, venture into the entryway. It is like an albergue run by aliens who have seen albergues on television. It suffices. The Way lightens my load, metaphorically and in reality. Thoughts, feelings, expectations, pills, pebbles, pages of maps. I make brief notations in my tiny travel-tracking journal. Laura calls it a "fetal Moleskine." What will it grow up to be?

The ascents and descents take out my big toenail at last and blacken a new nail on my right foot. Laura has bike envy; bicycles can be rented from Alto do Poio to Sarria, mostly downhill. In the retreat center Montán that echoes Manjarín, we stop for donativo juice and fruit, rest a little but decline an offer of soup, keep walking. We pass through small villages where cattle are driven in the streets; therefore the Camino is thick with fresh dung. Chickens and cats abound. House martins, a common cuckoo—finally, Euro-hototogisu!—many European robins, many hawks; cow bells clank in the fields and giant chestnut trees line the road.

> After walking all
> day through cow manure, Patxarana
> tastes gorgeous.

Ecce sapiens

Laura and I encounter a stela, maybe, or a shrine, or art, a short, irregular stone column incised "HOMO," a stone maybe-Jesus looking out through a dark metal grid. We don't check the back for ECCE or ANTECESSOR. We photograph each other beside it because, well, HOMO. *Homo sapiens sapiens homo.* Exponentially subspeciated, palindromically identified, ultreia. We stop for coffee near an enormous mosaic scallop shell.

> Martins hug the wires.
> A brown bird lofts. Cryptic, plane
> of the ecliptic.

In Sarria, where many begin a short Camino that still

qualifies for a compostela, young Japanese pilgrims dressed in traditional Japanese pilgrims' garb distribute fliers for a talk tonight about Kumano Kodo and Shikoku, the Camino de Santiago's sister pilgrimage routes. The albergues and hotels we try are full. We find bunks at the Monasterio de la Magdalena. The Camino is not a kimono. Shikoku haiku-*ka?*

> We await the late
> train. My friend leaves her walking
> stick. I amble on.

Camino sabi

"Cancer is a journey" is true yet reductive, an over-extended metaphor, a cliché. Hototogisu is an actual Japanese cuckoo, *Cuculus poliocephalus,* and also a country bumpkin, and also the longing that is sabi, the poignancy of a walked forest.

> Who do I see whom
> I'll never see again? Blood,
> wine, Matamoros.

I'm glad that Laura joined me. Her companionship refreshes me and helps me look forward to my last days of peregrinating. Today's route is more crowded, with peregrinxs, tourigrinxs, bicigrinxs, mounted police, Spanish families with cigarettes and boom boxes, their enormous dogs. The mood is different, though I enjoy it, walking with a nurse from York until we reach her hotel pick-up point. The Way is a tree-shaded dirt path, mossy stone walls to either side. The weather is sunny with a breeze and not too hot; the ascents and descent not bad; the walking surfaces varied. The hotel I reserved after yesterday's housing surprise has a large lawn and a bar with a shady patio. For lunch I have a lemon beer, *Caldo Gallego,* and a cup of Cebreiro farmers-style cheese with honey that is fantastic. I eat two titsy rolls with their knotted dough nipples, *Pan Gallego de Moña.* Yum. Pair with *Queso de Tetilla,* the titsy cheese.

A window at the hotel displays a magic square, another palindrome.

SATOR
AREPO
TENET
OPERA
ROTAS

Dinner is also excellent: Local red wine, gazpacho, rice salad, tortilla with mushrooms, Torta de Santiago with a little cream liqueur. A perfect pilgrimage day.

Walking forward, walking toward a destination. I prefer to have a goal, but I'm not too invested in the goal. No "everything will be wonderful when I get to Santiago." Having a destination frees me from the destination. I seek the heart of the labyrinth, knowing that when I arrive it will be empty, that I might sit awhile, then, if I am so fortunate, walk back out.

The Way is not like a squelching slog in manure. The Way is like a country lane. The interplay of light and shade through the leaves is called *komorebi* in Japanese.

A song for James the Moor-slayer

Hello, Santiago, Semite on the Way,
reclaiming right of Way.
Hello, Isabella,
greetings from the Holy Land.
Hello, Gallego brujas,
sisters under the Inquisition.
Omega to Alpha, here again,
still here.

Gone

I almost smell the sea. "If you are squeamish, don't prod the beach rubble," cautions Sappho, but I like the wreck and wrack, the pungency overtaking. I walk that way, solfège thundering around me, waves of warped air, dissolution. The hot blue sky ahead hints at the death of everything. I am not yet the age my grandmother was when I was born. All the memories she had by then in which I played no part! All the memories that I'm still forming now.

Consciousness is 60 years of noise. I walk and I become old. What a pile of pebbles, Cruz de Ferro, a heap of clattered wishes, warm to the touch at an ancient crossroad, safeguarding the liminal edge of everything, the susurrus of land approaching sea.

Into those delicious waves a white horse canters, touches the drop off at the earth's end, returns festooned in scallops, draped in kelp. It may be a sign or a puzzle. It may be nothing at the heart of nothing, no one home in the midst of someone. I might learn to be content with that.

I love the right-to-leftness of the Camino Francés, languages of the ancient east propelling us sunsetward. I walk with my sisters, stepping our vowels onto the land, tracking our origins into the earth, the women of Syria and Judaea, Pakistan and Persia. I imagine walking the Camino until I die, all its arteries pulsing. No need to send my dead meat back to Oregon.

I make an early start on a sometimes difficult but interesting path. I arrive in town to find no beds, *completo.* I reserve a hotel room then show up to learn that there has been a booking error, he is *désolé.* I know something will happen next, even if it is walking another 15 kilometers to Melide. The French proprietor makes some multilingual calls, finds me a room in a pension, *merci beaucoup!* As I walk to the pension, I see Rafael far downhill, following the waymarks out of town. I yell and run after him, I'd have shared my bed. But he doesn't turn, walking rapidly toward the setting sun.

The room is clean but has no windows except one to an airshaft that admits the lamp light from the next room. The bathroom is shared and I can't access the Wi-Fi. My boots smell none too great, either. I step out to find a signal and run into some Australian and British peregrinxs in a restaurant. They are busily booking out as well, though they have Spanish phone service and enough Spanish language, and therefore more options. They invite me to share their *pulpo á feira,* boiled octopus with salt and paprika, which I appreciate since I only want a taste, not a whole ración. I am pretty sure octopi are smarter than us and eating them makes me uneasy.

After a pilgrim meal of beer, gazpacho, chicken with chestnuts, and Torta de Santiago, I return to my room, scrape at my boot soles with a twig, and hang my washing every which way across the tiny room's diagonals, settle in for a hot, agriculturally redolent, but solitary night.

> I shout, my voice thin
> in the wind. He doesn't hear
> me; he's gone, gone on.

Green

I am a eucalypt in the hot, bright air, *verde, "que te quiero verde,"* wishing you too were green.

Pilgrimage is a rite to attain by process the empty center and mystery. An anti-catechism: "Who is there?" "No one is here." Who are you? "I Am Not That I Am Not." "Where am I?" "I am everywhere that is nowhere."

Shall I eat the dust of the Cathedral's renovation? Pulpo, *polvo, concha de vieira,* tentacles and claws. Chew spent candles, drink the wash water.

In a lovely caesura, my Camino is bracketed by floods of

singing children, this time not Basque but Gallego, wearing their own tee shirts, singing their own language.

> Sun-dazzle washout
> blotches obscure my vision
> *komorebi ya.*

I walk in the ambit of different pilgrims. I've seen several people I know in the last few days, but by breaking up a long stage, resting, I'm not likely to see them again. At a bar, I admire statues of enormous ants. I walk by a gigantic wall-mounted scallop shell, *hórreos* that evoke the raised graves among the rice fields of Vietnam.

> I'm back, Matamoros
> talking smack, Matamoros
>
> not smacking, Matamoros
> not attacking, not backing down
>
> Matamoros, my tomorrows
> are words not swords

The albergue is clean and spacious, top and bottom cotton sheets and a towel, so luxurious! I cry. My backpack has started to smell like socks and manure so I pick at my boots some more and machine-wash and dry my clothes. It is unbearably comforting; I cry a little in the laundry room as well. I re-encounter a woman I met the night before. She has a work meeting in Italy later in the week. She sends her huge suitcase of professional clothes and work paraphernalia ahead of her each day. I enjoy her company so I'm sorry she isn't free to join me for dinner. It rains overnight, a deeply lulling patter and chill.

I grow sad about the upcoming end of my Camino. I want to see my wife and cats, but otherwise I would be content to rest awhile, then continue on my Way.

> How many greens? Green

is illusory, no greens.
Still, so many greens.

Eucalypts

I walk through eucalyptus groves. It rains steadily, softening my feet and making my ankles and hips ache. I'm happy to walk more slowly in the rain. Galicia is green for a reason! At the hotel the water is only tepid, but a bath is a bath. I rub inside my boots with eucalyptus leaves, spicing the room.

I pass a field planted with "walking stick" cabbage, *Brassica oleracea var. longata.* I wonder if it would grow in my own garden.

> No birds heard in the
> non-native trees. At least Spain
> didn't farm bamboo.

Actually, Spain does farm bamboo, but I'm not walking through it.

Lentil soup

The pensión reeks of unpleasant fish. The Camino's challenges give me plenty of practice attending to both physical and emotional side effects, especially taking a few moments to breathe before turning to problem-solving. Enacting my anti-tamoxifen-induced-helplessness practice of finding satisfaction rather than bursting into frustrated tears, I search for another place to spend the night. No dice. So I walk down the Camino in the windy rain to the next pensión. It has no beds tonight, but does have a proper bar. I drink tea with sugar, eat lentil soup and a beautiful, 8-vegetable salad. That and my remaining handful of trail mix will hold me until morning. If the accommodation I've reserved tomorrow night is not satisfactory, I'm sacrificing the cost and pressing on to Santiago de Compostela, where even an awful room is still a room in Santiago, and an expensive room represents a triumph over adversity.

> I stumble through mud,
> strip eucalyptus leaves,
> again stuff my rank boots.

We should reinstitute the tradition of metal pilgrim badges. The patches on my backpack, penguin and scallop shell, are satisfactory, but what about the anthropomorphic penis and vulva badges I've seen in books? These would be a fine conversation starter.

"Ain't It Strange"

I see on the news that Patti Smith is playing in A Coruña tomorrow. That's about an hour north of here, and easy to get to from Santiago. However, since tomorrow is my entry to the city, I won't try to get a ticket, though I'm sorely tempted. Focus, focus; sing "Ain't It Strange" to split the difference between desire and intention.

This town boasts a rooster statue. Today's pensión is a thousand times better than last night's place, which still smelled overpoweringly of fish in the morning, as well as mold from the closed-up bathroom. It's a bit shabby and eccentric, but clean, light, and with cheerful colors. My clothes are whipping around on the line in a stiff breeze, the rain having stopped at about 9:00 AM. I shower in my non-moldy and private bathroom, and though I have no windows, there's a skylight. I sit in the common room by a wood stove, dry my boots stuffed with newspaper and eucalyptus leaves. The hospitalera shows me her compostela.

This is a peaceful green room. Things could be worse than having my clothes smell faintly of wood smoke as I enter Santiago tomorrow. I have a lovely dinner-long conversation with a professor from the northeast coast. Her name in Euskara means "joy." We have a long discussion about teaching, the Camino, and cats as we eat. She is gratified that I've read *Obabakoak* by Basque author Bernardo Atxaga. We have opposite meals of the two choices on the pilgrim menu —for me, salad and vegetable lasagna with sangria and yogurt with honey; for her, cream of zucchini soup and chicken with water and a cheese tart. This is the longest conversation I've ever had in Spanish.

> Always west,
> always overtaken
> by the sun.

Enough juice

Of course I'm both Orpheus and Eurydice, the masculine actor with strong internal locus of control and the feminine mute stubbornness that knows that if you rip the seeds from the soil, nothing can root. Images of celestial horror vacui. Is the thought of an empty heaven intolerable?

I awaken to overcast skies but no rain. My headlamp battery is failing, but has enough juice to get me and several other early risers through the dark wooded portion at the beginning of today's 19 kilometer walk. Though it sprinkles now and then, and is too misty to see the Cathedral from Monte de Gozo, it is a comfortable walk.

> Too cloudy to see
> the Cathedral from Monte
> de Gozo. It's there.

Pilgrim 823

I hear the bagpipes, sounding off the stones. In another age, I might hear the clang of chains being struck from the limbs of convicts as they complete their pilgrimage.

I am surprised to have an emotional reaction to the Praza Obradoiro. Part of it is probably the emotions of those around me, as well as the sense of completion. I am by myself, which feels odd, but there is a great sense of solidarity with the community. I head for the pilgrim office, receive my number. I will be the 823rd pilgrim today. I have lunch while I wait, a tapas scallop on the half shell in tomato sauce and a Coke Cero. On the whole, I prefer my mother's and Nancy's scallop preparation, but it's good to eat a local specialty. When I return to the pilgrim office, I light more candles in the chapel, visit the English speakers' welcome area for tea. In about 2½ hours, my number comes up and I receive my Latin compostela.

Off the map

Know what I don't want to eat? An octopus in any form, but especially in a bocadillo.

I have exhausted my Brierley terrain. Tomorrow I enter the unknown, sea serpents and mermaids in the corners of maps I don't own, milagros *y monstruos,* off the charts.

I wander back to the Cathedral. Frederic died on April 21st. This is also the feast of consecration and dedication of the Santiago Cathedral. It is under renovation for the holy year, under wraps, Camino kintsugi, bundled up like a Christo installation. The Cathedral is a shell within a shell, perhaps the bones of St. James at its core. I think about the difference between angels with scaffolds and scaffolds with angels. Perhaps it's a quantum state where both and neither are present. The statue of Queen Esther in the Portico de Gloria got the St. Águeda treatment, her breasts reduced. Queen Mother breasts are too lascivious, such that even statuary is unnecessarily arousing. Since everything is draped, I can't get a look at it, or at much of anything. Next time, next time. On impulse, I stand in the long, slow line to hug the icon of St. James. I wend past stonemason's marks, a depiction of stone boat. I hug the bejeweled golden statue, whisper "thank you" but not to it, not to St. James or a deity, gratitude scattered to anything receptive.

I came, I saw, I knew I would never understand, which is the point of all this effort.

> Muffled in plastic,
> sacred wonders. Angels we
> have heard are on high.

Getting to Q

Today takes me and I take myself to Finisterre, which, as its name proclaims, is the end of the earth. It's actually the second westernmost point on the continent, but hey, pretty close for ancient cartography! I have read the assertion that the pre-Christian pilgrimage followed the Milky Way to this edge to experience the miracle of the sun setting into the ocean. More recently, pilgrims would burn their clothes here, perhaps both as a fire and renewal ritual and to kill vermin. I don't figure that my technical gear's artificial fiber would burn cleanly, it would be carcinogenic, and I have the intention to donate much of it when I return to Santiago, so I choose the more ecological option of washing my Darn Toughs and Ex Officios instead.

My hotel room is large and clean. The bathroom is entirely blue, the floor, the tile walls, the decorative figured tiles blue-on-blue on the side of the tub, the tub itself, sink, bidet, toilet. I don't think this is what the character Estraven had in mind in *The Left Hand of Darkness* when s/he exclaimed, *"Blue—all blue... full of light."*

I walk a few kilometers on the Finisterre Camino to the lighthouse. In Virginia Woolf's novel, Mr. Ramsey can get to Q but never reach R. Z is not even part of this equation. I also can reach Q, questions, but R, *arrrnswer,* as a British classmate once argued, is beyond my knowing, at least for now.

Yesterday a restaurateur asked if I wanted Coke Cero or "Coke

Cero Cero," meaning without sugar or caffeine, similar to the Turkish coffee I brew with stevia and decaf. Kilometer Cero of the Camino is at the Cathedral, but what could be called Kilometer Cero Cero is at this lighthouse at the end of the Finisterre extension.

I scramble onto the rocks behind the lighthouse as far as vertigo and common sense allow. I play a Ladino Kaddish on my iPod and sit awhile in the center of the four elements, sun afire, brisk wind kicking the ocean into whitecaps, the ocean crashing into wet grey boulders below. The wind blows Frederic's molecules from across the Atlantic. I breathe in, I breathe out.

When it's time, I hurl Frederic's medallion into the unknowable void. Like the One Ring, the thing has a contrarian mind of its own and lofts back toward the rocks in the wind, an angel flying in that instant of grace. Someone on a different journey may receive it someday, as I once retrieved a small silver cross from a gutter. It is an ending but not climactic or conclusive, a part of the unknotting denouement. The Camino not an end, not revelatory, but confirmatory, a continuation. The climactic moment in this story is that in this moment, I am still walking, and I am still here. Negredo to albedo, *per aspera ad astra,* from compost to stars.

Frederic was my best friend. We had an instant and compelling bond. I have known no one as funny, as linguistically clever, as attuned to whatever my own essence may be. He had periods in which he was wrapped up in himself, cruel, mendacious, alcohol-abusing. I say this in order to give a more complete accounting of him. Like any of us, he was flawed, unintegrated, sometimes stupid with those he loved. Frederic died a quarter-century ago and I still miss him terribly. Releasing his angel doesn't change our relationship.

On my walk back to town I stop to see the sacred stones. One divinates by rocking, but I don't know which stone, or even if it is here or elsewhere on the bouldered coast of northern Iberia. Perhaps, therefore, all stones should be understood as holding meaning, not sad.

> Gull on a stone cross.
> Behind, shells of new houses.
> Before us, just sea.

Illumination

I run into several pilgrims I know, including a woman who was at my albergue in St.-Jean the first night and Hermann from Germany. We embrace; we have walked. Hermann beams. I hope he can carry a bit of his Camino peace back home, a pebble of joy in his pocket.

> I watch the planet
> turn, slow burn, a star, we are
> illuminated!

A thicket of walking sticks

On my return to Santiago de Compostela, I visit a Decathlon, indulge in the purchase of non-wool socks and a fresh tank top for my impending travel home, 5, 4, 3, 2, 1. On my walk to Egeria House, I take a photo of the enormous bright sun that turns the Cathedral to silhouette. Later, much played with and metamorphosized, it becomes my book cover, something changed, remade anew. Since Pilgrim House is closed this week, at Egeria I donate my pocket knife, scissors, well-worn but still-serviceable boots, my trekking poles, my daypack, a tiny fan, extra food, extra toiletries, extra bandages. Liberated, I walk to Alameda Park and the Chapel of St. Susana. St. Susana and I are both ultimately named for the Shoshannah of the apocrypha to the Book of Daniel. Her name traveled from Greek to the Romance languages, becoming Susan in English via the French Suzanne. I was named Shoshana because my father liked Shoshana Damari, a Yemeni-Israeli folk singer. She sang a song entitled "Shoshana, Shoshana, Shoshana," which I imagine my father thought was a love song about Shoshana and the handsome captain who is smuggling Jews into Palestine during the British Mandate, but as the notes from an album of Palmach army songs delicately describe it, Shoshana is a "camp follower." Perhaps this is my point of intersection with Rebekah Scott's novel *The Moorish Whore*.

I visit El Museo de las Peregrinaciones y de Santiago, where I enjoy the exhibits of pilgrim clothes through the ages, maps, Game of the Goose boards, and art made from walking sticks, a reiteration of my journey.

I buy a small bright *azabache* cabochon set in a silver circle for myself, a pair of azabache earrings for Nancy. This local jet or "black amber" is thought to confer protection. I thread my pendant, a mineral that is also a plant, onto the chain now vacated and made available by Frederic's absent angel. As I clasp the chain, I feel the Buddha's inner smile alight.

The Camino is like cancer because now I know what it is like. How to do it. I would like to walk another Camino. I would prefer not to have another cancer.

I eat an entirely yellow lunch. As I wait at the station for my bus to Lavacolla, two of the Korean pilgrims scream from across several bays and we run together for a final amoeba hug.

Ritual bath

"Lavacolla" refers to ancient pilgrims stopping at the stream here to wash their private parts before approaching the Cathedral. They're going the other way, but this still seems like a good idea. My hotel room does have a bathtub so I, too, may refresh myself, cleanse myself, for the long trip home.

> Because, because
> there was no wizard,
> not even some old man

purporting to be a mage and
writing his bestseller.

Charlemagne and I
missed each other by *this*
much; well, 13 centuries,
give or take.

Prester John commandeered my donkey,
John Frum brought it back,
an embarrassment of riches.

I fashion for St. Águeda
new breasts of scallop shells.

My handprints, too, my artifacts and bone.

Hototogisu

Don't take binoculars, they said. They're heavy and you won't
see many birds.

- Mallard
- Cattle egret
- Grey heron
- White stork
- Red kite
- Bearded vulture
- Egyptian vulture
- Griffon vulture
- Common buzzard
- Booted eagle
- Eurasian coot
- Muscovy duck
- Yellow-legged gull
- Rock dove (feral pigeon)
- Common wood pigeon
- Eurasian collared dove
- Great spotted woodpecker

- Common cuckoo
- Common swift
- Common kingfisher
- Woodlark
- Eurasian crag martin
- Common house martin
- Barn swallow
- White wagtail
- Winter wren
- European robin
- Black redstart
- Common redstart
- European stonechat
- Common blackbird (merula)
- Zitting cisticola
- Eurasian blackcap
- Western Bonelli's warbler
- Great tit
- Coal tit
- Short-toed treecreeper
- Southern grey shrike
- Azure-winged magpie
- Common magpie
- Carrion crow
- Northern raven
- Spotless starling
- Common starling
- House sparrow
- Rock sparrow
- European serin
- European goldfinch
- Common linnet
- Red crossbill
- Eurasian bullfinch
- Cirl bunting
- White nuthatch

The myth of the future

Walking planets, fading light, the light rekindling. Perturbations in the field of stars. Cancer and the Camino are alike because the stories for both can be told using narrative structures that include the Hero's Quest, a labyrinth, a meander, a map, the stages of grief, a memory palace, a list of birds. The myth of a knowable future. I stroke the foxed edges of my tiny journal. I am not a cancer survivor. I am a cancer pilgrim.

> I begin with one
> Camino story, gather
> more. I end with none.

POSTAMBLE: NO PEBBLE

Rilke's thimble

Back home after two months away, vacation and peregrination. Two toenails down, one to go. I reinstate my routine. It's a bit tricky to detach my self-esteem from my work but still stay engaged and present. I laid down my angst at the Cruz de Ferro, burned it out on the plains and mountains, the live and faded towns. What is left to untangle is the loose strands of grief.

Half a year later, we return from vacation, arriving at our almost-local airport in the evening. A perfect storm of weather and staff illness snarls air traffic from this point out, trapping us in the airport overnight without our luggage or food, jacketless, a chill winter downpour fogging the windows of baggage claim, gusting inside whenever anyone walks through or past the sliding doors. I stand in slow, goose-game customer service lines trying to book the 66-minute flight home; "Not tomorrow or the next day," sorry, completo. With nothing better to do, I try several lines over the hours. You never know. In the last line, jammed together in the boustrophedon labyrinth of tired, cold, and angry customers, I hear a woman crying. Though we are separated by many people, she is near at hand as the crow flies. I hear her explaining to an airline representative that her family member is dying and she has to get to him. Sympathetic nods, but there are no flights. She continues to stand in the line, sniffling and praying. I still have the brown metal cross on my waist pack, the gift of that pilgrim early in my Camino. I tease the knotted cord apart until I can unthread it from the zipper tab. I call to her across the stanchions and cordons. She looks up, startled. I duck under the belt and join her. When we have what privacy there is, I tell her that I heard her talking with the representative and that I am sorry for her upsetting situation. I hand her the cross and explain that it had been given to me when I was a pilgrim on the St. James Way that summer, and that I think she needs it now. She hesitates, saying it looks expensive. I reply that I think it isn't, but either way, it needs to be hers. She reaches out and takes it gladly, stowing it carefully in her purse, from which she then extracts a silver-colored thimble. She asks if I knew Rilke's story about the thimble. I know Rilke, but not this story. She presses the thimble into my hand. "Read it when you get home." I accept her gift, though I imagine that she intended to give it to a grandchild. I have to trust her reciprocity. We hug. The line shuffles forward and I return to my place. I hope she makes it to her family in time. I've given up the badge of Christianity. I read the Rilke.

I can no longer read some of my journal entries, written in other languages and codes I've forgotten. My memory smooths. I am no longer everywhere I've been.

On an international Zoom meeting, an African psychologist asserts, "Scientists have proved there's somebody up there." I'd like to see that proof, but it's sufficient for me that we are somebody down here. I am part and I am one. Is this a way to identify with the tripartite goddess or god? To embody the triquetra, earth, sea, sky; maiden, mother, crone. Cataracts halo every light, glow like a nimbus, aureole, gloriole. I'll bring the fire, ignite that barrier between mundane and celestial, wrap us in the vesica piscis, our interlocked mandorlas. It means "almonds." Almonds, right. That's the most important thing a mandorla looks like. You bring the little olives of St. Águeda.

Symbols are metaphorical comparisons, an image or idea standing in for another, borne and worn into our collective psychic grooves, the mechanism of the thought rooted in our brains and guts like the rooting reflex. We infer and question relatedness, if and how we should interpret it. Leaving aside the question of what constitutes enlightenment for an atheist, I am an atheist with icons and rites. I don't want to privilege my underlying deference to a Judaic monotheism I don't believe in over the possibility of many gods, of spirits, sprites, pixies and nixies, devils and demons. In my country, we foreigners have accreted only several hundred years of technology and myth, explanatory tales. The goddesses and animals, the sacred plants of Europe, are deep in my people's history, even if less-well syncretically adapted. I do not think they are real. I do think they are vessels for meaning, unconscious and collective, love and dread and longing.

A zombie apocalypse

I'm flying home, returning from an expert-in-residence week in Iowa. Nancy texts, "It's in Seattle." In Minneapolis-St. Paul airport, I pull a medical mask from my bag. Since the immunosuppression of chemotherapy, I don't travel without one. I wear it to Seattle, jog through SeaTac, then stick close to my sparsely populated gate.

My students look at me uneasily and at each other to signify that I'm insane as I take a few minutes in their last week of class to speculate about this new contagion, make suggestions that are alien to them, but not to me because I was there for AIDS and I've read Defoe, Boccaccio, Zinsser on the Bubonic Plague. It is the first week of March, still cold. As an abstraction in the frontal lobes, I love rats, contagion, and infectious disease, vectors and epidemiology. In my deep human monkey mind, I gibber and screech.

In Psalm 91 we are promised and betrayed: *There shall no evil befall thee, nor shall any plague come near thy tent.* We already lived through the plague of boils, the death of the first-born sons. My tent, our tent, has been visited already and again, notwithstanding the lamb's blood smeared on the tent gables with our trembling fistful of hyssop. Climbing into Frederic's hospital bed is not like COVID. It is a palliative, though not a cure. AIDS killed my friends and altered my future. It revealed the cultural disdain that some are now experiencing for the first time. I'm glad I don't know anyone who has died of COVID yet. Two decimations would be that much more to bear.

On not writing during a pandemic: I tried but didn't know what to say. Another journal of more plague years. I already wrote through a different pandemic. That one is still happening. Must I keep another vigil? Shouldn't there be some reciprocity? I'll write about COVID if you'll write about AIDS, how you ignored it, how our government gleefully buried my friends? In the brief hours as I ready the vegetable garden for spring, hacking at bamboo and blackberry, my arms running with fine threads of blood, another thousand are infected.

In Anno Camino 1, it is helpful to have secretly symbolic jewelry, which I wear every time I go to work or Zoom from home until I am offered a lousy contract during the COVID hiring freeze and say no. Now I wear my silver Camino earrings to oncology appointments. I don't believe they protect me. They are a locus for remembering stories about myself, an invocation of the St. James trance.

Election results are reported in waves, sometimes small and far between. The blue seep across the map evokes the ocean, neap tide discernable with patient observation. It's been hard to write. No journal, few poems, no articles, no chapters, no stories. I am tidally locked like the flat grey moon. Yes, I am in motion but you wouldn't know it. Yes, I run through phases but perceive little change. I am the rabbit in the moon, solitary. We cannot name what we do not know, the wild blue.

I drink Madame Liberté Brut, check the news and cry. Tears of relief, tears of distress. So many dead. I will not dance in the street, *sororité* tonight, the frenetic and fantastic tarantellas of the Great Mortality, saint-cursed, spider-bit, ergot-spelled, dancing to the death. I have my own plague routes to trudge. They beckon, Danse Macabre while sheltering in place. Wildfires, pestilence-dead, the Jews, the witches, anyone the wrong shape or color: This is a season of danger, a threat to both miracles and monsters.

Instead I walk the wave, not the enormous Hokusai curl, gateway of the floating world. The slow wave, seep dampening the sand. Through the plague lands, through the dream lands, walking west to another end of the earth.

COVID is like a zombie apocalypse. Our weapons are largely ineffective so we barricade ourselves inside. We do not want it to eat our brains. Then come the shortages, supply chain disruptions, fires. Accusations, "They got you! You're one of them!"

From roast chicken to our goose is cooked. Skeletal birds pick out a *Danza de la Muerte*.

Wildfires in a time of contagion. We keep our go-bags ready, our inadequate masks and nominally protective gear. COVID inspires a desire to separate from others, shack up, ensconce, encapsulate. We suit up as if for the radiation creep of *Level 7*, dash out for supplies as in "A Pail of Air," the science fiction of my childhood. Cancer prepared me for COVID: For danger out there, for the lack of answers, the mystery. The Camino prepared me for COVID: For vulnerability out there, for the lack of answers, the mystery. Eno on the iPod, no angel rests against my chest.

I dream of the sandstorm that excoriates, picks the bones clean. A hot, dry humor. In the Dominican Republic, my students and I had an early nighttime visit from the community, dogs barking on the porch of our dwelling, Santería, I don't know which orishas. I should have thought of Babalú Ayé, the sore-covered saint of diseases. I should have watched to see if the dogs held by his side like St. Rocco's or licked his legs.

I walk by cars, their windows grease-penciled as if citing bible verses: 12:10, 3:25. Psalms, Matthew? No, they are COVID vaccination times, marked in snaking lines, a temporary tattoo.

My cancer family was online in the moment and afterward. My Camino family was mostly afterward, the convergence of electrons. They are my sanghas, a worldwide tracery of relationships. Walking along and sitting together, we make new designs.

I see my chest vividly this morning, the stretch marks around the scars, the scars unfaded and reddened, uneven, still looking somewhat raw, drain scars and radiation burn that despite assurances haven't faded after more than 6 years. I don't mind the reminder, but it still looks unfinished, like an accident, a knife fight, emblem of detritus. My asymmetry, my body wabi-sabi, unhidden repair. Egon Schiele died of the so-called Spanish flu in 1918, so much younger than I am now.

5:15 AM. If this were the Camino, I'd already be walking. The albergues are closed. The Taj Mahal is closed. Easter Island is closed; we cancel our reservations. In the house, I lighten like a Black Virgin sanitized and rendered white, like the virgins of Rapa Nui sequestered in the caves. Pilgrimage foregrounds breathing. COVID takes the breath away. We should set a plague cross at the market outside the edge of town to reduce contagion. Then we could buy and sell our lentils and carrots, rinse our coins in the vinegar stone. We should erect a *Pestkreuz* while we're at it, or sew another enormous quilt, let the Fates inhabit us, snipping their threads. Now I am the plague doctor, walking out in my birdlike mask. Pilgrims, the rich, the flagellants, we carry the seeds from town to town. Is the mote in my eye a rat flea? Now I am lined up on the streets of Zamora to kiss the relics of St. Rocco in the influenza pandemic of a century ago. Shall I build a plague church? Is there such a thing as a plague synagogue? Now I, too, am dead on the road.

I think of those dead lesbian books. Books about self-discovery, enough to end with a kiss. But what then? What comes after the kiss?

> Wet COVID autumn.
> I harvest the last padróns.
> Cold rain. I miss Spain.

My students and I, my psychotherapy clients and I, know each other from the neck up. Sometimes my students are masked. Sometimes they are across the ocean. Sometimes their roommates walk by in their underwear, yawning loudly, Zoom albergue trance.

Glasses get spattered
as I write haibun, hop to
bathtub from old pond.

Zoom offers to prettify me, blur my lines and edges. I am an architectural grotesque, crouched on my corbel, a skeuomorph lacking a useful function. The comfort of the broken shape, the danger of the new way, the new thing. A journal is like a bag of rusty tools, jumbled.

I'm running out
of certain kinds of time.
The moon ascends,
rien, de rein. J'ai
besoin de something.

In adolescence, I fantasized about a room of one's own, and only one's own. What would I do with a space no one but me ever saw or entered? Now COVID creates this functional opportunity, albeit with a wife. My students, clients, and friends see the small window I've dressed for them, a sliver of room, oculus. It's an opportunity to ask how I want my private space to hold me.

Dry trees are leaved with sacred birds,
holy ponds thick-rimmed with rushes.
Young monkeys teach each other speech.
Their loss. After the fall and spring,
after the rapture, a rough slouch,
Prometheus re-binds himself,
convolvulus, fields of bindweed,
old wisteria. Recalls the eagle.

We swing from the vines at the primate zoo
freight train's a-rollin' and she's comin' soon
noise and signal, zombie virus clatter,
mutant cats cry to the full orange moon
under violet clouds, happy tails, *mew, mew.*

Synapses glitter, chitter-chatter.

Bricolage is a way of making, not violence. A bowl is not a woman, a text is not a woman. I reject that story of postmodernism, the gleeful smashing. Zombie kintsugi: I am not a monster but an assemblage, parts sometimes interestingly mismatched.

Will we walk again, ecstatic in the ordinary? I peregrinate by analog, circles around my circumscribed house. A Pilgrimage in Place is like kintsugi. COVID is like being a Lady of Port Lockroy, walking around and around the same penguins, admiring the mountains and sky.

> Step, no stepping stones.
> Deadheading dandelions,
> mint crushed underfoot.

COVID is like exile, like diaspora. We make place portable, shoo the god back out of the box. We are in the box; there is no room. We make the god modular through prayer, through study, by acts to repair the world. We follow, out of the box. We learn to do without it. This is a challenge similar to reaching O Cebreiro—a steep climb but attainable if we attend to the quality rather than speed of the endeavor, noticing our steps and appreciating our intentions.

> Cooking down quinces.
> Remember *membrillo.* Sweet
> earth, cool rain, cool stones.

We journal the plague, make art of it. Spatter wine on the page as a proxy. Catch ourselves smiling, just a little Buddha's smile.

I cultivate sufficient wonder. How wonderful it is to drink coffee! To bathe in hot water! How wonderful the Penzey's blend cinnamon, the Vietnamese cinnamon, the China Tung Hing cinnamon, the Indonesian cinnamon, the Ceylon cinnamon sticks. How marvelous to revel in such bounty! Such fine huge cats, such an excellent wife! So many books to read, though still fewer than Susan Sontag's vast collection. I am still here, not yet a dead breast cancer memoirist.

> Nuns fret not at their COVID's narrow room;
> And students are contented with their Zoom.

I ambulate in circles, large and small. I practice to be serene right now, to be in whatever this moment is. I walk across Spain with others who are there and elsewhere, constructing a fictional Iberia that exists because wherever we are, we are walking it together.

> Friends I've never met
> teach me to eat buttered toast,
> radishes and salt.

One great thing

"It's a good thing I already had the mastectomies, or that cat would have clawed my breasts right off!" I told the anesthesiologist. Or maybe not. That's some powerful medicine. But I know that's what I was thinking when I woke to yet another swaddled chest.

You don't expect to encounter a mountain lion. Rattlers, sure, I've seen them; skunks, I've only scented. Or maybe that was marijuana. I did once chase a raccoon out of the cat bathroom, both of us hissing as it hesitated over the water bowl, a dripping bit of dunked kibble in its paw. So I was prepared superficially but not adequately. Wake up!

I'd made the number one mistake when it comes to cougars, carrying an enormous fish on my back. It wasn't a fish, it was a hard-boiled egg, already peeled so I wouldn't have to pack out the fragments, though in the big picture I'm sure my shredded backpack and paperback copy of *Zen Flesh, Zen Bones* engendered a greater ecological burden than a few tesserae of shell. The plan, my plan, was to meditate in the redwoods, read about "The Mind Is Not Buddha," eat my egg with salt and intense mindful concentration: Slickness, sulfur, cream and jaundice. Watch little brown ants for a few hours, write a haiku about ants. With one thing and another, I've sorely lacked the time and attention necessary for really good ant-watching.

One great thing about a Buddhist retreat center is that a good loud shout doesn't get lost in a lot of background noise. I'd like to report that I cried out, "Lion! Namaste! I wish you speedy journey to your higher incarnation!" Instead, and I don't fault myself for this, I just screamed, and not a very good scream because I'd been on silent retreat for four days and my vocal cords were hoarse, out of practice. A strangulated scream sufficient, though, to startle the lion and roust a flock of monks and meditators, robed or in yoga pants and tie dye, urge them up the short trail that was not, strictly speaking, on the institute's land. I thought I saw monks flying, like a tale I'd read or a story I'd overheard. It made me wonder if there was a dollop of Yun-Shih in the yak butter tea.

As I tumbled down the slope, I admired a tiny pink blossom, like the monk who plucks a strawberry between the tiger and the chasm. As I hit, I thought this might be satori, but maybe it was shock. Who am I to expound on the physiological mechanisms of enlightenment?

I wish that lion well. It probably didn't inch toward epiphany. For me, it's just more scars and a good story that didn't happen. What I mean is that after that, there's not as much that scares me anymore. The cancer, I mean. The cancer was real.

Cuentos y recuentos

I fantasize about my next Camino. Now I know one way to do it. Now I know something of the rhythm of the walk, the heat hotter than a hot flash, relaxing, stretching into the swelter. At night, meditating on stray currents, near-motionless air, sweat slurring into the pools of my closed eyelids, plastic mattress heat radiating through my silk sleeping bag liner. Asleep for instants, draped in my blue cotton wrap. Then more walking, seeing, listening, more pleasurable motion.

My toes are still affected, by chemo, by Camino. More practice, more Masses, easier on the toenails.

Have I ever had an epiphany? I have had three dreams with that quality, luminous and true, a triptych of still lives. First, I was looking at a stained glass window, Madonna and Child. The colors were supersaturated, especially the blue. I felt great peace and fulfillment. The whole dream was the looking. Second, I was with Paula, flying on a magic carpet, laughing and laughing. The whole dream was the laughter, suspended overhead. Third, I was with Nancy and other friends, sitting together in a suffusion of good cheer and connection. The whole dream was the relationships.

I want to walk again. I want to enjoy coincidence and synchronicity, time alone, time with others, time alone, time with whatever emotions flower. Walking as repair of the world: Not fixing, not canonizing, breathing and walking. After I walked, years after, after reading more about pilgrimages to Jerusalem and the persistence of post-exilic pilgrimage from diaspora, the purpose shifting from an obligatory rite to lamentation, I asked to speak to a rabbi. She may be "my" rabbi, though I'm not a member of the congregation. We talked about pilgrimage. The rabbi suggested that visiting the Kotel was a personal intercessory experience, pointing to the notes and prayers stuffed between the huge blocks of stone. She talked about Mount Moriah as a sacred space, of cosmic power and access. The grave of Maimonides of the Almoravid Empire, born in Córdoba and buried in Tiberius. The High Holy Days are a form of pilgrimage, she said, as is cleansing the house of chametz for Passover. I asked about the Holocaust, Yad Vashem, the concentration camps. The rabbi thought not, said she saw these visits as attestation and defiance, memorial and remembrance, not pilgrimage. She spoke of slaves creating communities of liberation, of bearing compassionate witness.

I asked what she would suggest as I walk the Camino. Her response was simple: Don't take Communion. Don't go to the site of the Second Temple. Don't be seduced away from Judaism by the attractive rituals of other faiths.

I did not take Communion. I can say with confidence that I am as Jewish as I was before I walked, perhaps even more. Immersing myself in European Christianity inspired me to look inward as well as outward, to renew my curiosity about Jewish history and values in conjunction with opening myself to experiencing Catholic culture, the beauty of other traditions. I want to listen, join more deeply, engage more confidently with others' expressions of faith.

Breakage is opportunity, repair is another step. Accidents happen, change arises. This is normal, if sometimes tragic. Transmutation, lead to gold, and sometimes gold to gold, gold to lead. I can't write about cancer without writing about travel, nor the reverse. I can't say what my Camino would have been without it.

I'd rather not walk in a Holy Year. Pope Francis appeared in St. Peter's while we admired the Pietà. Escalating murmurs then cries of *"Papa! Papa!"* and a stampede of feet. We rushed forward with the rest, sighted him, saw that the people around us were crying and holding up their children, trying to give them a view. Nuns ran down staircases for a glimpse. So we stood back, let the crowd surge past. We were incidental to that story. Sometimes it's good to step out of the way.

I would like to be the slowest walker on the Camino. I doubt that I can. I would like to experience the tripartite Camino, body to psyche to soul. I doubt that will happen, either. I might be at James Fowler's "Conjunctive" stage of faith, but most of the phenomena he describes as preceding it are largely alien to my experience. Oh, well. I've never been good at sticking to stage theories.

I dream that Nancy and I are in line to board our flight when I suddenly realize I haven't brought my passport. What shall I do? I am out of practice.

What can I carry? is not the same question as *What do I want to carry?*

Not in the same stone boat

The Camino is a heuristic, a map, a guide. The thing itself is experiencing the thing. When I walk again, I will not pay a mason to chisel my crusader cross into the wall. I do not know if I will write as I walk, blurring the ink of my fetal Moleskine with my sweaty hands. I will not film or blog it. Though could I get a sponsor for writing up my exotica? Star in a series of commercials for cancer medications? Would I wear a backpack emblazoned "Upjohn"? Pimp for Lilly? Whatever the Camino needs to make of itself through me, it will make in its own way, in its own time.

Frederic of my memory is not person-Frederic but symbol-Frederic, similar and different, relational by other means. He visits in dreams, not a soul or spirit but the enactment of his relationship with me.

When I walk again, I will not be in the same boat, stone or sun. When I walk again, disease will still stalk the land, overwrite the old ways, sing its new song. The pilgrimage will still assert the symbolic over the cognitive, a longing for meanings that are not rational and yet make perfect sense. I will be in some pilgrim trance or a different one.

Tenga Stupi

On the Camino, I was impressed by how little people talked about jobs as identity. Most didn't ask. I didn't volunteer that I'm a faculty member and psychotherapist. I'm not happy that COVID diminishes travel, but this does lead me to reflect on disability, on my resources and my privilege to act in ways that may not be available to others.

Sometimes we are travelers and sometimes we steer the ferry, alternating between pilgrim and hospitalera, hero and companion. With intention, we know that we are always all of these.

I don't know what most of my students and clients look like, only their heads and shoulders visible. I teach one in-person class, on pilgrimage. We see each other's bodies, how we move in space, but no faces or emotions. Only the occasional nose slipped from a colorful mask. My students don't know that sometimes when I listen to them grappling with pilgrimage in the hypothetical, under my mask I smile the Buddha's smile, smile with the awareness of mystery, that the mystery is a mystery, that knowledge is not the only form of experience, that accruing evidence is just one way of being. As Anatole France said, "It is good to collect things, but it is better to go on walks."

A student confides, "I think maybe there is a tiny Buddha in me." This suffices.

I am a storytelling therapist. My *tabula rasa* is not a blank slate, but more like the Meseta. There is plenty to observe, a lot going on, but the focus is on my clients' interior experience. I have had cancer; most of my clients have, or have had, cancer. They say it's helpful to know that we share this, though our paths diverge, though we often find different meanings in it. It helps that I am both vulnerable and competent, acknowledge the fiction of safety, name the benefits of privilege. I have wandered here. I know many routes, can name their obstacles, bandits, unfordable rivers, what to try eating when you can't eat anything you can think of. I am trustworthy not because I have the answers, but because I've also had to ask the questions.

When I first shifted my psychotherapy practice to focus on the needs of people with cancer and other serious illness, I needed new business cards. When I looked at thousands of the graphics on offer, I was struck by how many featured a pair of round objects—two stars, two flowers, two faces of the map of the world, two drops of water clinging to a stem. This seemed like the wrong imagery for my breast cancer clients, a cruel joke. I decided to choose a better joke. My card has a bird on it. It's a little tit.

My own cancer treatment wasn't that bad, though I've learned that many of us minimize our diagnosis and treatment, at least through comparison: *I only have Stage III. They were able to take out the lymph nodes, so I really can't complain. Yes, it's metastatic but the lesions on my liver are small.* I'll say, rather, that cancer treatment was interesting. The fear, though—the fear is still beyond description.

The crab pinched Hercules's toes, so Juno exiled it to the sky. Can the goose exile my cancer? Cast it out?

We ring bells to chase off evil. My ears ring all the time. My little mote Xhi-Xhi is a diacritical mark that punctuates my vision, changes the meaning of what I see.

My dance classes are cancelled. I dance alone at home, then less, then not at all. I feel the lack of motion in my balance.

My students and clients who haven't had cancer don't know. At one time, many did. It is a part of my identity, not a secret but not what I lead with. In person, they may notice that my chest is flat, though I've found that in general, people don't. Working remotely, it's easy to disguise by intention or accident, pass by omission. Strange how the tilt of a camera can make the visible invisible. Some days I feel like FDR, beating the intrusive gaze of the camera through artful positioning.

COVID is like the Camino. The same two sets of clothing rotated, the plans and strategies for obtaining basic supplies.

My students and clients who study and discuss it favor the term "disability" over "physical challenge." We lack a word for "This could be a problem, but since I can accommodate or compensate for it, it's just a nuisance." My asthma usually falls into this latter bracket, as does my well-controlled diabetes. Before it was discovered and named, my cancer itself had not become debilitating; indeed, it was not even evident, subjectively unmanifested. Cancer treatment has caused its own noticeable sequelae. On the Camino, the kilo of medications and supplements I carried was a burden and a passport. The weight of my pack diminished by 23 grams a day, a good incentive for scrupulous adherence.

My state initially reports daily COVID deaths with the tag "S/ he had underlying medical conditions." What a reduction of complexity, what a knocking-down of personal identity.

Is cancer a disability? Is uncancer after treatment a disability? Is cancer ever un? Is a cancer diagnosis like being struck off your donkey? Will you ever be able to ride your donkey into Santiago? What is Santiago? Also: Is being struck off your donkey hilarious, a cosmic joke encompassing both tragedy and comedy?

Dying and not dying are both narratives of continuity. One of my clients with metastatic cancer outlives her estimates. It's clear the cancer is progressing and she is in increasingly worse health, but then there's another medication to try, or something palliative to increase her comfort or functioning. Another chapter is added, more incremental additions to the story, no clear closure. An end is in sight, but which end?

Death enacts Zeno's paradox of Achilles and the tortoise, in motion but apagogically still, *reductio ad absurdum.* We creep past death toward dissolution, atom to quanta, never entirely arriving.

How walking the Camino de Santiago made me a better psychotherapist for people with cancer:

- The Camino reinforced the allegory of walking with a companion, coming together, then parting ways
- It brought home viscerally, by analogy, that not everyone makes it as far as they think they will
- It increased my awareness of archetypes and the variants, modifications, adaptations, and versions of the Hero's Quest
- The wayside shrines, the history of war, and the icons and practices of Catholicism normalized death as an aspect of the cycle of life
- Daily life on the Camino permitted undistracted time to consider the questions, *What do you want? What do you want to be and do in the here and now?*
- I understood more deeply that sometimes the question is, *What do you hope your life will be?* and sometimes, *What do you hope your death will be?*
- It improved my willingness to ask my clients spiritual as well as existential questions, added to my vocabulary of and comfort with discussing the sacred
- It increased my facility in translating between spiritual and existential meaning-making
- I expanded my meditation
- I noticed what I tell myself more
- I was surprised by my own tentativeness, by my curling in, still covertly present several years after my own cancer
- I got better at noticing and stepping away from my tamoxifen frustration, and therefore, I am more able to be emotionally present rather than preoccupied,

> angry, and scared
> - As I walked, I looked outside myself to see the world, to see others on and near the Way, see us making similar and different decisions, choosing our paths, making history under the Milky Way's sea of stars.

The Camino makes me a better atheist, a better Jew, more integrated in Europe's past, knowing horrors and wonders may coincide.

Now when I sit down for therapy, I wear something symbolic, the scallop shell ring, the iron scallop pendant, my quartz mala bracelet, or my Camino earrings. I might touch my wrists with a drop of Frederic's Floris scent, light rose. When it is gone, it will be gone.

> To everything its season,
> seeding the air, silent root.

I should cut Susan Sontag more slack. I clung to my books, too, when I had cancer, even though I had no stamina to read them.

I am the ghost in the therapy machine. Yes, I'm wearing pants. If I am ever deposed, I want to be able to affirm this.

I dream that in the collected tractates is one called *Tenga Stupi,* whose topic is grieving your enlightened soul. I've read it over and over until the page edges are furred. In a macaronic bit of Spanish and Romanian, "Tenga Stupi" is "have beehives." I'm sure this isn't meaningful. Pretty sure.

Enacting the opposite of the rabbi's concerns, I light a yahrzeit candle, though a little early since I won't be home later. My mother says, "That's okay. It's almost sunset, and you're almost a Jew."

When I returned from my Camino, a client's cancer had metastasized. Just at the dawn of COVID, I visited him in hospice, masked, held his hand for an hour. Possible deaths sniffed at the thresholds and lintels but didn't find us this time.

My client was mostly asleep. This was the last time I touched a client, was able to sit with someone dying.

A client dies. I learn about it from an obituary. A client dies, the phone message tells me, the text message tells me. A client chooses the time and circumstances of her death. A client dies and I learn about it from Facebook posts, spanning our degrees of separation.

Mono no aware refers to empathy, sensitivity, the sadness we feel as we understand that everything is ephemeral. Kintsugi reminds us of change. Wabi-sabi reminds us of entropy.

Which aspect of the dream symbolically holds the disease? Which part of yourself is represented by the rats? How do we embrace both joy and sorrow, wrapped in each other's arms?

When we are on a spiral, metaphorically speaking, returning to the radius where we were before can appear to be "back to square one," being stuck, lack of motion. But we may well have moved, whatever that implies. We need to shift perspective, look back across the spiral's arm to see where we were, apprehend the relationship between the deep interior and unspooling exterior, to see ourselves in the context, weaving and unraveling into and out to infinity.

I consider the question of spiritual formation, the ways we shift in our religious experience. Do we move forward, or is that metaphor of progress too confining? Must formation be spiritual? What does existential formation look like for atheists? I don't know; it's too early to speculate. I play with the idea, consider what I might want to write about it, the next smooth stone in my pocket.

Aligned with the solstices

I usually know something. I never know nothing. Maybe next time around. I was here and am here now and may be here again. Reaching forward and backward, the supply chain of continuous experience.

I consider a photo, the front of a new calendar. It ought to be appealing: Smooth, stacked river stones on a raked sandy verge, blue water and sky behind it. Yet the effect is off-putting, artificial. Like many staged photos, its intended beauty lies in its reliance on a mechanical simulacrum of perfection. It does not depict a realistic calm or serene scene; it is a simplistic fantasy, a Barbie of a meditative moment. It lacks wabi-sabi. It feels wrong, claustrophobic. It makes a show of fullness, but it is jarringly empty, ultimately sterile. I feel uneasy. I feel hungry.

At Earth Sanctuary on Whidbey Island, I walk a labyrinth under the trees, scuffing through fallen leaves as I ambulate. I pass the standing stones with their inner circle of high basalt columns. I sit in the woods, watching nothing discernable happening in the crumbled heart of a large fallen limb. I observe the frogs at the edge of the water. I walk into a dolmen. A small black squirrel kuk-kuk-kuks and bolts. I admire a stacked cairn, inuksuk. I sit in the center of another stone circle, aligned with the solstices. The walkway to the stupa is lined with prayer wheels. I spin them, watch the unreadable alphabet blur off blessings into the sky. The prayer flags startle me, too big to be most birds. A grey whale skull, a medicine wheel. The artist asks that we think of our favorite song. The grey whales will hear us as they pass by the island. A triangle formed of Washington, Montreal, Antarctica, personal mythology meeting the collective, "Farewell to Tarwathie," ultreia.

A flock of waxwings

> drunk in the berry tree.
> I eat berries, too,
> at the stupa
> unripe, unsweet.

I contemplate burning the holy, the opposite of incinerating trash. I lie on my back, trace crown shyness against the sky.

I considered picking up a stone at the Cruz de Ferro. Taking the numinous out for a stroll, a field trip to Santiago de Compostela, walkabout to another continent. I didn't do it. I looked and didn't touch, didn't work my hands wrist-deep into the supplications and rubble of the crossroads. In my pocket is my next Camino stone, and also not. I always have some pebble in my pocket now, a black Japanese river stone, a bit of bluestone, a tiny agate from an Oregon beach. When I teach, I carry a stone. When I counsel, I carry a stone. I pick one from a pile in my home now and then, sometimes discovering several in my pockets at the end of the day. They are emblems of the collective unconscious, the shared stone identity. I have the urge to set one down at the medicine wheel, oriented to the sun, beside the white whale skull. This is not the time and place.

I approach a ley line installation, a row of driftwood uprights, charred. I don't believe in energetic patterns in the ground but I walk to the end of the row, position myself where the next burned stick would stand. I'm overcome by a shiver, a fizz, a drawing forward in the earth. Well, shit. There is always something new to learn.

Two days later, I drive to town for an early dinner, sitting alone outside. The server and I trade pleasantries. She says something about anxiety and I reply something about noticing it. She looks at me closely. "Are you a Buddhist psychotherapist?"

A sleepy, slit-eyed tabby on his porch perch, overlooking

the yard. Painfully bright purple delphinium blooms, golden oregano close to the dry ground, yellow bearded irises, spent rhododendron flower clumps. A tall, fuzzy fennel cloud that if left alone will dry and feed the chestnut-backed chickadees and bushtits this fall. Purple chive blossoms soon to dry white, soon to burst into seed.

Six winters ago.
Nothing grows—good news!—after
my last mammogram.

My nose itches. Fog on my reading glasses, breath made cataract, plague in my face. Through my mask, I smell toast. Real toast, not a stroke. I feel the lymph nodes under my ears, behind my jaw. Bilateral, that's usually good except when it happens that it isn't.

With my mask on, I can't get hotter than the Camino in high summer. I reframe hot flashes as the warmth of righteous anger and support for all those standing with me as we face life's challenges. A pebble is every pebble, a person is every molecule of being.

Giacommeti's "Tall Figure" is a woman, not the plump and fecund fertility goddess but a skinny column, a sacred pillar, a tree, a crone, the last loop of the triquetra I approach, the next entry. Ashera is a door.

I dream that my friend Cara, my colleague, consultant, writing partner, who died unexpectedly this summer, says "Hi." "Hi," I respond. "What's it like being dead?" "It's okay, a little boring." I relate this dream to Nancy, who says, "Well, that's good. The feathers aren't a problem." "Feathers?" "Of the angels," she clarifies, but my angels aren't fluffy. That hasn't changed.

It's about 2:00 AM. This is when a rebound medication effect wakes me, sweaty and alert, no matter what time I go to sleep. I'm not sure which medication or combination causes this, but it's been consistent in the 6 years since I finished what's called "active" cancer treatment. I already know there's nothing that will put me back to sleep for at least an hour, maybe two, maybe not at all. What I can do, though, is calm my thoughts, relax my body, listen to the moment.

I pick up my Camino memories, those long, sultry nights. Focusing on my breath, I attune to the sensations around me: Pilgrims breathing, sometimes snoring. Odors of soap, mint toothpaste, a little mildew from the shower drains, a little manure despite the prohibition on boots in the dorm room, damp wool socks, apples. Bedframes creak, a small truck grumbles past, a fly buzzes at the closed window. I concentrate on a faint cool draft against my feet, remember walking that morning in a light breeze, reaching the foot of the Cruz de Ferro.

I'm with my friend who joined me for part of this pilgrimage. We're old friends; we've walked together before. She has a stone in her hand, too. We set them down. We continue walking. We don't talk about what we released among all those others, the polished rocks, millstones, contributions to the cairn. We know each other well. We don't need to share our challenges and hopes, sorrows and intentions.

I breathe on the Camino, and I breathe at home. I am not comfortable, and I am at rest. Ultreia, no pebble in my shoe.

Water tiger return

No actual chickens were harmed in the filming of this episode, except insofar as the mayor had already eaten the chicken breasts by the time the Saint intervened. Like those chickens, I've been carved, marinated and flamed, yet dance all the more passionately for having survived it. To be alive is a sufficient miracle.

I would not remember dreaming about Cara except that I crystalized it into a story. A story is a heuristic and not the dream itself. The Camino is not the experience of the Camino.

While performing a check for diabetic neuropathy, my nurse practitioner spontaneously comments on my attractive feet. If they're attractive again, it must be time for another Camino.

I outlive my father. He has been dead as long as he was alive before I was born, and I am still here. Just weeks later is my seventh cancerversary. The calendar bifurcates, spins out alternate worlds, the elongated links of the months and years, *vinculaciones,* pendulum tracing discernible patterns, sometimes interrupted, sometimes something new. Next I must outlive the oldest albatross.

This year, the black water tiger returns, water tiger lily. Tiger stalks her cellular prey, pounces, rips that spiky mutant to shreds.

I see no peregrines, but a row of American kestrels on the telephone wires will do. I write this on Kalapuya land. Whose land was Spain, and when? What does it mean to be a part of a land?

My next Camino won't be what I fantasized about. I wanted to walk more slowly, detour, bring a bottle of wine to lengthy and convivial albergue dinners, attend more church services. Instead I'll probably walk longer distances, stretch my limits, stay in solitary hotel rooms. Each method has its ups and downs. Eventually, I'll do both. And I would like to walk in Portugal as well. I read that I can find nuns who make almond biscuits shaped like fish. A mandorla is an almond and a fish as well.

Dr. Luz tells me to back off on my Vitamin D dose and I think, *How many grams will that save on my next Camino?*

Reliquary bust; how do you house emptiness? But there's a stored tumor sample somewhere, though I'm not Henrietta Lacks. At this moment, it's being tested to determine whether additional years of tamoxifen will contribute to my longevity. Either way, thank you, Tamoxifen. I am about to outlive that albatross. Now I'll try to outlast Susan Sontag.

I should construct a Game of the Goose board depicting my life. Reaching square 63 is not an end but arrival in the present moment. We are always on square 63, then spiral out and in, discover fine-grained Mandelbrot Buddhas, algebra that never wraps up. What makes a pattern real? Perceiving it into being. My goose game has cuckoos and txori, undead chickens, misperceptions caused by eye-specks and stars, ley lines, airports, skulls and spiny creatures, angels fiery and benevolent. The instructions are in multiple languages, not all well-rendered. The game must be played in a trance or dream.

My perspective shifts. Suddenly an image leaps from my radiation positioning tattoos; the constellation on my body springs to life. It is not Icarus plunging toward the sea, though it could be. Feet together, head down, arms outstretched. It is not the hanged man. It is a woman restored to life, diving for handfuls of sea urchins and pearls. I no longer want to remove these glyphs that hold a story of my transmutation.

I will see the turbines slowly turning as I walk through their shadows. I will not see the same woodpecker feather, or Rafael and Hermann, the same Korean pilgrims. I touch the stone in my pocket. Today it is a smooth yellow fragment of a shell, sea-sanded, smoothed by the waves. This pebble that isn't a pebble but is like a pebble won't make it to the Cruz de Ferro. Some time, some pebble will.

> Guess my destiny,
> inconstant constellations
> whose stars are airplanes.

NOTES AND SOURCES

Citations include fair use quotations and permissions where noted. Some sources of inspiration that inform this memoir but are not quoted directly also appear below. My previous publications appear in this memoir either as they were originally published or in modified form. Unfamiliar words in other languages are translated on their first appearance if the context is not sufficiently explanatory. Additional brief notes appear below as well.

Preamble: Bright and Inexplicable Motifs

Shoshana D. Kerewsky, "Bright and Inexplicable Motifs," first presented at the Swarthmore College Class of 1983 Salon, 2018.

Bakshish: Bribe, schmear (Persian).

"A zoom like growl": Katherine Russell Rich, *Dreaming in Hindi: Coming Awake in Another Language,* Mariner, 2010.

Hijra: In India, a 3rd-gender person (Urdu).

Coracias benghalensis benghalensis: A bird, the Indian roller.

Namaste: The god(ess) in me salutes the god(ess) in you (Sanskrit via Hindi).

"I like this more than paint": Shoshana T. Daniel [Kerewsky], excerpted from "androgyne contrapposto II," *Common Speaking,* vol. 1, no. 1, 1981.

Origin Stories

Trylon and Perisphere: Symbol of the 1939 World's Fair.

Shoshana T. Daniel [Kerewsky], "Clay," in Catherine Reid (Ed.) & Holly Iglesias (Ed.), *Every Woman I've Ever Loved: Lesbian Writers on Their Mothers,* Cleis Press, 1997.

A Giacometti bronze: See Alberto Giacometti, "Tall Figure," Art Institute Chicago. See https://www.artic.edu/artworks/9567/tall-figure

Old Testament: Anne Edwards, Charles Front (Ill.), & David Christian (Ill.), *The Bible for Young Readers: The Old Testament,* Golden Press, 1967.

Afikoman: A piece of matzo hidden by children during the Passover seder (Hebrew via Greek).

Havdalah: The ritual that ends Shabbat (Hebrew).

"Mene, mene, tekel, upharsin": Numbered, numbered, weighed, divided. The writing on the wall in Daniel 5:25 (Hebrew).

Claude Steiner, *The Original Warm Fuzzy Tale,* Jalmar, 1977.

Landscape: Pieter Bruegel the Elder, "Landscape with the Fall of Icarus." See WikiArt: Visual Art Encyclopedia, https://www.wikiart.org/en/pieter-bruegel-the-elder/landscape-with-the-fall-of-icarus-1560

Mitzvah: A positive commandment, good deed (Hebrew). For a brief discussion of mapping mitzvot to body parts, see *Mi Yodeya,* https://judaism.stackexchange.com/questions/10406/is-there-a-list-of-mitzvot-and-their-corresponding-body-parts

Card XVIII: In a standard Tarot deck, The Moon.

Ram Das, *Be Here Now,* Harmony, 1971.

Tikkun olam: Repair of the world, both mystically and practically (Hebrew).

For more on Paleolithic cave art, see Bruno David, *Cave Art,* Thames & Hudson, 2017.

Sinister Wisdom: Multicultural Lesbian Literary & Art Journal, http://www.sinisterwisdom.org/

Federico García Lorca, "La Casada Infiel," *Romancero Gitano,* Revista de Occidente, 1928.

Cornell box: For examples, see *The Joseph Cornell Box,* https://www.josephcornellbox.com/

When They Come for the Jews

Shoshana T. Daniel [Kerewsky], "Parts," *Northeast Journal,* vol. 9, no. 1, 1993. The form is contemporary, unrhymed ghazal. See more about ghazals at https://poets.org/glossary/ghazal

Lort: A Cambodian noodle (Khmer).

Susan Sontag, "Trip to Hanoi," *Esquire,* December 1, 1968. Available: https://classic.esquire.com/article/1968/12/1/trip-to-hanoi

Shoshana D. Kerewsky, "Professional Travels and Ethical Travails: A Psychologist Abroad," *The Oregon Psychologist,* July/August, 2007.

Benjamin Moser, *Sontag: Her Life and Work,* Ecco, 2019.

Susan Sontag, "Pilgrimage: Tea with Thomas Mann," *The New Yorker,* December 21, 1987. Available: https://www.newyorker.com/magazine/1987/12/21/pilgrimage-susan-sontag

Joanna Scott, "Your Dinner with Susan Sontag," in Judy Sternlight (Ed.), *The Brown Reader: 50 Writers Remember College Hill,* Simon & Schuster, 2014.

George Bataille, *L'histoire de l'œil,* René Bonnel, 1928.

Pauline Réage, *Histoire d'O,* Editions Jean-Jacques Pauvert, 1954.

Amphetamine habit: Susan Sontag and David Rieff (Ed.), *As Consciousness is Harnessed to Flesh: Journals & Notebooks 1964-1980,* Picador, 2012.

Susan Sontag, *Illness as Metaphor,* Farrar, Straus and Giroux, 1978.

Thomas Mann & John E. Woods (Tr.), *The Magic Mountain,* Vintage, 1996.

"Afternoon interview": Thomas Mann, quoted in Benjamin Moser, *Sontag: Her Life and Work,* Ecco, 2019. Used by permission of HarperCollins and The Clegg Agency.

"I re-read, too": Susan Sontag and David Rieff (Ed.), *Reborn: Journals & Notebooks 1947-1963,* Picador, 2008.

"Fa": "Psycho Killer," Talking Heads, *Talking Heads '77,* Sire, 1977.

LIFE magazine: Penny Hinkle & Heinz Kluetmeier (photo.), "The Class of 1984," *LIFE Special Report,* Fall, 1977.

Unproductive: Carl Rollyson & Lisa Paddock, *Susan Sontag: The Making of an Icon,* W. W. Norton, 2000.

Susan Sontag, *AIDS and Its Metaphors,* Farrar, Straus and Giroux, 1989.

AIDS: See, for example, Jeramy Ashton, "World AIDS Day: Perseverance in a Pandemic of Prejudice," *The Arkansas Journal of Social Change and Justice,* November 27, 2021. Available: https://ualr.edu/socialchange/2021/11/27/world-aids-day-perseverance-in-a-pandemic-of-prejudice/

Judy Collins, "Albatross," *Wildflowers,* Elektra, 1967.

Judy Collins & traditional, "Farewell to Tarwathie," *Whales &*

Nightingales, Elektra, 1970.

Nón lá: Traditional Vietnamese conical hat made of palm leaves (Vietnamese).

A journal article: Shoshana D. Kerewsky, "The AIDS Memorial Quilt: Personal and Therapeutic Uses," *The Arts in Psychotherapy,* vol. 24, no. 5, 1997. Available: https://www.sciencedirect.com/science/article/abs/pii/S0197455697000191?via%3Dihub

"She who could talk": David Rieff, *Swimming in a Sea of Death: A Son's Memoir,* Simon & Schuster, 2008. Used by permission of Simon & Schuster.

Kim Phúc: For her own account, see Kim Phuc Phan Thi & Ashley Wiersma, *Fire Road: The Napalm Girl's Journey through the Horrors of War to Faith, Forgiveness, and Peace,* Tyndale Momentum, 2017.

J. Larry Jameson, Anthony S. Fauci, Dennis L. Kasper, Stephen L. Hauser, Dan L. Longo, Joseph Loscalzo, *Harrison's Principles of Internal Medicine,* (20th ed.). McGraw-Hill Education, 2018.

A biography: Carl Rollyson & Lisa Paddock, as above.

Hans Zinsser, *Rats, Lice and History: Being a Study in Biography, Which, After Twelve Preliminary Chapters Indispensable for the Preparation of the Lay Reader, Deals with the Life History of Typhus Fever,* Atlantic Monthly Press/Little, Brown, 1935.

C. W. Ceram & E. B. Garside (Tr.). *Gods, Graves and Scholars: The Story of Archaeology,* Alfred A. Knopf, 1952.

Thor Heyerdahl, *Aku-Aku* (11th ed.), Pocket Cardinal, 1967.

Swarthmore: A college in southeastern Pennsylvania. No, it was never an all-women's school. You're thinking of Skidmore.

Nước mắm nhỉ: Fish sauce (Vietnamese).

China: Susan Sontag and David Rieff (Ed.), *As Consciousness,* as above.

Nomen est omen: The name is the sign; naming summons the thing named (Latin).

Oryza sativa, var. glutinosa: Sticky rice.

"Things and people": Susan Sontag and David Rieff (Ed.), *As Consciousness,* as above.

"Spiked 'like a sea creature'": Quoted in Benjamin Moser, *Sontag: Her Life and Work,* Ecco, 2019. Used by permission of HarperCollins and The Clegg Agency.

Her son: David Rieff, as above.

"Whenever I travel": Susan Sontag, "Unguided Tour," *The New Yorker,* October 31, 1977. Available: https://www.newyorker.com/magazine/1977/10/31/unguided-tour

Odi, amo: After Catullus. Here, "I hate, I love" (Latin).

Verbs of Mutual Relationship

Aliyah: The act of obtaining Jewish Israeli citizenship (Hebrew).

Shmatte: Cloth, rag (Yiddish).

Har HaTzofim: Mt. Scopus, site of a campus of Hebrew University of Jerusalem (Hebrew).

Tzitzit: Ritual fringes on a prayer shawl (Hebrew).

Daven: Recite Jewish liturgy (Hebrew).

Madaba Map: A Jordanian mosaic map, the oldest known cartographic rendering of the region.

קירוסקאי: Kyrevskay or Kyroskay.

Mezuzot: Plural of mezuzah, the case and enclosed parchment

mounted on doorways in Jewish homes (Hebrew).

Siddur: Jewish daily prayer book (Hebrew).

Mishna and Gemara: The written record of Jewish oral law and rabbinical commentary, components of the Talmud.

Erev Shabbat: Eve of the Sabbath; Friday night (Hebrew).

Kibbutznik: Person who lives on a kibbutz (Hebrew).

Magen David: The Jewish star, originally a magical sign or amulet, later adapted by medieval Jewish and other mystics (Hebrew). See also the Seal of Solomon, from which it developed, https://en.wikipedia.org/wiki/Seal_of_Solomon

Spacebo: Thank you (Russian).

Motek Habibi: Sweetie beloved (Hebrew/Arabic).

Suq: Market (Arabic); in Hebrew, shuq.

Maleke: Limestone (Hebrew).

Mehitsa: Curtain used in some Jewish places of worship, typically the more traditional, to separate male and female congregants entirely or during song (Hebrew).

Halakhic: In accordance with Jewish law (Hebrew).

"Why can't I get": Violent Femmes, "Add It Up," *Violent Femmes,* Slash, 1983.

Geveret: Ms., Ma'am, Lady (Hebrew).

Punkistit: Punk rocker (f.) (Hebrew).

"The son": "Bread and Circuses," *Star Trek [The Original Series],* March 15, 1968.

"Who can tell": Author unknown, "In the Name of Jesus," original source and label unknown, date unknown. Available: https://divinehymns.com/lyrics/in-the-name-of-jesus-song-lyrics/

Moshav: A collective farm, similar to a kibbutz but economically based in family units rather than the larger commune (Hebrew).

Todah: Thank you (Hebrew).

Shukran: Thank you (Arabic).

Ful and shakshuka: Fava bean and egg-and-tomato dishes respectively (Arabic).

Shisha: Hookah, narghile, or water-pipe for smoking tobacco that is often flavored with fruit (Arabic).

Jellaba: Also djellaba, gallabiyah, a long, loose outer garment (Arabic).

Felucca: A traditional wooden boat rigged with lateen sails (Arabic).

Hajj: The pilgrimage to the Ka'bah in Mecca (Arabic).

Yom HaShoah: Holocaust Remembrance Day (Hebrew).

Ostraka: Potsherds (Greek).

The Buddha's Smile

Yeshiva: One of several types of Jewish school teaching sacred texts (Hebrew).

Midrasha: A Jewish institute of learning, similar to a yeshiva though sometimes with a cultural focus (Hebrew).

Shoshana D. Kerewsky, *HIV+ Gay Men's Processes of Making Their Own AIDS Memorial Quilt Panels,* #9809576, ProQuest Dissertations Publishing, 1997.

Orisha: Yoruba gods or avatars. A person may be possessed or "ridden" by an orisha (Yoruba).

The photo of Elie Wiesel: See https://encyclopedia.ushmm.org/content/en/photo/former-prisoners-of-the-little-camp-in-buchenwald

Shoshana T. Daniel [Kerewsky], "AIDS Quilt with Icarus Descending," *Calliope,* vol. 18, no. 2, 2015.

Meseta: The central tableland of northern Spain through which the Camino Francés passes (Spanish).

Hep!: An interjection to herd sheep and a rallying cry during European pogroms against the Jews. A probably apocryphal etymology understands it as an abbreviated form of Hierosolyma est perdita!, Jerusalem is lost, attributed to the Crusaders. Similarly, some believe that "Hip Hip Hooray" derives from Hep! and is thus anti-Semitic in origin, but there is scant evidence for this assertion.

Smalti: Hand-crafted mosaic tesserae made with gold or silver leaf.

Esteban Mayorga, "La Tenia," *Un Cuento Violento,* Casa de la Cultura Ecuatoriana Benjamín Carrión, 2007.

Diego Rivera, "Man, Controller of the Universe," 1934. See https://en.mxcity.mx/2016/12/man-controller-of-the-universe/

Themistocles Zammit and Karl Mayrhofer (Ill.), *Prehistoric Malta: Tarxien Temples and Saflieni Hypogeum* (English ed.), Interprint Limited (Malta), 1994.

Anastomus oscitans: Asian openbill stork.

Farang: A white European or foreigner (Thai).

Apsara: A female water or cloud spirit (Sanskrit).

Knife Fight with a Mermaid

Haibun: A writing form that includes juxtaposed prose poems

and haiku, popularized by Bashō (Japanese). See Matsuo Bashō and David Landis Barnhill (Tr.), *Bashō's Journey: The Literary Prose of Matuo Bashō,* State University of New York, 2005.

Ne Jupiter quidem omnibus placet: Not even Jupiter pleases everyone (Latin).

Rabbi Yohanan: *Babylonian Talmud, Tractate Shabbat,* Folio 12b, II 9.B.

"Kill the spare": J. K. Rowling & Mary GrandPré (Ill.), *Harry Potter and the Goblet of Fire. Scholastic, 2000.* I first encountered it at a Steimatzky book store in Haifa, Israel during the Lesbian Cruise to the Holy Land.

E. M. Forster, *Aspects of the Novel,* Mariner, 1956.

Timor mortis conturbat me: The fear of death disturbs me (Latin).

Meditation on a Corpse: A Buddhist practice. See https://blog.sevenponds.com/cultural-perspectives/corpse-meditation-a-buddhist-practice

Shoshana D. Kerewsky, "If cancer," was first presented at Telling a Life in Bricolage, Swarthmore College LGBTQ+ Alumnx Network, Café on the Crum, October 28, 2021.

Delenda est: [Carthage] must be destroyed, a repeated assertion of Cato the Elder (Latin).

Mickey Hart, *Planet Drum,* Ume, 1991.

David Fincher (Dir.), *Fight Club,* Twentieth Century Fox, 1999.

"Let's get on with it": Shoshana T. Daniel [Kerewsky],"In medias res," *The Newport Review,* vol. 4, no. 3, 1994.

"I like the nuisance birds": This haiku and those beginning "Moon rabbits return" and "Thank you, tiny white-" below appeared in slightly different form as Shoshana D. Kerewsky,

"Three Calm Haiku," *CURE (Oncology & Cancer News for Patients & Caregivers),* September 7, 2021. Available: https://www.curetoday.com/view/finding-acceptance-of-cancer

Her2 neu is +1: This is an example of the sort of nomenclature that travels with a cancer diagnosis.

Tanakh: The Jewish scripture (Hebrew).

She'ol: The Abode of the Dead (Hebrew).

Gog and Magog: Hostile nations in a prophecy of the end of days.

Two Jews: A Jewish aphorism. See https://www.barrypopik.com/index.php/new_york_city/entry/two_jews_three_opinions

Ursula K. Le Guin, *The Left Hand of Darkness,* Ace, 1969.

Terry Gilliam (Dir.) & Terry Jones (Dir.), *Monty Python and the Holy Grail,* Python (Monty) Pictures, 1975.

S'iz shver tsu zayn a Yid: A Yiddish aphorism, It's hard to be a Jew.

Leporidomorphized: I made this word up. The meaning should be clear from context.

"Our sages": Providence Hebrew Day School Rosh HaShana flier, 1986.

Michael Jackson, "Thriller," *Thriller,* Epic, 1982.

Netsuke: A decorative Japanese toggle, typically sculptural (Japanese).

Violet Beauregarde: Roald Dahl, *Charlie & the Chocolate Factory,* Knopf, 1964.

Ferron, "Snowin' in Brooklyn," *Shadows on a Dime,* Lucy Records, 1984.

Mrs. Doubtfire-style trouble: Chris Columbus (Dir.), *Mrs. Doubtfire,* Twentieth Century Fox, 1983. See https://www.youtube.com/watch?v=tGxxl7LOe_4

Brian Eno, *Music for Airports,* Polydor, 1979.

"I miss that old man": See https://en.wikipedia.org/wiki/There_once_was_a_man_from_Nantucket for the historical lineage of this limerick.

Sigourney Weaver: David Fincher (Dir.), *Alien 3,* Twentieth Century Fox, 1992. See https://www.imdb.com/title/tt0103644/mediaviewer/rm1009620992/

"Men burn to ashes": After Dorothy Parker.

Kishkes: Guts (Yiddish).

Siddhartha Mukherjee, *The Emperor of All Maladies: A Biography of Cancer,* Scribner, 2011.

Diving into the wreckage: References both Adrienne Rich, "Diving into the Wreck," *Diving into the Wreck,* W. W. Norton, 1973 and *The Satyricon* (next citation).

Naufragium: Shipwreck, as in "Si bene calculum ponas, ubique naufragium est," Gaius Petronius, *The Satyricon,* late 1st century CE. Available: http://thelatinlibrary.com/petronius1.html

Leonard Cohen, "Suzanne," *Songs of Leonard Cohen,* Columbia, 1967.

Milagro: Miracle, a religious healing charm usually made of metal (Spanish). Milagros typically depict the body part to be protected.

Yahrzeit: A memorial candle lit on the anniversary of a death. (Yiddish).

Yitga-this, v'yitka-that: The Kaddish, which is the Aramaic

mourner's prayer, begins, "Yit'gadal v'yit'kadash sh'mei raba," May His great Name grow exalted and sanctified (Aramaic).

Doctor's lady: A nude female doll used for diagnostic purposes. See https://en.wikipedia.org/wiki/Chinese_medical_doll

Sir Richard Francis Burton & Isabel Burton (Ed.), *Personal Narrative of a Pilgrimage to Al-Medinah and Meccah* (Memorial Ed.), Tylston and Edwards, 1893.

Mudra: A hand gesture used during meditation (Sanskrit).

Kintsugi, kintsukuroi: Functional synonyms meaning gold joinery or gold repair (Japanese). See https://traditionalkyoto.com/culture/kintsugi/. For an excellent example of bricolage as kintsugi, see Grace Eber, "Vibrant Tiled Mosaics by Ememem Repair Gouged Pavement and Fractured Sidewalks," *Colossal*, February 23, 2022. Available: https://www.thisiscolossal.com/2022/02/ememem-pavement-mosaics/?fbclid=IwAR3CvrquYSnLW6e2LZYkh-7XlyN1GC2k4K3JcVApMawuHhJG1hPnakKOKt8

Cheryl Strayed, *Wild: From Lost to Found on the Pacific Crest Trail,* Knopf, 2012.

Gail Gutradt, *In a Rocket Made of Ice: Among the Children of Wat Opot,* Knopf, 2014.

Katherine Russell Rich, as above.

Oliver Sacks, *On the Move: A Life,* Knopf, 2015.

Babalú-Ayé: The orisha of disease. What did you think Ricky Ricardo was singing about? See https://www.youtube.com/watch?v=rAV3bOJaQuY

Peter Trachtenberg, *Seven Tattoos: A Memoir in the Flesh,* Crown, 1997.

"No, Mr. Bond": Guy Hamilton (Dir.), *Goldfinger,* Eon

Productions, 1964.

Billy Joel, "We Didn't Start the Fire," *Storm Front,* Columbia, 1989.

Imagine Dragons, "Radioactive," *Continued Silence,* KidinaKorner/Interscope (2012).

"It rubs the lotion": Thomas Harris, *The Silence of the Lambs,* St. Martin's Griffin, 1988.

Tiresias: A male prophet who was changed into a woman for 7 years, then changed back into a man.

Four and a half hours: P. H. Graham, "Compression Prophylaxis May Increase the Potential for Flight-Associated Lymphoedema after Breast Cancer Treatment," *Breast,* Vol. 11, 2002.

Egon Schiele: An expressionist painter.

Batey: A community of sugar cane workers in the Dominican Republic (Caribbean Spanish).

E. L. James, *Fifty Shades of Grey*, self-published, 2011.

Negredo: Stages of alchemical transmutation adopted by C. G. Jung to describe personal transformative phenomena. See https://jungiancenter.org/jungs-prophetic-visions-part-2/

The Slow Fwmmp, Fwmmp of Enormous Wings

"These rocks": Pablo Neruda, "El Caminante," in Pablo Neruda & Ilan Stavans (Ed.), *The Poetry of Pablo Neruda,* Farrar, Straus and Giroux, 2003. This translation by Paula V. Smith, "To the Wanderer," *small craft warnings,* vol. 1, no. 2, Spring, 1981.

Satori: Sudden enlightenment (Japanese).

Gompa: Here, a Buddhist meditation room (Tibetan).

Hai: The Hebrew word for "life," frequently used as a motif on jewelry (Hebrew).

Nembutsu: A Pure Land Buddhist mindfulness chant and invocation in order to practice readiness for death (Japanese).

Stupa: A Buddhist reliquary structure, usually dome-shaped (Sanskrit).

Krama: A Cambodian scarf, traditionally often of gingham (Khmer).

Longyi: A sarong (Hindi via Persian).

Garuda: A divine sun-bird, a mix of eagle and human.

Kireji: See David Cobb (Ed.), *Haiku,* The British Museum Press, 2002.

Sangha: Community, people engaged in Buddhist practices together (Sanskrit).

A Buddhist monk: Matsuo Bashō and Sam Hamill (Tr.), *Narrow Road to the Interior,* Shambhala, 1991.

Suzanne Friedman, *Zen Cancer Wisdom: Tips for Making Each Day Better,* Wisdom Publications, 2014.

Dalai Lama XIV & Jeffrey Hopkins (Tr.), *How to See Yourself As You Really Are,* Atria Books, 2006.

Dalai Lama XIV & Jeffrey Hopkins (Tr.), *Advice on Dying: And Living a Better Life,* Atria Books, 2002.

The monk and novice: A slightly different version of this story appears as "14. Muddy Road," in Paul Reps (Compiler) & Nyogen Senzaki (Compiler), *Zen Flesh, Zen Bones: A Collection of Zen and Pre-Zen Writings,* Tuttle Publishing, 1985.

Samuel Beal (Tr.) & Kumarajiva (Tr.), *Vajra-chhediká, the "Kin Kong King," or Diamond Sútra,* Project Gutenberg eBook #64622, 2021. Available: https://gutenberg.org/files/64622/64622-h/64622-h.htm

Diamond Cutter Sutra: Dalai Lama XIV & Jeffrey Hopkins (Tr.), *Advice on Dying,* as above. The Diamond (Cutter) Sutra manuscript dates from 868 CE and is thought to be the earliest printed book where a date is indicated.

Bees: An important symbol in the Church of Jesus Christ of Latter-day Saints. See https://www.churchofjesuschrist.org/church/news/viewpoint-lesson-of-the-bees?lang=eng

Apsley Cherry-Garrard, *The Worst Journey in the World,* Constable & Company, 1922.

Pintado: Cape petrel (Spanish).

Cinclodes antarcticus: Tussock-bird.

Moai: Rapa Nui's giant stone figures (Rapanui).

Alfred Hitchcock (Dir.), *The Birds,* Alfred J. Hitchcock Productions, 1963.

"Our body": Thích Nhất Hạnh & Sherab Chodzin Kohn (Tr.), *You Are Here: Discovering the Magic of the Present Moment,* Shambhala, 2012.

Roast Chickens Re-feather

"Nel mezzo del cammin": Dante Alighieri & Stanley Lombardo (Tr.), *Purgatorio* (bilingual ed.), Hackett Publishing, 2016.

Albert Camus, *Caligula,* Éditions Gallimard, 1944.

Auto-da-fé: Act of faith, the Inquisition's imposition of public penance and burning of heretics (Spanish).

Limpieza de sangre: Blood purity, The Inquisition's judgement of people with Jewish ancestry who converted or were forced to convert to Catholicism (Spanish).

Quemadero: From a root word meaning "to burn," the site in Seville where the Inquisition executed heretics, including its

Jewish architect (Spanish).

Auto de los Reyes Magos: A medieval Spanish liturgical drama about the Epiphany (Spanish).

"Seda rasgada": Silk torn by ten knives, Federico García Lorca, "La Casada Infiel," *Romancero Gitano,* as above. Used by permission of Casanovas & Lynch Literary Agency S.L., Barcelona.

Albergue: A pilgrim hostel (Spanish).

Pensión: A 1- or 2-star guesthouse, often with shared restrooms (Spanish).

Bursts, bubbles, solrads, squeans, emanata, and briffit: The names of graphic comic and advertising symbols.

Peregrinxs: Peregrino/as, pilgrims referenced without gender (Spanish-ish).

Ladino: A Sephardic Jewish language, the Iberian analogue to Yiddish.

Gracias a la vida: Thanks to life (Spanish). Also the eponymous song by Violeto Parro, "Gracias a la Vida," *Gracias a la Vida,* RCA Victor, 1966.

Erlkönig: Elf-king. Johann Wolfgang von Goethe, "Erlkönig," 1782. Available: https://en.wikipedia.org/wiki/Erlkönig

The Turkish drink: Karl Gottlieb Hering, "C A F F E E (Kaffee)," *Die weiße Trommel,* 1934. Available: https://www.volksliederarchiv.de/c-a-f-f-e-e-kaffee/

"Mit Rosen bedacht": Johannes Brahms, "Wiegenlied," Op. 49, No. 4, 1868.

"Que te quiero": How I want you [green], Federico García Lorca, "Romance Sonámbulo," *Romancero Gitano,* Revista de Occidente, 1928. Used by permission of Casanovas & Lynch

Literary Agency S.L., Barcelona.

Heimlich, a canny valley: Freud used heimlich, psychologically familiar or canny, in contrast with unheimlich, uncanny (German). The uncanny valley refers the feeling of aversion or repulsion associated with almost-human phenomena, such as cyborgs or anime figures. I here reverse and extend the meaning to suggest familiarity with a literal valley.

"Quoth the raven": After Edgar Allan Poe, "The Raven," *The Raven and Other Poems,* Wiley and Putnam, 1845.

Credencial: The "pilgrim's passport" that permits access to albergues and, with sellos, qualifies a pilgrim to receive a compostela certificate (Spanish).

Sello: A stamp on the credencial, received at albergues, bars, churches, museums, and other Camino sites, demonstrating that the pilgrim has been walking the route (Spanish).

Portlandia: The Portland, Oregon chapter of American Pilgrims on the Camino.

Ultreia!: Let's go farther (Medieval French-ish Latin-ish). For origin and history, plus a hymn, see https://www.ultreia64.fr/en/ultreia-name/

Coercion theory: An explanation for the development of antisocial behaviors in children. See Justin D. Smith, Thomas J. Dishion, Daniel S. Shaw, Melvin N. Wilson, Charlotte C. Winter, & Gerald R. Patterson, "Coercive Family Process and Early-Onset Conduct Problems from Age 2 to School Entry," *Development and Psychopathology,* vol. 26 , no. 4/1 , 2014.

Gîte: A guest house (French).

"Frog in a new pond": A response to Bashō's most famous haiku, furuike ya/kawazu tobikomu/mizu no oto. See Steven Palme (Ed.), *The Classic Tradition of Haiku,* Dover, 1996.

La Chanson de Roland, 1115? See C. K. Scott Moncrieff (Tr.), The Song of Roland. Available: https://wps.ablongman.com/wps/media/objects/1497/1532958/songofroland.pdf

Ludovico Ariosto, *Orlando Furioso,* 1532.

Virginia Woolf, *Orlando: A Biography,* Hogarth, 1928.

"Learning to follow": This haiku and those beginning "That castle? Ruins," "Did the roast chickens," "I couldn't find St.," "Conversations in," "Standing in a stand," "A smoldering field," "God on the iPod," "Angels in angles," "I shout, my voice thin," Too cloudy to see," and "I begin with one" below appeared in slightly different form as Shoshana D. Kerewsky, *La Concha (American Pilgrims on the Camino Magazine),* Summer, 2021. Available: https://americanpilgrims.org/wp-content/uploads/2021/07/la_concha_2106.pdf. The sequence of all haiku in this chapter, in this order, is entitled "Waymarks."

Las flechas amarillas: The yellow arrows, a common waymark on the Camino (Spanish).

San Fermín: The fiesta associated with Pamplona's running of the bulls.

ESTO NO ES: This is not Spain (Spanish). HAU/ EUSKAL HERRIA DA!: This is the Basque country! (Euskara).

Cave cancrem: Beware of the cancer, following the Pompeiian mosaic at the House of the Tragic Poet, cave canem, beware of the dog (Latin).

Gora San Fermín!: An exclamation associated with the San Fermín festivities (Euskara).

Mozos: Young men (Spanish).

Hospitalera: Albergue host (f.) (Spanish).

Az-zubana: The Claw(s), part of a larger Arabic constellation, the Scorpion (Arabic).

Vía Láctea: Milky Way.

Ser compuesta: To be composed of billions of stars (Spanish).

Hidrógeno, algo, nada, caminar: Hydrogen, something, nothing, to walk (Spanish).

Homo sapiens sapiens: Contemporary homo sapiens, the only remaining subgroup of this genus and species.

Shirley MacLaine, *The Camino: A Journey of the Spirit,* Atria Books, 2000.

Paulo Coelho & Alan R. Clarke (Tr.), *The Pilgrimage: A Contemporary Quest for Ancient Wisdom,* HarperOne, 1995.

The hanged boy: For a good summary and photos, see Beth Jusino, "The Chickens of Santo Domingo de la Calzada," *camino times two: walking together on the way of saint james,* March 17, 2017. Available: https://caminotimestwo.com/2017/03/17/the-chickens-of-santo-domingo-de-la-calzada/

Matamoros: Moor-slayer, St. James's bellicose persona (Spanish).

John Brierley, *A Pilgrim's Guide to the Camino de Santiago (Camino Francés): St. Jean Pied de Port to Santiago de Compostela* (18th ed.), Camino Guides, 2021.

John Ruskin's scary wife: See Sarah Begley, "The Unsettling Legend behind the Broken Marriage in Effie Gray," *TIME,* April 2, 2015. Available: https://time.com/3765841/effie-gray/

El pulpo: The octopus (Spanish).

Mr. Johnson: James Boswell, *The Life of Samuel Johnson, L.L.D.* (New Edition), W. P. Nimmo, Hay, & Mitchell, 1890.

Mirabile dictu: Wonderful to relate! It's a miracle! (Latin).

"Swisser Swatter": John Aubrey & Andrew Clark (Ed.), *Aubrey's Brief Lives,* Project Gutenberg eBook #47787, 2014.

Available: https://www.gutenberg.org/files/47787/47787-h/47787-h.htm In Aubrey, this is a cry of ecstasy ("Sweet Sir Walter" becoming "Swisser Swatter"), but in Seamus Heaney's retelling, this is a rape (and metaphorically, the rape of Ireland by England). "Ocean's Love to Ireland," *North,* Faber and Faber 1975.

"Batter my heart": John Donne, "Divine Poems XIV," *Poems,* M. F. for J. Marriott, 1639.

Diario de un Mago: See *The Pilgrimage,* above.

Geoffrey Chaucer, A. Kent Hieatt (Ed.), & Constance Hieatt (Ed.), *The Canterbury Tales: A Bantam Dual-Language Book,* Bantam, 1964.

Galice at Seint-Jame: Spain at Santiago.

"A small cross": This section and those beginning "I pass as something," "I once took," "I pound across Spain," "We seek the fractal edges," "I almost smell the sea," "Consciousness," and "Into those delicious waves" below were first presented in slightly different form as Shoshana D. Kerewsky, "Passing Through," Telling A Life in Bricolage, Swarthmore College LGBTQ+ Alumnx Network, Cafe on the Crum, October 28, 2021.

Shema: Hear O Israel, the Lord our God, the Lord is One, the central Jewish assertion of monotheistic faith (Hebrew).

Abecedario: Alphabet (Spanish).

Shoshana D. Kerewsky, "Breathing in," *La Concha (American Pilgrims on the Camino Magazine),* Summer, 2021. Available: https://americanpilgrims.org/wp-content/uploads/2021/07/la_concha_2106.pdf

Vino tinto: Red wine (Spanish).

Bicigrino: Bicycling peregrino (Spanish).

Chinches: Bedbugs (Spanish).

Fuente de Irache: A wine and water fountain on the Camino at Bodegas Irache.

"How shall I send thee?": African-American traditional, "Children Go Where I Send Thee," Roud Folk Song Index #133.

Juego de la oca: The Game of the Goose, a medieval board game that may be linked to the Camino and the Roman goddess Juno, among others (Spanish). See Beebe Bahrami, *The Way of the Wild Goose: Three Pilgrimages Following Geese, Stars, and Hunches on the Camino de Santiago,* Monkfish, 2022.

The vizcacha: Charles Darwin, *The Voyage of the Beagle: The Illustrated Edition of Charles Darwin's Travel Memoir and Field Journal,* Zenith Press, 2015.

Ungeziefer: Vermin (German). The term describing Gregor Samsa in Franz Kafka & David Wyllie (Tr.), *The Metamorphosis,* Classix Press, 2009.

Matsuo Bashō and Sam Hamill (Tr.), as above.

Pastelería: Bakery (Spanish).

Gallinitas del santo: The saint's little chickens (Spanish).

St. Águeda: St. Agatha of Sicily.

So mucho depends: A parody of William Carlos Williams, "The Red Wheelbarrow" (poem XXII), *Spring and All,* Contact Publishing/Maurice Darantière, 1923.

Reconquista: The retaking of al-Andalus by Christian forces.

Encierro: The Running of the Bulls (Spanish).

Mochila, chanclas, saco de dormir de seda: Backpack, flip-flops, silk sleep-sack (Spanish).

Sarria: The closest town on the Camino Francés from which

a pilgrim can walk to Santiago de Compostela and earn a compostela certificate. Popular with Spanish families.

¡Buen Camino!: The pilgrim greeting in Spain (Spanish).

María Rosa Menocal (Ed.) & Burton Raffel (Tr.), *The Song of the Cid: A Dual-Language Edition with Parallel Text,* Penguin Classics, 2009.

Queso-y-jamón: Ham 'n' cheese (Spanish).

Antecessor or Heidelbergensis: Ancient hominid species.

Sopa de ajo: Garlic soup (Spanish).

Minne di Sant'Agata: Breasts of St. Agatha, a Sicilian pastry. See https://en.wikipedia.org/wiki/Cassatella_di_sant'Agata for a photo.

Juif: Jew (French).

Yersinia pestis: Bacterium causing the Bubonic plague.

Long-tailed tit ff: These are the common tits of Spain.

Khao Nom Sao: Female Breast Mountain (Thai).

Codex Calixtinus: A 12th-century manuscript on Santiago de Compostela and related matters, including the first guidebook for pilgrims.

A Lacanian phallus: In response to Freud, psychoanalyst Jacques Lacan understood the "phallus" as a signifier of something longed for and not an actual penis. As one of my instructors commented, "A man has a penis, so he gets tricked into thinking he can actually obtain the phallus."

A humoral explanation: The four humors is a theory based on bodily fluids and their (im)balance first articulated by Hippocrates. It was the basis of Galenic medicine, and indeed still pervades much of our contemporary thinking about health, bodies, physical harmony, and symmetry of systems.

Humoral and similar theories were and are widespread across cultures.

Queen, "Bohemian Rhapsody," *A Night at the Opera,* EMI, 1975.

Lulav and etrog: Citron and date palm frond, which with myrtle and willow constitute the Four Species, which are held together and waved as part of the harvest festival of Sukkot (Hebrew).

Chabadniks: A Hasidic, Orthodox Jewish group. Gentiles are not invited to participate in the waving of the Four Species, but Chabad does encourage all Jews to participate (Hebrew).

Noche estrellada: Starry night (Spanish).

Gustave Doré, "Le Juif Errant," 1856. See https://commons.wikimedia.org/wiki/Gustave_Doré#/media/File:Wandering_jew.jpg

Chelm: Though Chelm is a real town in Poland, Eastern European Jewish writers referred to it jocularly and fictively as an imaginary town of fools.

Las cruces: Big and little crosses, passing. I walk the Camino with a cross (Spanish).

S'vivotekhem: All around you (Hebrew), Deuteronomy 6:14.

Michael Jackson, "Smooth Criminal," *Bad,* Epic, 1988.

Jean Claude Benazet, "Le chant des pèlerins de Compostelle (Tous les matins... Ultreïa)," SACEM, 1989.

"Atom Ant!": Catchphrase from *The Atom Ant Show,* Hanna-Barbera, 1965-1968.

Vanity of vanities: Ecclesiastes 1:2.

MUL.AL.LUL: The Crab. Babylonian name for the constellation Cancer.

Jedidiah Jenkins, *To Shake the Sleeping Self: A Journey from Oregon to Patagonia, and a Quest for a Life with No Regret,* Convergent Books, 2018.

Bill Bryson, *A Walk in the Woods: Rediscovering America on the Appalachian Trail,* Anchor, 1998.

Miguel de Cervantes & Edith Grossman (Author, Tr.), *Don Quixote,* HarperCollins 2009.

Aeroglyph: I created this word to refer to marks in the sky that can be interpreted (clouds, contrails, shooting stars, vitreous floaters, Ezekiel Saw the Wheel, etc.). As it turns out, so did artist Ruben Wu, who uses long-exposure photography to capture "temporary geometries" made by lighted drones. See "Aeroglyph: Illuminated Symbols Hover Above the Horizon in New Light Drawings by Reuben Wu," Colossal, https://www.thisiscolossal.com/2018/08/aeroglyph-drawings-by-reuben-wu/

Galla Placida: A chapel in Ravenna, Italy the interior of which is largely decorated with mosaics, including a spangled ceiling. For more detail, see Matthew Gabriele & David M. Perry, *The Bright Ages: A New History of Medieval Europe,* Harper, 2021.

Anaphora to epistrophe: The rhetorical or poetic use of repeated words at the beginnings or ends of phrases.

Horror vacui: Fear of emptiness (Latin). In relation to manuscripts, the practice of filling in the page with decorative features. A carpet page, for example, includes no writing and often no representational images, but fills the space with complex geometrical designs.

Welcome the Sabbath Bride: The opening of the Friday night prayer service includes a song welcoming the Sabbath as a bride.

Bocadillo: A baguette with sliced meat (Spanish). On the

Camino, often prepared with a slice of cured ham and, if you're lucky, the bread may be rubbed with a cut tomato.

Pato: Duck (Spanish).

Patos almizclados: Muscovy ducks (Spanish).

Ubi o ubi: Ubi o ubi est mea sub ubi? is a macaronic Latin jingle, Where o where is my under-where?

Ubificated: As far as I know, there was no such word until I used it.

Jerusalem Syndrome: A religious mania, often Messianic, that overtakes some visitors to holy sites.

Minyan: A quorum for communal worship (Hebrew).

Gam sa ham ni da!: Thank you! (Korean).

Ensalada con atún: Salad with tuna (Spanish). On the Camino, Pilgrim's Menu salads often come with a dollop of tuna unless "sin atún" (without tuna) is requested.

Tohu v'vohu: Without form and void (Hebrew), Genesis 1:2.

"The nature of the body is to disintegrate." Dalai Lama XIV & Jeffrey Hopkins (Tr.), *Advice on Dying,* as above.

Xanthocephalus xanthocephalus: Yellow-headed blackbird.

A rough Fibbonacci-ish: A joke about W. B. Yeats, "The Second Coming," *The Dial,* 1920. Martha points out that the poem is connected to the 1918 influenza pandemic. See https://en.wikipedia.org/wiki/The_Second_Coming_(poem)

"Ha dado la marcha": Violeto Parro, as above.

Casa Rural: A type of accommodation (Spanish).

Karen Armstrong, *The Case for God* (reprint ed.), Anchor, 2010.

A cowgirl: After Ishmael Reed, "I Am a Cowboy in the Boat

of Ra," *New and Collected Poems, 1964-2006,* Carroll & Graf Publishers, 1972.

Ferō, ferre, tulī, lātum: The irregular conjugation of the Latin verb for "carry," whence "ferry."

An unknown pilgrim: M. Broshi & G. Barkay, "Excavations in the Chapel of St. Vartan in the Holy Sepulchre," *Israel Exploration Journal,* vol. 35, no. 2/3, 1985.

Stone boats abound: Fernando Alonso Romero, *La Barca de Piedra de San Juan de la Misarela: Características, Paralelos y Origen de Una Embarcación Legendaria,* Cuadernos de Estudios Gallegos, Tomo xxxix, Fascículo 104, 1991.

Inuksuk: A stacked stone figure, roughly shaped like a human, used as an indicator or landmark, both spiritual and mundane (Inuit).

The moon rock: A stained glass and lunar rock bricolage. See Elody R. Crimi, Diane Ney, & Ken Cobb (Photos), *Jewels of Light: The Stained Glass of Washington National Cathedral,* Washington National Cathedral, 2017.

Sea of Trees, ghost-home: Names for Japan's Aokigahara, a dense forest known as the site of many suicides.

"One who boards": *Śrīmad-Bhāgavatam (Bhāgavata Purāṇa),* Canto 6, SB 6.7.14. Available: https://prabhupadabooks.com/sb/6/7/14

A virgin blackened: For more on the Black Virgin, see Ean Begg, *The Cult of the Black Virgin* (Revised and Expanded Ed.), Arkana, 1996.

Hostal: A type of accommodation (Spain).

Susan Sontag: For her lists, see Susan Sontag and David Rieff (Ed.), *As Consciousness,* above.

Prester John: A legendary or mythic Nestorian Christian king, contemporaneous with Pope Calixtinus II. A purported letter from him, wildly popular, borrows liberally from other works.

John Frum: The central figure associated with the cargo cult of Vanuatu.

Laplap, tuluk. kava: Traditional foods and intoxicant of Vanuatu.

Kenophobia: Fear of empty spaces, more generally than horror vacui.

Glyphosate: A herbicide, Roundup being an example.

Jeanne-Paule Marie Deckers (Soeur Sourire), *The Singing Nun*, Phillips, 1963.

"You look down": My loose translation of Jeanne-Paule Marie Deckers, "Complainte pour Marie-Jacques," as above.

"Les routes vagabondant": I went wandering on all the roads (French), Jeanne-Paule Marie Deckers, "Alléluia," as above.

Abaciscus, abaculus, vitreous, ceramic, gold, mirrored, stained, pebbles. Opus vermiculatum: Specialized vocabulary related to tesserae and mosaics.

Adonai s'fatai tiftach: God, open my lips (Hebrew).

E sus eia! Deus adjuva nos: With "ultreia," Let us go further! and higher! with God's help (medieval Latin). Popularized by Benazet, above.

Azulejos: Glazed Iberian tiles, especially in Portugal, often with figurative blue tin-based glaze. The word derives from Arabic zillīj, a mosaic style. Interestingly, the word azul, blue, is from the Persian via Arabic for "lapis lazuli." I don't know if these two terms ultimately have a common etymology. I assume on the basis of no evidence that many believe the word azulejo refers to the blue glaze.

Glass bead game: Hermann Hesse, Richard Winston (Tr.), & Clara Winston (Tr.), *The Glass Bead Game,* Picador, 2002.

Darwin reports: Charles Darwin, as above.

Donativo: Pay what you can; also used for a table or box where pilgrims may leave their discarded gear for others to take (Spanish).

Beebe Bahrami, *Moon Camino de Santiago: Sacred Sites, Historic Villages, Local Food & Wine* (rev. & updated ed.), Moon Travel, 2022.

Bulbul, bulbil, pilpul: A bird family, axillary bulblet, subtle and sometimes-quibbling Talmudic rhetorical discourse (Hebrew).

Ahavat Olam: Eternal love, a prayer in the evening service (Hebrew).

Tikkun haguf, tikkun shaddaim: Repair of the body, repair of the breasts (Hebrew).

Narrative therapy: The kind I practice, heavy on personal meaning-making, metaphors, and restorying. See https://dulwichcentre.com.au/

Quelle dommage: What a pity (French).

M. C. Escher was highly influenced by the geometric decorative motifs of Mudéjar architecture, presumably zillīj and similar styles. See https://en.wikipedia.org/wiki/M._C._Escher

Obama worm: No relation. See https://www.thelocal.es/20190723/obama-worm-flesh-eating-flatworm-with-hundreds-of-eyes-poses-new-threat-to-spanish-wildlife/

Cama baja: Bottom bunk, also used for a non-bunk bed (Spanish).

Davka: "Both in fact" and "to the contrary" (Hebrew).

"Bienvenido a Villa Cero": Welcome to Zeroville (Spanish).

Paul Quenon, *In Praise of the Useless Life: A Monk's Memoir,* Ave Maria Press, 2018.

"The Sign" uses Edward FitzGerald's "Rubaiyat Quatrain" form.

Kahlil Gibran, *The Prophet,* Knopf, 1923.

T. S. Eliot, *Four Quartets,* Harcourt, 1943.

Cancer sisters and Chemosabes: Two member-organized breast cancer support groups.

Cinconia ciconia: European white stork.

Raciones: Tapas (Spanish).

Wat: A Buddhist temple (Sanskrit).

Ladyboy: A trans, cross-dressing, or feminine male, sometimes gay. In Thai, kathoey.

Anassa kata: Queen, descend, I invoke you, fair one. Hail, hail, hail, victory! (Greek). The Bryn Mawr College cheer.

Audiating chants: The lists that follow are forms of solfège (syllables assigned to musical tones, such as do, re, mi) from different cultures and musical traditions. The Guidonian hand is a mnemonic that associates notes to parts of the hand.

Caminante: Walker, there is no path (Spanish). Antonio Machado, "Extracto de Proverbios y cantares (XXIX)," *Campos de Castilla,* Editorial Renacimiento, 1912.

Bodhi: Enlightenment (Sanskrit).

Elgin Marbles: A number of sculptures removed from the Parthenon and in the possession of the British Museum.

My my, hey hey, necesito mas café: After Neil Young, "Rust Never Sleeps (Out of the Blue)," *Rust Never Sleeps,* Reprise, 1979.

Mudéjar: Architecture of medieval Spain that is influenced by Islamic style.

Convivencia: Co-existence (Spanish). As a proper noun, the period from the early 8th to late 15th centuries CE when Muslims, Christians, and Jews made up much of the population (lasting from the Muslim conquest to the expulsion of the Jews).

Alf Laylah Wa Laylah: *A Thousand Nights and a Night* (Arabic).

Matryoshka: Nesting dolls (Russian).

"My trousers rolled": T. S. Eliot, "The Love Song of J. Alfred Prufrock," *Collected Poems, 1909-1962,* Faber & Faber, 2020.

Pimientos de padrón: Padrón peppers seared in olive oil and tossed with coarse salt (Spanish).

Lo ira ra: I will fear no evil (Hebrew), Psalm 23:4.

Sappho's fragment: I paraphrase a translation issue. See, for example, https://greek_english.en-academic.com/70996

On this rock: Matthew 16:18.

These rocks: Pablo Neruda and Paula V. Smith (Tr.), as above.

Sappho: μὴ κίνη χέραδος (Greek) (my translation).

Bruja: Witch (Spanish).

Palloza: A type of traditional round stone building (Spanish).

Patxarana: A liqueur made of sloe berries.

Tourigrinxs: Tourist pilgrims.

Caldo Gallego: A hearty white bean soup from the Galicia region (Spanish).

Omega to Alpha: Bahrami's *Moon Tour* guide, as above, notes that the reversal may signify that the stonemason was Jewish or Arabic and carved the letters right to left.

Mary Barnard, *Sappho: A New Translation*, University of California Press, 1958. Used by permission of University of California Press.

A white horse canters: A story about Santiago features a white horse that plunges into the sea and returns draped in scallop shells, Santiago's symbol.

Completo: Full (Spanish).

Désolé: Sorry (French).

"Que te quiero": How I want you [green], Federico García Lorca, "Romance Sonámbulo," *Romancero Gitano,* as above. Used by permission of Casanovas & Lynch Literary Agency S.L., Barcelona.

Polvo: Dust (Spanish).

Concha de vieira: Scallop shell (Spanish).

Hórreo: A raised granary (Spanish).

"Walking stick" cabbage: For more on the taxonomy of the Camino's flora, see Lyndon Penner, *The Way of the Gardener: Lost in the Weeds along the Camino de Santiago,* University of Regina, 2021.

Patti Smith Group, "Ain't It Strange," *Radio Ethiopia,* Arista, 1976.

Bernardo Atxaga & Margaret Jull Costa (Tr.), *Obabakoak: Stories from a Village,* Graywolf Press, 2010.

Monstruos: Monsters (Spanish).

Queen Esther: "Viaje al Centro del Queso de Tetilla: El Origen de Este Manjar Gallego," *Quincemil,* 23/2/2021. Available: https://www.elespanol.com/quincemil/articulos/cultura/viaje-al-centro-del-queso-de-tetilla-el-origen-de-este-manjar-gallego

Christo: Artist who wrapped buildings in fabric.

Ursula K. Le Guin, as above.

Virginia Woolf, *To the Lighthouse,* Hogarth, 1927.

One Ring: See https://en.wikipedia.org/wiki/One_Ring

Per aspera ad astra: Through difficulties to the stars (Latin).

Decathlon: A sporting goods store with several branches on the Camino.

Shoshana Damari, "Shoshana, Shoshana, Shoshana," *Songs of Israel,* CBS, 1968.

Rebekah Scott, *The Moorish Whore: A Novel,* Peaceable Publishing, 2012.

Azabache: The mineraloid jet (Spanish). Interestingly, this is also the Spanish name for the coal tit.

Postamble: No Pebble

Rainer Marie Rilke & M. D. Herter Norton, "How the Thimble Came to be God," *Stories of God,* W. W. Norton, 1992.

Vesica piscis: The intersecting area of two circles, used as a form of halo.

Daniel Defoe, *A Journal of the Plague Year: Being Observations or Memorials, of the Most Remarkable Occurrences, as Well Publick as Private, Which Happened in London During the Last Great Visitation in 1665,* E. Nutt, J. Roberts, A. Dodd, J. Graves, 1722.

Danza de la Muerte: Danse Macabre (Spanish).

Mordecai Roshwald, *Level 7,* McGraw Hill, 1959.

Fritz Lieber, "A Pail of Air," *The Best of Fritz Leiber,* Doubleday, 1974.

Spanish flu: For an overview of the Influenza Pandemic of 1918, See Laura Spinney, *Pale Rider: The Spanish Flu of 1918 and How It Changed the World,* PublicAffairs, 2017. Written prior to the COVID-19 pandemic, it shows how little our approach to and beliefs about contagious disease have changed in a hundred years.

Vinegar stone: A large stone or plinth of a cross with a depression filled with vinegar. Coins were placed in the depression and goods were left nearby in a form of sanitizing and social distancing during the Plague. See Charles Merrell, "Plague stones: Social distancing during pandemics over 400 years ago," *Academia,* 2020. Available: https://www.academia.edu/43479702/Plague_Stones_social_distancing_during_pandemics_400_years_ago

Pilgrimage in Place: An online group.

Membrillo: Quince paste (Spanish).

"Nuns fret not": Parody of William Wordsworth, "Nuns Fret Not at Their Convent's Narrow Room," *Poems, in Two Volumes,* Longman, Hurst, Rees, and Orme, 1807.

A strawberry: A slightly different version of this story appears as "18. A Parable," in Paul Reps (Compiler) & Nyogen Senzaki (Compiler), as above.

Faith Development Theory: James W. Fowler, "Faith Development Theory and the Postmodern Challenges," *The International Journal for the Psychology of Religion,* vol. 11, no. 3, 2001.

Anatole France: Source unknown, quoted in Bruce Chatwin, *The Songlines,* Penguin, 1988.

Earth Sanctuary: See https://earthsanctuary.org/

"It's about 2:00 AM": This section and those

immediately following appeared in slightly different form as Shoshana D. Kerewsky, "No Pebble," *La Concha (American Pilgrims on the Camino Magazine),* Autumn, 2021. Available: https://americanpilgrims.org/wp-content/uploads/2021/09/La-Concha-2109.pdf

Vinculaciones: Links, connections (Spanish).

Henrietta Lacks: Rebecca Skloot: *The Immortal Life of Henrietta Lacks,* Crown, 2011.

Mandelbrot: A fractal set that looks something like a seated Buddha. See https://fractal.institute/introduction-to-fractals/how-to-generate-the-mandelbrot-set/

ACKNOWLEDGEMENTS

My heartfelt thanks to Nancy Taylor Kemp, Laura Gulley, and Arlene Berrol. Scott from Nova Scotia: I wouldn't have had the guts to take the bus if it weren't for you.

I continue to appreciate and benefit from my relationships with Bhavia Wagner and Friendship with Cambodia, Annie O'Neil and the Pilgrimage in Place members, the Confraternity of St. James/Camino Pilgrims, American Pilgrims on the Camino, American Pilgrims on the Camino Portlandia Chapter, and the staff and community members of BreastCancer.org, especially my Sisters and Chemosabes.

Diane Wilder, Cara DiMarco, Suzanne Feldman, Lisa Fortin, Maria Simson, and Sybille Yates offered writing support, critique, and technical assistance on this and other projects.

Paula V. Smith and Paul Tjossem, my family, Swarthmore College, and Brown University generously provided funding over time to support my writing. Jim Sorrentino commissioned me to write a series of erotic haiku when I was a starving graduate student. His tattoo of a Japanese sword guard in the form of a crane appears as a haiku in this memoir.

Sara Tjossem made me a silver scallop shell pendant that opens to reveal tiny representations of a bee, a pearl, and this memoir. Thank you for this astonishing and lovely gift.

Cindy Smith, Meg Hamilton, Robert Schauer, Katharine Barford, Merideth Wendland, Martha Reilly, Christina Karcher, Carma Douglas, Wendy Maris, and Debra Rachelle: Thanks for keeping me alive and in the best shape possible.

Lillian Winkler-Rios, thank you for your warmth, your optimism, your kindness, and your boundless enthusiasm. I miss you.

* * *

Shoshana D. Kerewsky's work has appeared in such varied publications as *fiction international, Which Lilith?: Feminist Writers Re-Create the World's First Woman, The Psychology of Harry Potter, Responsible Travel Guide Cambodia: Improving Lives through Thoughtful Travel Choices, Journal of Human Services, Professional Psychology: Research and Practice,* and professional handbooks. She now eschews the 5-paragraph essay and returns to lyrical prose, poetry, and short fiction.

Cover design by Shoshana D. Kerewsky

Author photo by Laura J. Gulley

Made in the USA
Monee, IL
21 January 2024

51672050R00208